DATE DUE

the accounting process

a program for self-instruction

the accounting process

a program for self-instruction

Gerald O. Wentworth
Associate Professor of Accounting,
Stanford University Graduate School of Business

A. Thompson Montgomery
Management Consultant and
Ph.D. candidate in Business, Stanford University

James A. Gowen
Ph.D. candidate in English,
Stanford University

Thomas W. Harrell
Professor of Applied Psychology, Stanford University
Graduate School of Business

mc graw-hill book company, inc.
new york   san francisco   toronto   london

preface

This text offers the beginning student an efficient means of learning
the fundamental concepts of the accounting process. The self-teaching
characteristics of its programmed form permit the instructor using it to
economize class and conference time spent on fundamentals and thereby
to concentrate his important efforts on the more sophisticated aspects
of accounting. The instructor can assign the program as part of an
introductory unit to accounting courses, or he can assign its individual parts
at appropriate intervals during the course. Students who have difficulty
with the fundamental concepts will find it useful as the basis for a
thorough review. In addition, anyone who needs to know how accounting
is used in business, or anyone who needs a basic understanding of
accounting in preparation for courses such as business finance, will find
this program useful for his independent study.

An accounting system is usually thought of as a set of procedures
designed both to maintain a record of the firm's properties and to classify
financial data in some meaningful way. In this program we have expanded
the definition to include our reader as an integral part of the system.
This inclusion allows greater freedom in discussing accounting activities
and eliminates the issue of whether a system or an individual performs
the operations required to achieve the desired results. Particularly in the
case of accounting, the effectiveness and efficiency of the system must
depend on the people who operate it.

The presentation of a generalized system of which the reader is a
part will facilitate the reader's identification with the specific system of
which he will become, or is now, a part. The inclusion of purpose and the
initial emphasis on inputs and outputs is intended to provide both a
frame of reference for understanding and a motivation for learning the
accounting concepts and techniques as they are introduced. Parts 1 to 11
present accounting concepts and the accounting cycle, with a minimum
of bookkeeping detail. Part 12 contains additional practice in journalizing
for those who desire it. A primary objective is to enable the reader to

understand accounting fundamentals quickly and easily. The corporate form of ownership is therefore used throughout, since the transition to other forms presents little difficulty. Similarly, materials and techniques not contributing to a grasp of the fundamentals have been omitted.

The authors wish to express their gratitude to the International Business Machines Corporation, whose support led to an earlier version of this program designed for its use. Thanks are also due to Professors Robert Jaedicke and Alexander Robichek of Stanford University, Professor Herbert E. Miller of Michigan State University, and Dr. Robert Mager of Varian Associates, Palo Alto, Calif., for their valuable advice and suggestions.

Gerald O. Wentworth
A. Thompson Montgomery
James A. Gowen
Thomas W. Harrell

September, 1962

contents

PART 1
introduction

what this text is about

This is a text about the process of accounting. However, it is unlike most standard accounting textbooks. Too often students interested in learning the function of accounting systems are obliged to begin by memorizing a whole series of bookkeeping rules which may seem unnecessarily complicated. Initial emphasis on detailed bookkeeping problems often obscures the fact that accounting practices have a fundamental logical simplicity when viewed in the light of their purpose and utility.

Accounting is called the basis of business decisions. In order to offer you a clear understanding of the way in which accounting serves business management in making decisions, this text presents the accounting system as a functional whole. As you read, you will discover the logic underlying the accounting process and the utility of accounting practices in providing management with vital information.

When you have finished this text, you will have gained an understanding of how an accounting system operates and an appreciation of the uses made of accounting by modern business. You may later wish to master the more complex details of accounting and bookkeeping theory required of the practicing accountant. Standard accounting texts[1] will be found useful for further study.

[1] For example, W. B Meigs and C. E. Johnson, *Accounting: The Basis for Business Decisions*, McGraw-Hill Book Company, Inc., 1962; H. A. Finney and H. E. Miller, *Principles of Accounting: Introduction*, 6th ed., Prentice-Hall, Inc., Englewood Cliffs, N. J., 1963; H. S. Noble and C. R. Niswonger, *Accounting Principles*, 8th ed., South-Western Publishing Company, Cincinnati, 1961; H. A. Black and J. E. Champion, *Accounting in Business Decisions: Theory, Method, and Use*, Prentice-Hall, Inc., Englewood Cliffs, N. J., 1961; W. H. Childs, *Accounting for Management Control*, Simmons-Boardman Publishing Corporation, New York, 1960; and R. N. Anthony, *Management Accounting: Text and Cases*, 2d ed., Richard D. Irwin, Inc., Homewood, Ill., 1960.

what you will learn

At the end of this introductory part is a brief portion dealing
with the purpose of accounting and its importance in supplying information to all concerned with the financial position
of a firm.

In Part 2 you will learn about the "end products" of the
accounting process, called outputs. As you proceed, you will
be surprised to discover how much you already know about
accounting. The payroll check, with which you are undoubt-
edly familiar, is one output, and the chances are that you
know something about the other nine as well.

In Part 3 you will learn about inputs, the "raw materials"
from which the accounting system produces its outputs. A
"bill," or invoice, is one input you will recognize. There
are six types in all, and each has a specific use in the accounting system's activities.

Part 4 describes the three major accounting responsibilities—processing and recording, financial reporting, and control reporting. This presentation gives you simple subdivisions of accounting activities to make your learning easier.

With this background you will be introduced in Parts 5
and 6 to the techniques of accounting. You will learn the
meanings of specialized accounting terms such as "entry,"
"journalize," and "account." You will discover that what-
ever air of mystery and confusion you may have associated
with debits and credits and with double-entry bookkeeping is
unfounded. A magician is no longer awe-inspiring when you
see his tricks performed step by step in slow motion.

In Parts 7 and 8 you will put your knowledge of outputs,
inputs, functions, and techniques together to gain a clear
understanding of the process by which inputs lead to outputs.

You probably realize how important cost control is in
business management. Entire courses are devoted to the
problems of cost accounting. In Parts 9 and 10 you will
learn some of the fundamental concepts of cost allocation,
as well as some of the basic methods of cost analysis.

Part 11 covers additional concepts, such as those involving depreciation and accrual. While these are not essential
to your understanding of bookkeeping practices, they com-

plete the general picture of the accounting process. In addition, you will learn some of the criteria managers use in determining which accounting activities can best be handled by data-processing machines, together with the advantages of such equipment.

Part 12 is designed for those students desiring a review of basic bookkeeping. It covers representative entries involved in the accounting cycle.

This text uses a consistent vocabulary. However, accounting terminology is not wholly standardized, and you may hear other terms used as synonyms for those you encounter here. At the end of the text is a Glossary which supplies definitions along with common synonyms. You will find it useful in solving any problems of terminology that might arise.

what kind of text this is

This text is a *programmed text*, which we think you will find more satisfactory than a standard textbook. The programmed text has been developed only recently, but it has undergone more scientific scrutiny than other educative forms. Tried and proved in comparative studies, this kind. of text has immense advantages, as we hope you will discover for yourself.

First, the programmed text permits the reader to participate *actively* in the learning process. When you consider the kind of text you have used in the past, you will realize how much of an advantage this is. In addition, the programmed text has a built-in aid to concentration. The memory process it encourages makes memorization part of learning rather than a painful exercise.

You will find the program easy to use—quite a bit easier than the standard text. In order to use it effectively, follow the directions provided below.

how to read the program

Thumb through the program briefly. Notice that the text is divided into paragraphs, called frames, which furnish information and require completion answers. The correct responses will be found in the right-hand portion of each frame.

The reason for this form is quite simple. We learn any new subject best step by step; in programmed learning, each frame provides the information necessary for the next logical step in the learning sequence. Your ability to complete a frame assures you at each step that you have mastered the material to that point and can confidently proceed.

Before you begin, locate the twenty-five illustrative panels at the end of the program. The text will refer you to these panels as you proceed.

When you begin, read the first frame and *write in* the missing terms before continuing to the next frame. The act of writing the proper response is crucial to your participation in the learning process. If you skip through the pages filling in the blanks mentally, you may nullify the built-in aid to learning this text offers. In addition, some frames require you to do some simple figuring. Keep a piece of scratch paper handy so that you can take advantage of these useful problems.

You will probably find that having an answer so close to your range of vision is distracting. If so, use an envelope or small file card to cover the answer column. When you have completed a frame, check immediately to see that you are correct.

Each blank space represents one missing word. The few exceptions are self-evident. Synonyms are acceptable completions in some frames, and since all possible synonyms are not listed, use your own good judgment in determining whether you have completed a frame successfully.

The program is organized so that the reader can complete each of the twelve parts at one time. Plan your study accordingly. Since each part is an integral unit, breaking in the middle will make resumption of that part difficult.

You will find brief review quizzes between parts. In studying a new part, first take the quiz on the preceding part for review and self-evaluation. After completing the quiz, check your performance against the answers provided at the end of the program. If you answer all questions successfully, proceed to the new part. If you miss a question, do not begin the new part until you have uncovered the source of your difficulty. First consult the Glossary for those terms you missed or whose meaning is unclear. If you need further clarification, most Glossary items carry index references to specific frames. Turn to these frames and review as much of the sequence as necessary. After completing your review, proceed with the new part.

An advantage of the programmed text is that the reader can choose his own speed. We suggest you proceed slowly at first, speeding up when you find the rate that suits you best. If you have difficulty completing a frame, do not guess. Review mentally the preceding material and reread the frame. The answer will probably occur to you. In some cases you may find it helpful to review preceding frames. Don't hesitate to do so when necessary. Of course it is possible to look ahead for the right answer, but since this is not a test but an aid to learning, it will be of no advantage to do so. If you should make a mistake, go over the frame again, supplying the correct answer before proceeding.

Begin now with the brief programmed sequence below. Concentrate, and complete each frame in turn.

1-1 Managers make most of their business decisions based on data supplied by the accounting system. Knowing this, you can see how much management depends on those responsible for their firm's _____.

accounting

1-2 The affairs of most businesses are too involved for prudent decisions based on memory. An efficient accounting system is therefore essential to provide data for business_____.

decisions

1-3 In general, all business decisions in some way concern the two major goals of any firm: to make a profit and to remain solvent. The first of these is obvious. Certainly the owners of any firm started their business with the intention of earning a_____.

profit

1-4 The second goal is related to the first. To stay in business, a firm must always have available enough funds to pay its bills when due. In other words, a firm must remain _____.

solvent

1-5 When you say that a firm is solvent, you mean that _____
_____.
(Answer in your own words.)

a firm has available enough funds to pay its bills when due

1-6 To review briefly, the information supplied by the accounting system is the foundation for _____ _____.

business decisions

1-7 In considering such information, managers have in mind two major goals: to _____ a _____ and to _____ _____ .

earn [a] profit

remain solvent

1-8 The accounting system records the "events" affecting the financial position of a firm. The purchase of inventory and the sale of a finished product are two examples of "events" which affect a firm's _____ position.

financial

1-9 Managers periodically consider the need to borrow or otherwise obtain new funds and also the availability of earnings for distribution to owners. They base their decisions on the firm's financial position as reported by the _____ system.

accounting

1-10 To purchase more inventory, to obtain new equipment, or to expand the business are examples of countless _____ _____ necessarily based on information supplied by the accounting system.

business decisions

1-11 In assessing the effectiveness of their management, the owners of a firm consult accounting records and reports. Owners as well as managers are therefore concerned with their firm's _____ _____ .

financial position

1-12 Creditors lend money to a firm only after examining the firm's financial position. The records and reports that the accounting system provides are therefore of interest to a firm's creditors, as well as to its _____ and

_____ .

managers [and] owners

1-13 All firms have tax obligations and must report data following methods established by law. Consequently, government agencies—Federal, state, and local—are also interested in the records and reports showing the firm's

_____ _____ .

financial position

1-14 An accounting system consists of a series of concepts, procedures, and documents established and maintained to provide at least four separate groups with information about a firm's financial position and the "events" affecting it. These four groups are:

1. _____
2. _____
3. _____
4. _____ _____

1. managers
2. owners
3. creditors
4. government agencies (Federal, state, and local)

1-15 Even after this brief description, you can better see why it is accurate to say that the accounting system provides the foundation for_____ _____ .

business decisions

1-16 You also know that managers make business decisions keeping in mind two primary goals: to_____ a _____ and to _____ _____ .

earn [a] profit

remain solvent

1-17 The accounting system fulfills its responsibilities by maintaining records and preparing reports that reflect the firm's _____ _____ and the "events" affecting it.

financial position

1-18 The records and reports, or "end products," of the accounting system are known as outputs. In making decisions, management would therefore refer to the _____ of the accounting system.

outputs

1-19 The "raw materials," or documents, which supply the accounting system with information concerning the various events affecting a firm's financial position, are known as inputs. The accounting system itself can be thought of as a process which takes various _____ and converts them into _____.

inputs

outputs

1-20 Interested parties need more than just the data supplied by the accounting system; they must be able to evaluate its significance. To do this effectively, they must understand the sources of the information and the way it is put together. In other words, they must have a general understanding of the process of_____.

accounting

1-21 To understand accounting, you must therefore know the sources of information, the_____; the procedures for processing data; and the final records and reports, the_____.

inputs

outputs

End of Part 1. Turn to the next page for the Review Quiz only when you are ready to complete Part 2.

1. An accounting system provides data used by managers in making _____
   _____.
2. The two ultimate goals of business decision making are (a) to _____ a _____
   and (b) to _____ _____.
3. When a firm can pay its bills when due, it is _____.
4. The accounting system accounts for, or records, the " _____ " or activities affecting the _____ _____ of a firm.
5. Four distinct groups or agencies have an interest in the financial activities and position
   of a firm. List these groups below:
   (a) _____
   (b) _____
   (c) _____
   (d) _____
6. Documents from which the accounting system obtains necessary information about the
   various events affecting the firm's financial position are called _____.
7. The records and reports prepared by the accounting system in fulfilling its functions
   are called _____.

PART 2
outputs

2-1 It is helpful to think of the accounting system of any modern business as a kind of machine performing a number of important and highly specialized functions. The "end products" produced by the _____ _____ often include ten specific documents called outputs.

accounting system

2-2 You are probably already familiar with most of the outputs prepared by the accounting system. The Payroll Check, for instance, is one example of an_____.

output

2-3 Besides the Payroll Check, the accounting system produces other reports, records, and checks from information provided it. All ten of these documents are called

_____.

outputs

2-4 This section describes the outputs in accounting terms to help you identify them as they relate to the accounting system. One output both salaried and hourly paid employees receive as payment for work performed is the

_____ _____.

Payroll Check

2-5 Generally speaking, Payroll Checks are of two kinds: those issued to salaried employees and those issued to hourly paid employees. Because they do not work for an hourly wage, Payroll Checks for _____ employees are issued only once or twice a month, depending on company practice.

salaried

10

2-6 For convenience, hourly paid employees are issued
Payroll Checks weekly or every other week, again depending upon company practice. Whether a Payroll Check is issued to a salaried or an hourly paid employee, it is an
"end product" of the accounting system and is called an
_____.

output

2-7 A second kind of output is also a check. It is called a
Check to Creditor and is issued to pay for materials and
services that the firm has received. A business must pay
its bills, and to do so, the accounting system issues
_____ to_____.

Checks [to]
Creditors

2-8 Both the Payroll Check and the Check to Creditor,
since they are "end products" of the accounting system,
are called _____.

outputs

2-9 In the normal course of business the firm receives
invoices, or "bills," from its suppliers. When these are
approved, the accounting system settles the debts these
invoices represent by issuing _____ to_____.

Checks [to]
Creditors

2-10 The procedure followed in issuing Checks to Creditors varies. Some firms accumulate invoices for a periodic run, as in the case of Payroll Checks. Other firms
pay approved invoices daily. In this case, these outputs are
prepared every_____.

day

2-11 Other firms prefer to accumulate, or batch, the approved invoices for periodic processing. For instance,
Checks to Creditors may be prepared weekly, monthly, or
at other specific times, such as on the tenth and twenty-
fifth of each month. This practice of accumulating approved
invoices for periodic payment is called_____.

batching

2-12 The two major outputs of the accounting system that
are in the form of checks are the _____ _____
and the _____ to _____.

Payroll Check

Check [to] Credi-
tor

2-13 The third kind of output is the Customer Invoice, often referred to as a "bill." The firm sends a customer an invoice to advise him of the amount he owes for materials or services that the firm has supplied him. When the firm "bills" a customer, it sends him an output called a

_____ _____ .

Customer Invoice

2-14 In advising customers of amounts they owe for materials or services, Customer Invoices include two major items of information: (1) a description of materials shipped or services performed and (2) the_____ owed.

amount (price)

2-15 Besides the amount owed, a Customer Invoice also includes a _____ of the materials shipped or services performed.

description

2-16 Generally, the accounting system prepares Customer Invoices daily; these contain a _____ of the materials shipped or services performed and the_____ owed.

description

amount

2-17 The accounting system usually prepares Customer Invoices every day, as soon as possible after the shipments are made or services performed. Therefore, this output is prepared on a continuing, or _____, basis.

daily

2-18 The output by which a firm "bills" its customers for materials or services is called the_____ _____ .

Customer Invoice

2-19 The Sales Performance Analysis is a fourth kind of output. In order to evaluate the performance of a firm's sales organization, management requires information about *orders received* or *shipments made*. This is provided on an output called the_____ _____ _____ .

Sales Performance Analysis

2-20 Sales Performance Analyses provide information about a firm's sales performance; these are based on either_____ _____ or_____ _____ .

orders received

shipments made

2-21 Management needs sales information in terms of dollars or quantities, or both. A Sales Performance Analysis covering the sale of outboard motors may therefore be expressed in terms of the _____ value or the _____ of outboard motors sold.

dollar

quantity (number)

2-22 When managers require information on the firm's sales performance during a particular period, they will refer to outputs called _____ _____ _____.

Sales Perform-
ance Analyses

2-23 A firm may require a variety of Sales Performance Analyses, and according to particular needs, the information on each will be expressed in _____ or _____ , or both.

dollars

quantities

2-24 Sales Performance Analyses are prepared to cover specified periods (week, month, quarter, season, year) as needed. If a firm has found a seasonal analysis desirable, the accounting system would prepare a _____ _____ _____ for each specific season.

Sales Perform-
ance Analysis

2-25 In addition, a firm might find it useful to examine sales performance by comparing orders shipped every month and every quarter during the year with similar periods in preceding years. In this case, sales management would require Sales Performance Analyses for each _____ and each _____ of the year.

month

quarter

2-26 Sales Performance Analyses are simply records of sales organized in meaningful ways. For instance, sales management may find it useful to examine sales performance by sales territory. In this case, the accounting system would provide Sales Performance Analyses reflecting the firm's sales performance in every _____ _____.

sales territory

2-27 Management may also desire to examine sales performance by product, by customer, or, perhaps, even by salesman. In such circumstances the accounting system would provide Sales Performance Analyses for every _____, for every_____, or for every _____.

product

customer

salesman

2-28 Four ways in which sales information can be meaningfully organized are by salesman, by sales territory, by product, and by customer. Sales information organized in these meaningful divisions is reported on outputs called _____ _____ _____.

Sales Performance Analyses

2-29 The information on Sales Performance Analyses is based on either orders received or shipments made and is expressed in terms of _____ or_____ , or both.

dollars

quantities

2-30 The accounting system prepares Sales Performance Analyses periodically by organizing sales information in ways that allow management to evaluate the firm's sales efforts. They may cover such periods as the week, month, quarter, season, or year. They may categorize sales by _____ _____ , by_____ , by_____ , or by_____.

sales territory

salesman

product

customer

2-31 You have been introduced to four of the accounting system's ten outputs. List them here.

1. _____ _____
2. _____ to _____
3. _____ _____
4. _____ _____ _____

1. Payroll Check

2. Check [to] Creditor

3. Customer Invoice

4. Sales Performance Analysis

2-32 Another kind of output is the Inventory Control Record (sometimes called the Stock Control Record). This
output always shows the quantities of inventory items on
hand. Inventory Control Records may also show quantities
on order, but in every case they show quantities _____
_____ .

on hand

2-33 In determining quantities of goods available for sale
as well as quantities needed to replenish stocks, material
control personnel refer to outputs called _____
_____ _____.

Inventory Control
Records

2-34 In addition, some firms find it useful to include on
Inventory Control Records the *forecasted* customer requirements. In modern business, management must plan
purchasing and production well in advance. In order to do
so successfully, it may require Inventory Control Records, which carry _____ customer requirements
as well as on-hand and on-order quantities.

forecasted

2-35 Material control personnel are able to schedule
additional production or purchasing on the basis of information provided by_____ _____ _____.

Inventory Control
Records

2-36 Inventory Control Records show quantities on
_____ and sometimes quantities on _____;
they may also show quantities of _____ customer
requirements.

hand

order

forecasted

2-37 Inventory Control Records may be updated continuously. When each change in inventory stock levels is recorded as soon as it occurs, Inventory Control Records are
said to be updated _____ .

continuously

2-38 For convenience, Inventory Control Records are
sometimes updated periodically (every week or month)
rather than continuously. Therefore, when changes in inventory stock are accumulated and recorded every week or
every month, Inventory Control Records are said to be
_____ _____.

updated
periodically

2-39 Inventory Control Records, then, always carry quantities on _____ and sometimes quantities on _____; they also may carry quantities of _____ customer requirements. According to a particular firm's needs, they may be updated either _____ or _____.

hand

order

forecasted

continuously

periodically

2-40 The Cost Analysis Report is another kind of output. For a number of reasons, management must know the cost of producing, storing, selling, and shipping the firm's various products. This information is provided on outputs called _____ _____ _____.

Cost Analysis
Reports

2-41 The *profitability* of a firm's products is a crucial consideration in business planning. The costs involved in the production and sale of a product determine to a large extent the profit the firm can realize from the product. Management consequently refers to Cost Analysis Reports when studying the _____ of its products.

profitability

2-42 Cost reduction is obviously one way that a firm can increase the profitability of a product. However, in order to examine the possibility of cost reduction on a particular product, management must know all the cost factors involved in its production and sale. For this information, management refers to the _____ _____ _____ prepared for the product.

Cost Analysis
Report

2-43 Cost Analysis Reports, then, provide management with detailed information on the costs of products. These are the bases for _____ reduction programs by which management strives to increase the _____ of the firm's products.

cost

profitability

2-44 Suppose that an automobile manufacturer wished to examine the profitability of its ten standard models. The managers would probably request that the accounting system prepare at least one _____ _____ _____ covering each model.

Cost Analysis
Report

2-45 The Budget is another output of the accounting system. You would find a fully integrated projection of future operations expressed in terms of anticipated *revenues* and *expenses* contained in the _____ .

Budget

2-46 A Budget may be prepared for each *responsibility center* (division, department, section, and so on). The Budgets for those responsibility centers that do not sell products or services would have no revenue. Budget outputs for such centers report only the planned _____ .

expenses

2-47 Responsibility centers that sell products or services have revenues and are called *profit centers*. Budgets for profit centers would therefore contain both planned _____ and _____ .

revenues

expenses

2-48 A responsibility center whose operations involve both revenues and expenses is called a _____ _____ .

profit center

2-49 Budgets are usually prepared annually to cover either *monthly* or *quarterly* periods of the year for each _____ center.

responsibility (profit)

2-50 Budgets provide management with the necessary information about planned revenues and expenses and are prepared annually in advance to cover either _____ or _____ periods.

monthly

quarterly

2-51 Assume that you are the manager of a responsibility center, such as a department. To ensure that your decisions are in accord with the coordinated operating plan for the company, you would refer to the _____ covering your responsibility center.

Budget

2-52 In order to guide them in making decisions which will correspond to an integrated plan, managers of all responsibility centers are provided with a Budget covering each _____ or each _____ of the year.

month

quarter

2-53 The Budget Performance Analysis is another kind of output prepared by the accounting system. Since it records information dealing with the Budget, the _____ _____ _____ is prepared either monthly or quarterly to cover the same period as the Budget.

Budget Perform-
ance Analysis

2-54 The Budget Performance Analysis is used to compare the *actual* revenues and expenses with the *budgeted* revenues and expenses of the various profit centers. It is prepared for each budget period, either _____ or _____.

monthly

quarterly

2-55 In order to permit evaluation of budget planning and performance for each responsibility center, the Budget Performance Analysis contains, for comparison, both the _____ and the planned, or _____, revenues and expenses.

actual

budgeted

2-56 For control of a business, the first step is the adoption of a coordinated plan, the Budget. However, unless performance is related to plan, management cannot exercise adequate control. The second step, therefore, is the comparison of budgeted and actual revenues and expenses, and for this management refers to the _____ _____ _____.

Budget Perform-
ance Analysis

2-57 For instance, if a manager responsible for a department discovered that actual expenses for that department exceeded budgeted expenses, he would know that corrective measures might be required. Thus the Budget Performance Analysis serves as a periodic guide to planning and control by providing a _____ between actual and budgeted revenues and expenses for each budget period.

comparison

2-58 The Balance Sheet is another important output. By reporting the firm's *assets* and *equities*, the _____ _____ is a record of the firm's *financial position* at a given date.

Balance Sheet

2-59 Assets are properties owned by the firm. Equities are liabilities and other claims against, or sources of, these same assets. In reflecting the financial position, the Balance Sheet lists the firm's _____ and _____ on a given date.

assets

equities

2-60 Although you may hear the term *liabilities* applied to all claims against or sources of assets, *liabilities* more precisely refers to creditors' claims. The term used here to apply to total claims and sources, including liabilities, is _____ .

equities

2-61 The Balance Sheet is always prepared *yearly* and is often prepared *monthly*. It is basically a record of the firm's _____ _____ at a given_____ .

financial
position

date

2-62 The Balance Sheet lists in detail the firm's assets and equities as of a particular date. It is prepared periodically—always _____ and often _____ .

yearly

monthly

2-63 The Balance Sheet is a report of the firm's financial position at the time of its preparation. It lists in detail the firm's_____ and _____ .

assets

equities

2-64 Another output produced by the accounting system, the Income Statement, is related to the Balance Sheet. Recall that the _____ _____ lists the firm's assets and equities.

Balance Sheet

2-65 Successive Balance Sheets show changes in the firm's financial position, many of them the result of regular business operations. For information on the changes arising out of regular business operations, management must therefore refer to an output related to the Balance Sheet, the _____ _____ .

Income
Statement

2-66 Recall that the Balance Sheet does not cover a period
of time but instead shows the financial position as of a
particular date. In contrast, the Income Statement reports
changes in the financial position between successive
Balance Sheets and therefore covers a _____ of
time.

period

2-67 If Balance Sheets are prepared at the end of each
month, the Income Statement, prepared at the same time,
covers the preceding _____.

month

2-68 The Income Statement lists in detail all *revenues* and
expenses, as well as the difference between them, the *profit*
or *loss*. The Income Statement in this way records factors
that change the firm's financial _____ during the
period.

position

2-69 In order to show changes in the firm's financial position during a particular period, the Income Statement lists
all revenues and expenses and the difference between them,
the _____ or _____.

profit

loss

2-70 The Balance Sheet, which records assets and equities, shows the firm's financial position at a particular
time. The Income Statement, on the other hand, records
factors which _____ the firm's financial position
during the period between Balance Sheets.

change

2-71 The Income Statement, in order to show the factors
which change the financial position of a firm during a particular period, lists all_____ and _____ and the
difference between them, the _____ or_____.

revenues

expenses

profit

loss

2-72 The Income Statement is the last of ten major outputs prepared by the _____ _____.

accounting

system

2-73 Recall that two outputs are in the form of checks. These are _____ _____ and _____ to _____.

Payroll Checks

Checks [to] Creditors

2-74 Payroll Checks are issued to both _____ and _____ paid employees.

salaried

hourly

2-75 The firm issues Checks to Creditors in response to _____ received from suppliers covering goods or services provided the firm.

invoices

2-76 Some firms issue Checks to Creditors the same _____ that invoices are approved. Others issue them periodically, a practice called _____.

day

batching

2-77 Another output is often called a "bill." A firm advises a customer of the amount owed for goods or services by sending a _____ _____.

Customer Invoice

2-78 Usually firms follow the practice of preparing Customer Invoices on the same _____ that goods are shipped or services completed.

day

2-79 Customer Invoices include two major items of information:

1. A _____ of materials shipped or services performed
2. The _____ owed

1. description

2. amount

2-80 When management wishes to examine the sales performance of its organization, it refers to an output called the _____ _____ _____ .

Sales Performance Analysis

2-81 Sales information on the Sales Performance Analysis is expressed in terms of _____ or _____ , or both.

dollars

quantities

2-82 Sales Performance Analyses list sales in a variety of meaningful categories. What are four of these categories?

1. _____ _____
2. _____
3. _____
4. _____

1. sales territory
2. salesman
3. product
4. customer

2-83 The output which records the quantities of inventory items on hand, and sometimes the quantities on order, is called the _____ _____ _____ .

Inventory Control Record

2-84 Besides listing quantities of inventory items on _____ and sometimes on _____ , Inventory Control Records may also list _____ customer requirements.

hand

order

forecasted

2-85 If Inventory Control Records are altered to reflect changes affecting the stock balances as soon as these changes occur, they are said to be updated _____ .

continuously

2-86 On the other hand, if changes are accumulated and recorded every week or every month, Inventory Control Records are said to be _____ _____ .

updated
    periodically

2-87 The outputs which list all costs of particular items produced by a firm are called _____ _____ _____ .

Cost Analysis Reports

2-88 Management refers to the Cost Analysis Report covering a particular product when examining the _____ of that product.

profitability

2-89 The output which is a plan listing the anticipated revenues and expenses for each profit center within the firm is the _____ .

Budget

2-90 The Budget is prepared annually to cover the forth-
coming year, which is divided into _____ or
_____ periods. Each of these periods is called a
_____ _____ .

monthly

quarterly

budget period

2-91 The Budget provides the manager of each
_____ _____ with the planned _____
and _____ affecting his department or section.

profit center

revenues

expenses

2-92 The output related to the Budget that provides a comparison between _____ and actual revenues and expenses is the _____ _____ _____ .

budgeted (planned)

Budget Perform-
    ance Analysis

2-93 The Budget Performance Analysis covers the same
period as the _____ and is therefore prepared for
every _____ or every _____ of the year.

Budget

month

quarter

2-94 The output that lists a firm's assets and equities in
recording the firm's financial position at a particular date
is the _____ _____ .

Balance Sheet

2-95 The Balance Sheet shows the _____
_____ of the firm by listing the firm's _____
and _____ as of a particular date.

financial
    position

assets

equities

2-96 A related output, covering the same period as the
Balance Sheet and showing factors which change the firm's
financial position during the period, is the _____
_____ .

Income Statement

2-97 The Income Statement shows factors changing the firm's financial position by listing all the firm's _____ and _____ and the difference between them, the _____ or _____.

revenues

expenses

profit

loss

End of Part 2. Turn to the next page for the Review Quiz only when you are ready to complete Part 3.

review quiz on part 2

After each of the following descriptions place the letter corresponding to the appropriate output.

A	Balance Sheet	F	Check to Creditor
B	Cost Analysis Report	G	Inventory Control Record
C	Income Statement	H	Sales Performance Analysis
D	Payroll Check	I	Budget
E	Customer Invoice	J	Budget Performance Analysis

1. Settles the firm's financial obligations to its employees: _____
2. Settles the firm's liabilities to its outside creditors: _____
3. Reports details of labor and material costs, often by product: _____
4. Reports the firm's financial position as of a given date: _____
5. Contains a plan for future operations expressed in terms of revenues and expenses: _____
6. Contains net prices and descriptions of goods and services that the firm has shipped or provided to a customer: _____
7. Provides management with revenue and expense details for the period between one Balance Sheet date and another: _____
8. Provides management with a comparison between planned and actual performance: _____
9. Reports data on either an orders-received or a shipments-made basis: _____
10. Records balances in units of stock on hand: _____

Complete the following sentences.

11. Sales Performance Analyses carry data expressed in terms of _____ , _____ , or both.
12. Sales information on a Sales Performance Analysis may be grouped according to different categories. List three possible groups below:
    (a) By _____
    (b) By _____
    (c) By _____
13. Inventory Control Records carry stock balances expressed in _____ rather than in dollars.
14. In addition to carrying balances of stock on hand, Inventory Control Records may also carry amounts _____ _____ and amounts _____ .
15. Budgets are often prepared for each _____ _____ within the firm.
16. The Balance Sheet reports a firm's financial position as of a specific _____ , rather than over a period of time.
17. The Balance Sheet is a listing of the firm's _____ and _____ .
18. The Income Statement reports revenues and expenses leading to a profit or loss over a _____ of _____ , not as of a specific date.

3-1 The "raw material" from which the accounting sys-   outputs
tem prepares its "end products" called _____ is
data contained on documents called inputs. This part
will introduce you to these inputs and show which of the
outputs covered in Part 2 they affect.

3-2 Specifically, the documents that the accounting system   outputs
uses as sources of information in preparing _____
are called _____ .   inputs

3-3 The accounting system requires various kinds of   outputs
specific information in order to prepare_____. Refer to Panel A. Keep it in front of you as you proceed
through this chapter in order to see clearly the relationship of the outputs and inputs covered here.

3-4 The Payroll Check is one of the _____ of the   outputs
accounting system.

3-5 To prepare the Payroll Check, accountants use data   inputs
called *payroll information*, which is provided by two
_____ , the Timecard and the Salary List.

3-6 The Timecard, submitted by hourly paid employees   payroll
either daily or weekly, is one of two inputs which provide   information
the accounting system with data called _____

_____ .

3-7 You know that the accounting system produces two   salaried
kinds of Payroll Checks: those issued to hourly paid employees and those issued to _____ employees.

3-8   The accounting system prepares Payroll Checks for salaried employees from _____ _____ provided by the input called the Salary List.

payroll
   information

3-9   The Salary List is simply an authorized listing of payroll information for those employees who receive regular salaries. This input provides the accounting system with the information used to prepare the _____ _____ issued to salaried employees.

Payroll Checks

3-10   To review, the two inputs which provide the accounting system with payroll information are the _____ and the _____ _____ .

Timecard

Salary List

3-11   The Cost Analysis Report, the Balance Sheet, and the Income Statement are three other _____ which use payroll information.

outputs

3-12   Labor costs are an important part of operational costs. Payroll information is therefore used in preparing the output which lists costs for analysis, the _____ _____ _____ .

Cost Analysis
   Report

3-13   When the firm incurs obligations to pay wages or salaries, its financial position is changed. Timecards and Salary Lists, therefore, also affect another output, the _____ _____ , which reports the firm's financial position.

Balance Sheet

3-14   The output that lists the firm's total revenues and expenses and the resultant profit or loss is the _____ _____ .

Income
   Statement

3-15   Labor costs are part of a firm's total expenses and therefore affect income. The Income Statement, consequently, must account for labor costs derived from data called _____ _____ , which is supplied on Timecards and Salary Lists.

payroll
   information

3-16 The Payroll Check, the Cost Analysis Report, the
Balance Sheet, and the Income Statement are four outputs
affected by payroll information. The two inputs which provide the accounting system with payroll information are the
_____ and the_____ _____ .

Timecard

Salary List

3-17 Payroll information affects four outputs:

1._____ _____
2._____ _____ _____
3._____ _____
4._____ _____

1. Payroll Check

2. Cost Analysis
   Report

3. Balance Sheet

4. Income
   Statement

3-18 Another kind of data required to prepare a number of
important outputs is purchase information. When the firm
buys materials, such transactions must be accounted for.
To do so the accounting system needs data called

_____ _____ .

purchase
information

3-19 All materials purchased by a firm must be accounted
for in a variety of ways. The accounting system is able to
do this from data called_____ _____ , pro-
vided by three related inputs.

purchase
information

3-20 The Purchase Order Copy is one of three related
_____ which provide the accounting system with purchase information.

inputs

3-21 Purchase orders are generally prepared in several
copies, each of which has a specific use. The copy that the
firm retains for accounting purposes becomes an input
called the_____ _____ _____ .

Purchase Order
Copy

3-22 Along with the Purchase Order Copy, the Receiving
Record provides the accounting system with data called
purchase information. Receipt of materials purchased from
suppliers is recorded on the input called the_____
_____ .

Receiving
Record

3-23 The Incoming Invoice is the third input that provides the accounting system with purchase information. Any "bill" which the firm receives from a creditor becomes an input called an _____ _____.

Incoming Invoice

3-24 Incoming Invoices are of two kinds: Materials Invoices and Other Incoming Invoices. As you would expect, the Incoming Invoice which is a bill for materials received into inventory is the _____ _____.

Materials Invoice

3-25 Other Incoming Invoices include bills for such items as services and employee expense-account vouchers. A phone bill is one example of an Incoming Invoice which is referred to as an _____ _____ Invoice.

Other Incoming

3-26 The Purchase Order Copy, the Receiving Record, and the Incoming Invoice—both Materials and Other—are the three inputs which provide the accounting system with _____ information.

purchase

3-27 The copy of the completed purchase order retained by the company for accounting purposes is the input called the _____ _____ _____.

Purchase Order Copy

3-28 Recall that the output which records quantities of inventory items on hand and sometimes also the quantities demanded and on order is the _____ _____ _____.

Inventory Control Record

3-29 If a firm's Inventory Control Records carry *on-order* balances, these are updated according to purchase information provided by the _____ _____ _____.

Purchase Order Copy

3-30 The Purchase Order Copy provides the purchase information used to increase the on- _____ balances on Inventory Control Records when they carry such balances.

order

3-31 The Inventory Control Record is also affected by the input which lists materials received from suppliers, the _____ Record.

Receiving

3-32 When the firm receives materials which have been ordered from a supplier, Inventory Control Records must be updated accordingly. The on-order balances, when carried, are reduced, and the on-_____balances are increased.

hand

3-33 The *on-hand* balances are increased and the *on-order* balances, when carried, are reduced on the Inventory Control Record according to purchase information provided by the _____ _____.

Receiving Record

3-34 The accounting system has three inputs covering each purchase of inventory: the Purchase Order Copy, the Receiving Record, and one kind of Incoming Invoice called the _____ Invoice.

Materials

3-35 Materials received and held in inventory become part of the firm's assets. Simultaneously, amounts owed to suppliers become claims against the firm's assets and therefore increase equities. Purchase information, consequently, has an ultimate effect on the output that records the firm's assets and equities, the _____ _____.

Balance Sheet

3-36 The Balance Sheet is one of the outputs affected by purchase information concerning inventory. In preparing the Balance Sheet, the accounting system uses purchase information provided by the _____ _____, as verified by its related inputs, the Purchase Order Copy and the Receiving Record.

Materials Invoice

3-37 Verified Materials Invoices act as inputs in the preparation of still another output, the check which pays the "bill" for materials purchased. This output is the _____ to_____.

Check [to] Creditor

3-38 In preparing Checks to Creditors for materials received into inventory, the accounting system uses the verified _____ _____ .

Materials Invoice

3-39 Recall that other kinds of invoices, called Other Incoming Invoices, include invoices which report purchase information other than inventory. An example is a bill for office supplies; in paying this, the accounting system also issues a _____ to _____ .

Check [to]
Creditor

3-40 The two kinds of invoices leading to the preparation of Checks to Creditors are _____ and _____ Incoming Invoices.

Materials

Other

3-41 Other Incoming Invoices are "bills" for goods which may be new assets or for goods and services chargeable as operating expenses. Other Incoming Invoices may therefore affect both the Balance Sheet and the output that records total revenues and expenses, the _____ _____ .

Income Statement

3-42 To review, the accounting system obtains purchase information from three related inputs: the _____ _____ _____ ; the _____ _____ ; and the _____ _____ , both Materials and Other.

Purchase Order
  Copy

Receiving Record

Incoming Invoice

3-43 The accounting system uses the Purchase Order Copy for two purposes. Together with the Receiving Record, it verifies the legitimacy of the Incoming Invoice called the _____ _____ .

Materials Invoice

3-44 If Inventory Control Records carry on-order balances, the _____ _____ _____ also provides purchase information used to update this output.

Purchase Order
  Copy

3-45 The Receiving Record also has two uses. Together with the Purchase Order Copy, it verifies the legitimacy of the _____ _____ .

Materials Invoice

3-46 Also, since all Inventory Control Records carry *on-hand* balances, the accounting system uses the _____ _____ to increase these balances.

Receiving Record

3-47 Incoming Invoices are of two kinds: _____ and _____ _____ Invoices.

Materials

Other Incoming

3-48 Both kinds of Incoming Invoices lead to the preparation of the outputs by which the firm pays its "bills," the _____ to _____.

Checks [to]
Creditors

3-49 When they are verified, the accounting system uses the Materials Invoice to increase both asset and equity figures carried on the _____ _____.

Balance Sheet

3-50 Other Incoming Invoices may represent new noninventory assets, such as a truck the firm purchased for its use. They always represent new equities, i.e., the liability which is the amount owed to the supplier. Consequently, Other Incoming Invoices also affect the _____ _____.

Balance Sheet

3-51 Some Other Incoming Invoices, such as a phone bill, do not represent new assets, but they do represent new equities, the amount owed. They also represent new expenses. Consequently, Other Incoming Invoices covering expenses affect both the _____ _____ and the _____ _____.

Balance Sheet

Income Statement

3-52 Materials Invoices and Other Incoming Invoices for expenses both involve costs of running the business. Therefore, these inputs also affect the output concerned with costs, the _____ _____ _____.

Cost Analysis
Report

3-53 To review, Materials Invoices have three uses: They ultimately lead to the preparation of _____ to _____ and they affect both the _____ _____ and the _____ _____ Report.

Checks [to]
Creditors

Balance Sheet

Cost Analysis

3-54 Other Incoming Invoices also lead to the ultimate preparation of _____ to _____. In addition, they may affect three other outputs: the _____ _____, the _____ _____, and the _____ _____ _____.

Checks [to]
   Creditors

Balance Sheet

Income Statement

Cost Analysis
   Report

3-55 Sales information is another kind of data used to prepare outputs. Each sales transaction must be accounted for in a variety of ways. To accomplish this, the accounting system uses _____ _____ provided by two inputs, the Customer Order and the Shipping Notice.

sales
   information

3-56 Recall that the Sales Performance Analysis, an output, can be based on either _____ received or shipments made, whichever is more convenient.

orders

3-57 Suppose that a firm required Sales Performance Analyses based on orders received. In this case the accounting system would prepare them from sales information carried on _____ _____.

Customer Orders

3-58 The accounting system generally uses the Customer Order in preparing only one output, the _____ _____ _____, and only if this output is based on _____ _____.

Sales Perform-
   ance Analysis

orders received

3-59 The shipping department makes a record of every shipment to a customer. This record is the second input that provides sales information, the _____ _____.

Shipping Notice

3-60 The Shipping Notice provides sales information used on the Sales Performance Analysis when this is based on _____ made.

shipments

3-61 If based on orders received, Sales Performance Analyses are prepared by the accounting system from sales information provided by the _____ _____. If based on shipments made, Sales Performance Analyses are prepared from information provided on the

_____ _____.

Customer Order

Shipping Notice

3-62 Most firms find it more convenient to prepare _____ _____ _____ on the basis of shipments made. Thus the _____ _____ , rather than the_____ _____ , is the more common source for sales information used on these outputs.

Sales Perform-
ance Analyses

Shipping Notice

Customer Order

3-63 Whenever materials are shipped to a customer, the Inventory Control Record must reflect a corresponding reduction of stock on hand. The Inventory Control Record, then, is another output affected by the input called the

_____ _____.

Shipping Notice

3-64 According to sales information provided by the Shipping Notice, the on-hand balances of the_____ _____ _____ are reduced.

Inventory Control
Record

3-65 If the Inventory Control Record carries a forecasted customer requirement balance, this is also reduced according to sales information provided by the_____

_____.

Shipping Notice

3-66 The Shipping Notice can affect the Inventory Control Record in two ways. According to the sales information provided by the Shipping Notice, the accounting system reduces both the customer requirement and the on-_____ balances of the Inventory Control Record.

[on-] hand

3-67 The Customer Invoice is another output which the accounting system prepares from the Shipping Notice. When the firm ships materials to a customer, the accounting system prepares the Customer Invoice from sales information carried on the _____ _____.

Shipping Notice

3-68 The "bill" which the firm sends to the customer for materials shipped to him is prepared from the Shipping Notice. This output is the _____ _____ .

Customer Invoice

3-69 Shipments to customers represent revenues, with a corresponding increase of an asset, accounts receivable (amounts that customers owe the firm). Therefore, the Shipping Notice ultimately affects an output that reports assets, the _____ _____ , and an output that records revenues, the _____ _____ .

Balance Sheet

Income Statement

3-70 Shipments also represent reductions of another asset, inventory, and an expense, the cost of goods sold. Thus, in a second way, the Shipping Notice affects the same two outputs, the _____ _____ and the

_____ _____ .

Balance Sheet

Income Statement

3-71 The Customer Invoice, the Inventory Control Record, the Sales Performance Analysis, the Balance Sheet, and the Income Statement are outputs affected by the _____

_____ .

Shipping Notice

3-72 The two inputs that provide the accounting system with data called sales information are the _____ _____ and the _____ _____ .

Customer Order

Shipping Notice

3-73 The accounting system uses the Customer Order in preparing one output, the _____ _____

_____ , but only when this is based on _____

_____ .

Sales Perform-
ance Analysis

orders received

3-74 The accounting system uses the Shipping Notice in preparing two outputs, the _____ _____ Analysis (when this is based on shipments made) and the _____ Invoice.

Sales
Performance

Customer

3-75 Within the accounting system, the Shipping Notice also affects three other outputs:

1. _____ _____ Records
2. The _____ _____
3. The _____ _____

1. Inventory Control
2. Balance Sheet
3. Income Statement

3-76 Another kind of input data is inventory transfer information. So far we have discussed only the receipt of inventory and its shipment to customers. However, inventory may move from one control area to another within the firm itself. To account for such movements, the accounting system requires data called _____ _____ _____.

inventory transfer information

3-77 Firms establish control areas, such as raw materials stores, production, and finished goods, and each has separate Inventory Control Records for inventory under its responsibility. Inventory transfer information is necessary to update Inventory Control Records for each _____ _____ involved in the transfer of inventory.

control area

3-78 Internal movements are recorded on some form of movement document, which becomes the input providing inventory transfer information. If the production department of a firm requisitions raw materials using a Stores Requisition, this document would be the input carrying the _____ _____ information required to update the _____ _____ _____ for raw materials stores and production.

inventory transfer

Inventory Control Records

3-79 If production then ships goods to the finished goods storeroom, the storeskeeper might issue a Stores Receipt to record the transfer. The Stores Receipt, then, like the _____ _____ , is an input carrying inventory transfer information.

Stores Requisition

3-80 The difference between these two documents lies only in the direction of movement of the material. For this reason most firms use a single form for recording internal transfers. We shall call this document simply a Stores Requisition. It is the input that provides data called _____ _____ _____ , which is used to update the_____ _____ _____ for each control area affected by a transfer of inventory.

inventory transfer information

Inventory Control Record

3-81 In manufacturing, particularly, costs are added to inventory as it progresses through the various control areas, thus changing its value. Inventory asset values are reported on the Balance Sheet, and therefore the inventory transfer information provided on the _____ _____ may also affect the Balance Sheet.

Stores Requisition

3-82 The Stores Requisition will always affect the _____ _____ _____ for each control area. If inventory values are derived from quantities re-corded on these outputs, the Stores Requisition will also affect the output recording assets, the _____ _____ .

Inventory Control Records

Balance Sheet

3-83 The Stores Requisition, then, provides _____ _____ _____ which may affect the_____ _____ . In all cases, this data affects the_____ _____ _____ for each control area.

inventory transfer information

Balance Sheet

Inventory Control Records

3-84 Inventory transfer information is also recorded on the Scrap Notice, a document issued whenever inventory has to be discarded or scrapped as unusable. Since the Scrap Notice, like the Stores Requisition, records the movement of inventory, the information it carries will af-fect the _____ _____ _____ of the con-trol area involved.

Inventory Control Record

3-85 Unlike the Stores Requisition, which may record inventory movements without any change in quantities or value, the Scrap Notice always records a loss of inventory, an asset. Thus the _____ _____ will always affect the output recording assets, the _____ _____ , as well as the Inventory Control Records.

3-86 Losses of inventory due to scrapping involve an asset reduction, which is also an expense of doing business. The asset reduction reported on the Scrap Notice is reflected on the _____ _____ and the equivalent expense is reflected on the output which lists expenses, the _____ _____ .

3-87 A cost analysis must take into account any scrap losses. The Cost Analysis Report, then, must reflect the data provided by the _____ _____ .

3-88 Thus the Scrap Notice provides inventory transfer information, an inventory reduction due to scrapping. This input, then, will affect inventory values reported on the _____ _____ , expenses reported on the _____ _____ , costs analyzed in the _____ _____ , and quantities carried on the _____ _____ _____ .

3-89 To review, the Stores Requisition and the Scrap Notice are two _____ which provide data called _____ _____ _____ .

3-90 The Inventory Control Records maintained for each _____ _____ within the firm will always be affected by the inventory transfer information provided by the _____ _____ and the _____ _____ .

3-91 When the asset values of inventory are derived from quantities carried on Inventory Control Records, the Stores Requisition will affect the output reflecting assets, the

_____ _____ .

Balance Sheet

3-92 Since it records a loss of inventory, the _____ _____ , unlike the Stores Requisition, will always affect the Balance Sheet, as well as the Income Statement and the Cost Analysis Report.

Scrap Notice

3-93 The Stores Requisition, then, may affect two outputs, the _____ _____ _____ and the

_____ _____ .

Inventory Control Record

Balance Sheet

3-94 The Scrap Notice, on the other hand, affects four outputs:

1. _____ _____ _____
2. _____ _____
3. _____ _____
4. _____ _____ _____

1. Inventory Control Record

2. Balance Sheet

3. Income Statement

4. Cost Analysis Report

3-95 The cash and cash reconciliation inputs are another important group of inputs. When the firm receives a Check from Customer in settlement of his account, this check becomes an input in the group called the _____ and _____ _____ inputs.

cash [and] cash reconciliation

3-96 Before a Check from Customer is deposited in the bank, it must be accounted for as an increase in cash and a decrease in the accounts receivable, two assets recorded on the _____ _____ .

Balance Sheet

3-97 Occasionally a customer may be allowed a cash discount for prompt payment. The amount of the discount is a reduction of revenues. In such cases a Check from Customer may also affect the output reporting revenues and expenses, the _____ _____ .

Income Statement

3-98 The two outputs possibly affected by a Check from Customer are the _____ _____ and the _____ _____ .

Balance Sheet

Income Statement

3-99 The Check from Customer is one input in the group called the _____ and_____ _____ inputs.

cash [and] cash
reconciliation

3-100 The other two inputs in this group are Canceled Checks returned and Bank Statements. Since they do not directly affect outputs but are used instead to *reconcile and verify* existing records, _____ _____ and _____ _____ may be considered together.

Canceled Checks

Bank Statements

3-101 Canceled Checks and Bank Statements, two of the cash and cash reconciliation inputs, do not affect outputs directly. Instead they are used to _____ and _____ existing records.

reconcile [and]
verify

3-102 In the same way that a person verifies the accuracy of his checkbook-stub balance, the firm uses _____ _____ and _____ _____ to ensure that the firm's accounting records are correct.

Canceled Checks

Bank Statements

3-103 Checks from Customers, Canceled Checks, and Bank Statements are three inputs in the group called the _____ and _____ _____ inputs.

cash [and] cash
reconciliation

3-104 Budget Information completes the list of the kinds of data used to prepare outputs. Since inputs related to the Budget carry the same kind of data, they may be considered as a single input, which provides _____ _____ .

Budget
Information

3-105 Recall that the Budget is an output that lists the anticipated _____ and _____ for each profit center within the firm.

revenues

expenses

3-106 Annually, those responsible for the profit centers within the firm submit approved plans of anticipated revenues and expenses for each budget period of the coming year. These plans are the inputs which provide data called _____ _____ .

Budget
    Information

3-107 Budget Information, then, is provided by the approved plans submitted for each profit center. These plans list, for all profit centers, the anticipated revenues and expenses for each _____ _____ of the coming year.

budget period

3-108 Budget Information is summarized and published for the firm as a whole and for each _____ _____. These summaries together constitute the output called the _____ .

profit center

Budget

3-109 Recall that the output that compares the actual and budgeted revenues and expenses is the _____ _____ _____ .

Budget
    Performance
    Analysis

3-110 The planned revenues and expenses shown on the Budget Performance Analysis are the same as those shown on the Budget and are therefore provided by inputs which carry data called _____ _____ .

Budget
    Information

3-111 The two outputs affected by Budget Information are the _____ and the _____ _____ _____ .

Budget

Budget
    Performance
    Analysis

3-112 Budget Information provides the planned revenue and expense figures for the Budget Performance Analysis. Actual revenue and expense figures are derived from most of the _____ which have just been introduced.

inputs

3-113 Before continuing, review mentally the accounting system's inputs grouped according to the kind of data they provide. The first kind of data is payroll information: This is carried on two inputs, the _____ and the _____ _____ .

Timecard

Salary List

3-114 In your own words, describe briefly the content of the Timecard. _____ _____ _____

A record of the hours worked by an hourly paid employee

3-115 Describe the content of the Salary List._____ _____ _____ _____ _____

A list of those employees authorized to receive regular salaries

3-116 Three inputs provide data called purchase information:

1. _____ _____ _____
2. _____ _____
3. _____ _____ , both Materials and Other

1. Purchase Order Copy

2. Receiving Record

3. Incoming Invoice

3-117 The input called the Purchase Order Copy is one of several possible copies of the completed _____ _____ , which the firm retains for accounting purposes.

purchase order

3-118 Describe the content of a Receiving Record._____ _____ _____

A list of items received from a supplier prepared at the time the items are received and accepted

3-119 Describe the content of an Incoming Invoice, both Materials and Other. _____ _____ _____

An itemized "bill" covering materials or services provided by a supplier

3-120 What is the difference between Materials Invoices and Other Incoming Invoices? _____ _____ _____

Materials Invoices cover inventory items received from suppliers; Other Incoming Invoices cover noninventory items

3-121 The two inputs which carry sales information are the _____ _____ and the _____ _____.

Customer Order

Shipping Notice

3-122 The Customer Order is self-explanatory. Describe the content of a Shipping Notice. _____ _____ _____

The record of a shipment to a particular customer

3-123 The two inputs which carry internal transfer information are the _____ _____ and the _____ _____.

Stores Requisition

Scrap Notice

3-124 The Stores Requisition serves what purpose? _____ _____ _____

To record the movement of inventory items from one control area within the firm to another

3-125 Describe the Scrap Notice. _____

_____

_____

A record of inventory items scrapped or discarded as unusable

3-126 Three cash and cash reconciliation inputs are _____ from _____, _____ _____, and _____ _____.

Checks [from] Customers

Canceled Checks

Bank Statements

3-127 The accounting system prepares the Budget and Budget Performance Analyses from input data called Budget Information. Describe this data. _____

_____

_____

Approved plans concerning anticipated revenues and expenses submitted for the firm as a whole and for each profit center

End of Part 3. Turn to the next page for the Review Quiz only when you are ready to complete Part 4.

review quiz on part 3

Identify each of the following as either an input (I) or an output (O).

1. Balance Sheet _____
2. Budget _____
3. Materials Invoice _____
4. Customer Invoice _____
5. Other Incoming Invoice _____
6. Salary List _____
7. Payroll Check _____
8. Timecard _____
9. Inventory Control Record _____
10. Budget Performance Analysis _____
11. Purchase Order Copy _____
12. Budget Information _____
13. Cash and cash reconciliation items _____
14. Sales Performance Analysis _____
15. Receiving Record _____
16. Shipping Notice (prepared by shipping department) _____
17. Cost Analysis Report _____
18. Scrap Notice _____
19. Income Statement _____
20. Stores Requisition _____
21. Check to Creditor _____
22. Customer Order _____
23. Check from Customer _____

After each of the following descriptions place the letter or letters corresponding to the appropriate inputs. (An item may be used more than once.)

A Timecard	G Stores Requisition
B Salary List	H Scrap Notice
C Materials Invoice	I Shipping Notice
D Purchase Order Copy	J Customer Order
E Receiving Record	K Budget Information
F Other Incoming Invoice	L Check from Customer

24. Received in settlement of a customer's account: _____
25. Contains descriptions of items shipped to customers: _____
26. A "bill" for goods (other than inventory) or services provided by suppliers: _____
27. A listing of employees authorized to receive salaries: _____
28. Contains data concerning future plans for the company's operations: _____
29. Descriptions of goods or services desired by a customer: _____
30. A record of hours worked by an hourly paid employee: _____
31. Description of inventory item which must be disposed of as unusable: _____
32. Description of items ordered from suppliers: _____

33. A record of items transferred from one control area within a firm to another: _____
34. A "bill" for inventory shipped to the firm by a supplier: _____
35. A notice of the arrival of material from a supplier: _____
36. Provide payroll information: _____, _____
37. Provide purchase information: _____, _____, _____, _____
38. Provide sales information: _____, _____
39. Provide inventory transfer information: _____, _____
40. Matched with Materials Invoice to verify its legitimacy: _____, _____

PART 4
major accounting responsibilities

4-1 You have seen that inputs provide the information from which the accounting system prepares its "end products" called _____.

outputs

4-2 Accounting includes the methods whereby the data provided on _____ is processed to lead to the preparation of useful documents called _____.

inputs

outputs

4-3 A knowledge of the principles and procedures that accountants use in preparing outputs from inputs is a knowledge of _____.

accounting

4-4 The accounting system has three major responsibilities: processing and recording, financial reporting, and control reporting. Refer to Panel B; keep the table in front of you as you proceed through Part 4. You see listed on Panel B the accounting system's responsibilities:

1. _____ and _____
2. _____ _____
3. _____ _____

1. processing [and] recording

2. financial reporting

3. control reporting

4-5 The first accounting responsibility is to process and record all "events" which affect the status of the firm's assets and equities. For instance, if the firm purchased a fleet of cars, you know that the accounting system must _____ and _____ this event.

process

record

4-6 A transaction is any event which affects the status of the firm's assets and equities. The accounting system's responsibility, then, is to process and record _____.

transactions

4-7 For instance, when the firm issues a Check to Creditor, this event is a transaction because it affects both an asset (Cash) and an equity (Accounts Payable, a liability). The accounting system is therefore responsible for_____ and _____this transaction.

processing

recording

4-8 When the firm receives a check in payment from a customer, the accounting system must also process and record this _____.

transaction

4-9 Because it records both a sale and a shipment of products from inventory, a Customer Invoice records a change in the status of the firm's _____ and _____.

assets

equities

4-10 When the firm ships materials from inventory this affects two assets: It reduces Inventory and increases Accounts Receivable. Preparing Customer Invoices is therefore part of _____ and _____ changes in the status of the firm's assets and equities.

processing

recording

4-11 Another accounting responsibility is financial reporting. The firm's managers, owners, and creditors need information about the firm's financial position and the factors changing it, and they depend upon the accounting system to perform this _____ _____ function.

financial

reporting

4-12 The Balance Sheet and the Income Statement are related to financial reporting. The output which records the firm's assets and equities and provides a record of the financial position as of a specific date is the _____ _____.

Balance Sheet

4-13 The Balance Sheet does not include the factors which changed the firm's financial position between successive Balance Sheets. Some of these factors are shown on the related output, the _____ _____.

Income Statement

4-14 When considering the Balance Sheet and the Income
Statement, you know that these two outputs are prepared to
fulfill a second major accounting responsibility, that of
_____ _____ .

financial
reporting

4-15 A third major accounting responsibility is control reporting. For instance, in preparing Inventory Control Records the accounting system fulfills a part of its responsibility
of _____ _____ .

control
reporting

4-16 Sales Performance Analyses and Cost Analysis Reports are two other outputs besides _____ _____
_____ which the accounting system prepares for control reporting.

Inventory
Control
Records

4-17 Budgets and Budget Performance Analyses are also
outputs prepared to fulfill the responsibility of _____
_____ .

control
reporting

4-18 Control reporting provides management with detailed
records that permit control of the internal operation of the
firm. For instance, in order to plan inventory procurement,
material control personnel refer to _____ _____
_____ .

Inventory
Control
Records

4-19 Control reporting also provides detailed reports on
both sales and costs. The two outputs that management refers to for information about sales and costs are _____
_____ _____ and _____ _____
_____ .

Sales Performance
Analyses

Cost Analysis
Reports

4-20 Budgeting is another method of internal control. To
provide management with the tools for budgetary control,
the accounting system prepares two outputs, _____
and _____ _____ _____ .

Budgets

Budget
Performance
Analyses

4-21 The accounting system has three major responsibilities: processing and recording transactions, financial reporting, and _____ _____ .

control
reporting

4-22 Processing and recording involves several distinct activities, one of which is the payroll activity. When the accounting system calculates employees' gross earnings, deductions, and take-home pay from Timecards and Salary Lists and then issues Payroll Checks, it performs the

_____ _____.

payroll activity

4-23 The two inputs that the accounting system uses in the payroll activity are the _____ and the _____

_____.

Timecard
Salary List

4-24 Calculating employees' gross earnings, deductions, and take-home pay is part of the accounting function called the _____ _____.

payroll activity

4-25 The outputs resulting from the payroll activity are the _____ _____ , issued in the amounts of each employee's take-home pay.

Payroll Checks

4-26 Processing and recording includes another activity, the billing activity. The accounting system prepares Customer Invoices from Shipping Notices in performing the

_____ _____.

billing activity

4-27 The accounting system uses input information provided on _____ _____ to prepare Customer Invoices.

Shipping Notices

4-28 Determining prices for each item and calculating total prices for all items in a particular shipment are parts of the _____ _____.

billing activity

4-29 After calculation of the total price of a shipment, an output called the _____ _____ is prepared.

Customer Invoice

4-30 Processing and recording involves five distinct activities. Among them are the two just discussed, the_____ _____ and the _____ _____.

payroll activity
billing activity

4-31 Processing and recording also includes the payables activity. When the firm issues Checks to Creditors, you know that this is the result of the _____ _____ .

payables activity

4-32 Remember that two kinds of Incoming Invoices--Materials and Other--lead to the preparation of _____ to _____ .

Checks [to] Creditors

4-33 The accounting system verifies Materials Invoices by comparing them with Purchase Order Copies and Receiving Records, and then issues Checks to Creditors. This processing and recording function is part of the _____ _____ .

payables activity

4-34 The accounting system must also verify Other Incoming Invoices, such as invoices covering office supplies, before preparing the _____ to _____ that pay these invoices.

Checks [to] Creditors

4-35 You know that the accounting system must verify all Incoming Invoices as part of the _____ _____ .

payables activity

4-36 The processing and recording responsibility includes another activity, cash receipt and reconciliation. In processing and recording the receipt of Checks from Customers and reconciling the firm's records with the bank's, the accounting system is performing the _____ _____ and _____ activity.

cash receipt [and] reconciliation

4-37 No outputs result from the cash receipt and reconciliation activity. However, the accounting system must record payment of the Customer Invoice when it receives a _____ from _____ .

Check [from] Customer

4-38 When the firm receives Canceled Checks along with the Bank Statement, it must reconcile its own records with the bank's. This too is part of the _____ _____ and _____ activity.

cash receipt [and] reconciliation

4-39 The bookkeeping activity is the last of five separate activities by which the accounting system fulfills one of its major responsibilities, that of _____ and _____ transactions.

processing

recording

4-40 The bookkeeping activity involves the recording of all events affecting the financial position of the firm. For instance, recording a cash receipt from a customer, which would increase the firm's Cash assets and correspondingly decrease its Accounts Receivable assets, is part of the _____ activity.

bookkeeping

4-41 The bookkeeping activity involves recording the financial effects of all other processing and recording activities. This includes recording payroll expenses, cash paid to employees, and earnings withheld for payment to the government. This data is computed by another activity, the _____ activity.

payroll

4-42 When the firm issues Checks to Creditors, the bookkeeping activity records the reduction of cash assets and the corresponding reduction of the creditors' claims, or equities. Issuing Checks to Creditors is part of the _____ activity.

payables

4-43 The bookkeeping activity also records sales to customers and the resulting increases in the Accounts Receivable from Customer Invoices prepared by the _____ activity.

billing

4-44 Recording all events affecting the financial position of the firm is the function of the fifth activity of processing and recording, the _____ activity.

bookkeeping

4-45 A second major accounting responsibility is financial reporting. Recall that this involves preparing two outputs, the _____ _____ and the _____ _____.

Balance Sheet

Income Statement

4-46 In preparing the Balance Sheet and the Income Statement, you would *abstract* and *summarize* data from the
"books," or Ledgers. This activity is necessary to fulfill
the responsibility of _____ _____.

financial
reporting

4-47 Financial reporting includes the preparation of the
Balance Sheet and the Income Statement from data which is
_____ and _____ from the "books," or Ledgers.

abstracted
summarized

4-48 In accounting terminology, the "books," or Ledgers,
are in a sense the inputs in the financial reporting function;
yet they are in another sense the outputs of the bookkeeping
activity. However, since they do not introduce data from
outside the accounting system and since they are not true
"end products," you do not refer to them either as
_____ or _____.

outputs
inputs

4-49 The function of the Ledgers is really quite simple.
For instance, you learned earlier that purchase inputs affect the Balance Sheet. However, purchase inputs first affect
the Ledgers. Data from the Ledgers are in turn _____
and _____ for use on the Balance Sheet.

abstracted
summarized

4-50 Similarly, all input data which affects the financial reports first appears on intermediate records, the_____.

Ledgers

4-51 Financial reporting, in simple terms, involves abstracting and summarizing data from the Ledgers and recording this data on two outputs, the_____
_____ and the _____ _____.

Balance Sheet
Income Statement

4-52 A third accounting responsibility is control reporting.
This responsibility is best understood in terms of specific
activities, each of which has a particular "end product," or
_____.

output

4-53 Control reporting includes the inventory control activity. Maintenance of a perpetual record of units of stock
on hand, together with customer demand and on-order information, is known as the _____ _____ activity.

inventory
control

4-54 Note that the Inventory Control Record contains balances for each separate item in quantities or units rather than in dollars. This differs from the recording of the total dollar cost of inventory assets, which is part of the _____ activity.

bookkeeping

4-55 Maintaining perpetual Inventory Control Records involves three kinds of input data: purchase information, sales information, and internal transfer information. You remember that on-order balances of Inventory Control Records are increased from data contained on one of the inputs carrying purchase information, the _____ _____ _____.

Purchase Order
Copy

4-56 On-order balances are reduced on the basis of another input providing purchase information, the _____ _____.

Receiving
Record

4-57 In addition to reducing on-order balances, the purchase information contained on the Receiving Record also increases the on-_____ balances of Inventory Control Records.

[on-] hand

4-58 The Shipping Notice (providing sales information) and the Stores Requisition and Scrap Notice (providing internal transfer information) affect the _____ _____ _____ by decreasing the on-_____ balances of these records.

Inventory Control
Records

[on-] hand

4-59 The Stores Requisition, when used as a receipt, increases the on-_____ balance of Inventory Control Records for the receiving control area.

[on-] hand

4-60 Finally, a Customer Order may increase a customer requirement figure, while the _____ _____ reduces this figure after the requirement is satisfied by shipment.

Shipping Notice

4-61 Of course, Inventory Control Records are not maintained as a clerical exercise. Management uses them to determine needs for additional purchasing and production. Thus, in maintaining perpetual Inventory Control Records from purchase, sales, and inventory transfer information, the accounting system fulfills one of its control reporting activities, the _____ _____ activity.

inventory control

4-62 The second control reporting activity is the preparation of Sales Performance Analyses. If sales management analyzes sales on an orders-received basis, you would prepare Sales Performance Analyses from sales information contained on the input called the _____ _____.

Customer Order

4-63 If management analyzes sales on a shipments basis, you would prepare Sales Performance Analyses from another input providing sales information, the _____ _____.

Shipping Notice

4-64 Abstracting and summarizing sales information into meaningful categories, such as sales territory, product, and customer, is a control reporting activity leading to the preparation of _____ _____ _____.

Sales Performance Analyses

4-65 The third control reporting activity leads to the preparation of the Cost Analysis Report. Abstracting and summarizing payroll cost and purchase cost information is part of the control reporting responsibility known as the _____ _____ activity.

cost analysis

4-66 Labor costs are available from the earnings figures calculated as part of the _____ activity.

payroll

4-67 Material and operating costs are abstracted and summarized from data contained on Incoming Invoices and recorded as part of the _____ activity.

payables

4-68 Abstracting and summarizing cost figures calculated as part of both the payroll and the payables activity is called the _____ _____ activity.

cost analysis

4-69 Control reporting involves activities leading to the preparation of five specific outputs. Three of these just considered are:

1. _____ _____ Record
2. _____ _____ Analysis
3. _____ _____ Report

1. Inventory Control
2. Sales Performance
3. Cost Analysis

4-70 The last two control reporting activities deal with budgeting. They involve the preparation of two specific outputs, the _____ and the _____ _____ _____ .

Budget

Budget Performance Analysis

4-71 Management submits Budget Information, the planned revenues and expenses for the firm as a whole and for each profit center within the firm. From this input data, the accounting system prepares the _____ .

Budget

4-72 In preparing the Budget, the accounting system records and summarizes the profit plans—planned revenues and expenses—which management provides in the form of input data called _____ _____ .

Budget Information

4-73 Budget Information, summarized for the Budget, and information recorded by the bookkeeping activity on actual revenues and expenses, serve as the basis for the output related to the Budget, the Budget _____ _____ .

Performance Analysis

4-74 The Budget Performance Analysis records planned revenues and expenses, together with_____ revenues and expenses.

actual

4-75 In preparing the Budget Performance Analysis, it would be necessary for you to abstract and summarize information recorded in the_____ activity and report it together with input data called _____ information.

bookkeeping

Budget

4-76 Control reporting, then, consists in accounting activities leading to five specific outputs. These are:

1. _____ _____ _____
2. _____ _____ _____
3. _____ _____ _____
4. _____ _____ _____
5. _____

1. Inventory Control Record
2. Sales Performance Analysis
3. Cost Analysis Report
4. Budget
5. Budget Performance Analysis

4-77 To review, list the three *major* objectives or responsibilities of the accounting system.

1. _____ and _____
2. _____   _____
3. _____   _____

1. processing [and] recording
2. financial reporting
3. control reporting

4-78 Can you recall the five activities related to processing and recording?

1. _____
2. _____
3. _____
4. _____ _____ and _____
5. _____

1. payroll
2. payables
3. billing
4. cash receipt [and] reconciliation
5. bookkeeping

4-79 List here two outputs that the accounting system prepares to fulfill the responsibility of financial reporting.

1. _____ _____
2. _____ _____

1. Balance Sheet
2. Income Statement

End of Part 4. Turn to the next page for the Review Quiz only when you are ready to complete Part 5.

review quiz on part 4

Complete the following sentences.

1. The three major responsibilities of the accounting system are:
   (a) _____ and _____
   (b) _____ reporting
   (c) _____ reporting

After each of the following activities or outputs, indicate by abbreviation the related responsibility.

   PR Processing and recording
   FR Financial reporting
   CR Control reporting

2. Budget Performance Analysis _____
3. Balance Sheet _____
4. Bookkeeping activity _____
5. Cash receipt and reconciliation activity _____
6. Income Statement _____
7. Cost Analysis Report _____
8. Sales Performance Analysis _____
9. Billing activity _____
10. Inventory Control Record _____
11. Payroll activity _____
12. Payables activity _____
13. Budget _____

Complete the following sentences.

14. The _____ activity uses two inputs, the Timecard and the Salary List, in preparing its primary output, the _____ _____.
15. The _____ activity uses the Shipping Notice as an input in preparing its primary output, the _____ _____.
16. The _____ activity involves processing Incoming Invoices and, after verification and approval, issuing _____ to _____.
17. The inputs to the _____ _____ and _____ activity are Checks from Customers, Canceled Checks, and _____ _____.
18. The _____ _____ responsibility involves abstracting and summarizing data from the Ledger and preparing the _____ _____ and the Income Statement.
19. Budgets and Budget Performance Analyses both list data from the input data called _____ _____.
20. The Budget Performance Analysis lists the _____ revenues and expenses shown on the Budget, together with the _____ revenues and expenses for the budget period.

PART 5
accounting records

5-1 In fulfilling the financial reporting responsibility, the accounting system prepares two reports that are of great importance in financial planning. Whenever management needs to see the financial position of the firm and some of the factors affecting it, it refers to these two outputs, the Balance Sheet and the Income Statement.

No response required

5-2 Part 5 deals with the basic concepts you need to know in order to see how the accounting system fulfills its responsibility dealing with the Balance Sheet and the Income Statement, the _____ _____ responsibility.

financial reporting

5-3 All the figures listed on the Balance Sheet and the Income Statement are in dollar amounts. Since data from inputs may be in pounds, hours, units, and so forth, they must be converted to _____ equivalents for use on the Balance Sheet and the Income Statement.

dollar

5-4 In order to be meaningful, the dollar amounts listed on the Balance Sheet and the Income Statement are classified by accounts. When you refer to these outputs, you will see such classifications as Cash, Inventory, Sales, and Cost of Goods Sold. These classifications are called_____.

accounts

5-5 Cash and Inventory are examples of accounts shown on the Balance Sheet. Sales and Cost of Goods Sold are examples of_____ shown on the Income Statement.

accounts

5-6 The total amount remaining in any account is called the balance. For instance, the dollar amount listed after Cash on the Balance Sheet is the_____ in the Cash account.

balance

5-7 The dollar amounts are listed on the Balance Sheet and the Income Statement according to meaningful classifications called _____.

accounts

5-8 The total amount in any account listed on the Balance Sheet or the Income Statement is called the _____ in that account.

balance

5-9 For instance, if you saw on the Balance Sheet the listing

Cash $2,000

you would know that the _____ account had a balance of $_____.

Cash

$2,000

5-10 If you saw the listing

Inventory $5,000

you would know that the Inventory _____ had a _____ of $5,000.

account

balance

5-11 Accountants therefore categorize and store information in individual accounts—as many as required to classify properly the data affecting the firm. Accountants call the file in which all accounts are kept the Ledger. When preparing the Balance Sheet, you would obtain the balance in each separate account from the _____.

Ledger

5-12 The Ledger is a file containing separate storage records called _____.

accounts

5-13 When preparing the Balance Sheet and the Income Statement, accountants find the data on each account in the

_____.

Ledger

5-14 The figures that change account balances result from business "events," or transactions. Since transactions affect different accounts, you would analyze each _____ to see which _____ it affects.

transaction

accounts

5-15 The detailed instructions listing the accounts affected by a transaction and the amounts affecting these accounts is called an entry. After analyzing a transaction, you would make an _____ to the appropriate accounts.

5-16 An entry is said to be posted when the accountant has transferred the entry amounts to the proper accounts in the

_____.

5-17 When someone says, "The posting is completed," you know that all the _____ amounts have been _____ to their respective accounts in the Ledger.

5-18 Transferring an entry amount to an account in the Ledger is called _____.

5-19 An entry is said to be posted when the amounts have been entered under the proper accounts in the Ledger, thus changing the _____ in those _____.

5-20 For example, the receipt of a customer's check for $450 is an "event" that affects the firm's assets and is therefore a transaction. Its effect is to increase the balance in the Cash account by $_____; at the same time it reduces the balance in the Accounts Receivable account by $_____.

5-21 The purchase and receipt of inventory costing $900 is another type of transaction. When the firm receives the goods and the invoice, the accountant must make an entry. He will [increase/reduce]_____ the Inventory account balance by $900; at the same time he will increase the balance in the account recording the amounts owed to suppliers, called Accounts Payable, by $_____.

5-22 The payment of the $900 invoiced for the goods purchased is another transaction. The balance in the Cash account must be _____ by $900, while at the same time the balance in the Accounts Payable account must be _____ by $_____.

5-23 Think for a moment of all the daily transactions which affect the balance in an account such as Cash. Since the volume of these transactions is enormous, it may be impractical to_____the entries to the Ledger accounts as soon as the transactions occur.

post

5-24 Accounting is usually more efficient when entries can be stored temporarily for posting at some more convenient time. Accountants therefore use a temporary file known as a Journal to store_____for later posting.

entries

5-25 The process of analyzing transactions and recording the proper entries in a temporary file called a _____ is known as *journalizing*.

Journal

5-26 If you received several transactions at one time, you would not post the entries directly to the Ledger. For convenience, you would journalize them. This means that you would analyze the_____ and store the resulting _____ temporarily in the_____.

transactions

entries

Journal

5-27 The first step in accounting procedure, from the receipt of the transaction inputs to the preparation of the Balance Sheet and the Income Statement, is that the accountant analyzes transactions and stores the resulting entries temporarily in the Journal. This procedure is called _____.

journalizing

5-28 At a more convenient time the entries accumulated in the Journal are posted to the _____.

Ledger

5-29 The Ledger contains each separate account, with all posted entries included in their respective accounts. By taking the beginning balance of an account and by adding or subtracting subsequent entries, the accountant can determine the current_____in any account.

balance

5-30 Only the account balances appear on the Balance Sheet. When preparing the Balance Sheet, you would determine the balance of each account from the_____.

Ledger

5-31 Accountants always prepare the Balance Sheet *yearly.* Some firms also require it *monthly.* If you were responsible for preparing the Balance Sheet, you would know that your firm would certainly require one at least every_____ and, in addition, might require one every_____.

year

month

5-32 The Balance Sheet shows the financial position of the firm as of a particular *date.* When making major financial decisions, management will refer to the most recent Balance Sheet in order to see the firm's _____

_____.

financial
    position

5-33 The Balance Sheet lists assets and equities, thereby showing the firm's financial position at the_____of the statement.

date

5-34 In reviewing the firm's financial position, management refers to the Balance Sheet for a listing of the firm's _____ and _____.

assets

equities

5-35 Now refer to Panel C. You see there a listing of Balance Sheet accounts in the conventional order. Assets are properties having a monetary value, and in the United States, assets are always listed on the _____ side of the Balance Sheet.

left

5-36 Properties which have a monetary value to the firm are listed as_____on the left side of the Balance Sheet.

assets

5-37 In preparing a conventional report of the firm's financial position, you would list the account balances for properties as assets on the_____ side of the _____ _____.

left

Balance Sheet

5-38 The asset accounts, you will notice, are grouped in divisions. The first, Current Assets, includes the accounts for cash and properties which, in the normal course of business, will be converted to cash within a *year.* Inventories, then, are_____ Assets.

Current

5-39 You would list account balances for the Cash account and other accounts for properties which will be converted to cash within a_____under Current Assets.

year

5-40 As you might suspect, Fixed and Other Assets are those which, in the normal course of business, will *not* be converted to cash within a year. Current, Fixed, and Other Assets are listed on the_____ side of the _____
_____.

left

Balance Sheet

5-41 Refer to Panel C and see that this simplified Balance Sheet has no Other Assets accounts listed. Panel C shows only Current and Fixed Assets, but it is important to remember that many Balance Sheets carry a third division of assets called_____Assets.

Other

5-42 Fixed and Other Assets are those which normally will not be converted to cash within a_____of the Balance Sheet date.

year

5-43 It is easy to see that account balances for such long-lasting properties as plant and equipment will be grouped under the division of_____Assets.

Fixed

5-44 When preparing the Balance Sheet, you would list assets on the left side in three divisions:_____Assets;
_____ Assets; and one not shown on Panel C,
_____ Assets.

Current

Fixed

Other

5-45 The Current Asset account whose balance is the total amount of cash on hand and in banks as of the Balance Sheet date is the_____ account.

Cash

5-46 The total of all unpaid Customer Invoices represents the amount of the customers' obligations to the firm. This amount is the balance of the Current Asset account called
_____ _____.

Accounts
Receivable

5-47 The balance of the Accounts Receivable account is the total of all _____ _____ unpaid at the date of the Balance Sheet.

Customer
Invoices

5-48 The total *cost* of merchandise that the firm has on hand or to which it has legal title is the balance of another Current Asset account, _____.

Inventory

5-49 The balance of the Inventory account is the total _____ of merchandise that the firm has on hand or to which it has legal title.

cost

5-50 Since properties listed under Cash, Accounts Receivable, and Inventory will, in the normal course of business, be converted to cash within a year, these are called _____ _____ accounts.

Current Asset

5-51 Remember that besides Current Assets, two other groups of assets are recorded on the Balance Sheet. These are _____ Assets and _____ Assets (not shown on Panel C).

Fixed
Other

5-52 The balance of the first Fixed Asset account on Panel C represents the total *cost* of real property owned by the firm. This is the _____ account.

Land

5-53 The balance of the Fixed Asset account called Land represents the total _____ of real property that the firm owns.

cost

5-54 The balances of the two other Fixed Asset accounts are also cost figures. These accounts are _____ and _____.

Buildings
Equipment

5-55 The balances of the Buildings and Equipment accounts represent the total _____ of such assets.

cost

5-56   Later on in this text you will learn that some Fixed
Assets are "depreciated." For the time being remember
that the balances of both the _____ and the _____
accounts represent the total _____ of these assets.

Buildings

Equipment

cost

5-57   Land, Buildings, and Equipment, since they are *not,*
in the normal course of business, converted to cash within
a year, are _____ _____ accounts.

Fixed Asset

5-58   Refer again to Panel C. On the right is a list of the
firm's equities. Equity account balances are claims against,
or sources of, the assets, and they are customarily listed on
the _____ side of the Balance Sheet.

right

5-59   It is important to remember that equity account balances represent claims against assets. In other words, the
properties listed as assets are owned or claimed by someone, in the amounts listed on the right side of the Balance
Sheet as _____ .

equities

5-60   Notice on Panel C that one of the accounts under equities is Wages and Salaries Payable. The balance in this account is $ _____ .

$5,000

5-61   What this means in accounting terms is simply that,
at the time this Balance Sheet was prepared, the firm's employees had claims for their wages and salaries against the
firm's total _____ amounting to $5,000.

assets

5-62   You can see that all the accounts listed on the right
side of the Balance Sheet under _____ may be viewed
as claims against total assets.

equities

5-63   Assets, then, are properties to which the firm has
legal title at the date of the Balance Sheet. Equities, on the
other hand, are _____ against the firm's total
_____ at this same date.

claims

assets

5-64 It is important to notice that no single equity account matches a single asset account. Each equity account balance is a claim, not against a particular asset, but rather against the amount listed at the bottom of the left side as_____ _____.

Total Assets

5-65 It will help you to understand the nature of equities if you think of the Balance Sheet as representing two sides of the same coin. The coin in this case is the properties. Accountants list the properties themselves on the left side of the Balance Sheet under_____; they list the various sources of assets, or claims against them, on the right side under_____.

assets

equities

5-66 Since all the firm's assets are listed in one column and all the sources of these assets listed in another column, you can probably guess why this output is called the _____Sheet.

Balance

5-67 Equity accounts are also divided into meaningful groups. The first major group includes the liabilities, or creditors' claims, that the firm must settle within a year of the Balance Sheet date. The accounts in this group are called Current_____.

Liabilities

5-68 Equity account balances listed as Current Liabilities are creditors' claims that the firm must settle within a _____of the Balance Sheet date.

year

5-69 In general, creditors' claims are legally collectible. The firm is "liable" for them, and they are therefore called _____.

liabilities

5-70 Liabilities which the firm must settle within a year of the Balance Sheet date are called _____ _____.

Current
Liabilities

5-71 Obviously the balance of the Wages and Salaries Payable account must be settled within a year of the_____ _____date; therefore, the Wages and Salaries Payable account is a _____ _____ account.

Balance Sheet

Current
Liability

5-72 The account balances grouped together as Current Liabilities are amounts of creditors' claims. These are listed on the _____ side of the Balance Sheet under the general title_____.

right

equities

5-73 Frequently firms obtain funds from creditors on a long-term basis and thus incur long-term debts. Management needs to know, of course, which debts the firm must pay within a year (the Current Liabilities). It also needs to know which debts are not due within a year (the_____-_____ Debt).

Long-term

5-74 As you can see on Panel C, Mortgage Payable is an example of a _____-_____ _____ account.

Long-term Debt

5-75 Liabilities, then, represent creditors' claims against total assets. The two groups of liabilities are_____ _____ and _____-_____ _____.

Current
Liabilities
Long-term Debt

5-76 The first Current Liability account is Accounts Payable. At the Balance Sheet date, all existing obligations payable within one year to creditors for goods and services that the firm has received are represented by the balance in the _____ _____ account.

Accounts
Payable

5-77 The balance in the Accounts Payable account represents all existing obligations of the firm payable within one year to its _____ for goods and services which the firm has received.

creditors

5-78 The second Current Liability account is Wages and Salaries Payable. At the date of the Balance Sheet, all unpaid obligations which the firm has to its employees for services rendered are represented by the balance in the _____ and _____ _____ account.

Wages [and]
Salaries
Payable

5-79 The Wages and Salaries Payable account balance represents the firm's unpaid obligations to its _____ at the Balance Sheet date.

employees

5-80 The third kind of Current Liability account shown on Panel C is Notes Payable. Often firms will borrow money on notes due in less than a year. The amount still due on such notes at the Balance Sheet date is represented by the balance in the _____ _____ account.

Notes Payable

5-81 The firm of course must pay its taxes within a year of the Balance Sheet date. Another Current Liability account, whose balance represents unpaid taxes at the Balance Sheet date, is the _____ _____ account.

Taxes Payable

5-82 You know that the balances in Current Liability accounts represent the firm's obligations to creditors which must be paid within a _____ of the _____ _____ date.

year

Balance Sheet

5-83 Four Current Liability accounts representing creditors' claims that the firm must settle within a year are:

1. _____ _____
2. _____ and _____ _____
3. _____ _____
4. _____ _____

1. Accounts Payable
2. Wages [and] Salaries Payable
3. Notes Payable
4. Taxes Payable

5-84 The two groups of liabilities shown on Panel C are _____ _____ and _____ - _____ Debt.

Current Liabilities

Long-term

5-85 Long-term Debts are creditors' claims which the firm is not obliged to pay within a _____.

year

5-86 The balance in the only Long-term Debt account shown on Panel C represents the balance due on outstanding mortgages. This account is called _____ _____.

Mortgage Payable

5-87 The balance in the Mortgage Payable account represents the amount due on an outstanding mortgage at the date __/__/__.

12/31/196B

5-88 You can distinguish between Current Liability accounts and Long-term Debt accounts if you know whether or not the balance of a particular account must be paid within a _____ of the Balance Sheet _____.

year

date

5-89 For instance, if a note or debt is *not* due until five years from the date of the Balance Sheet, you would list it on the Balance Sheet as a _____-_____ _____.

Long-term Debt

5-90 The balances of the two groups of liabilities listed on the Balance Sheet—Current Liabilities and Long-term Debt— are totaled on the Balance Sheet as_____ _____.

Total
   Liabilities

5-91 The Total Liabilities figure represents the total amount of the claims which the firm's creditors have against Total _____.

Assets

5-92 The third group of equity accounts do *not* represent legal liabilities. This group includes the accounts which together are the Owners' Equity, or Net Worth. The balances in these accounts are subtotaled after the caption Total _____ _____.

Net Worth

5-93 If a person invested $1,000 in the stock of the firm, he would not be a creditor, but an owner. Consequently, the amount listed as Total Net Worth is the amount of the owners' claim against the assets; it is also called the _____ Equity.

Owners'

5-94 It is obvious from this that the two terms Net Worth and _____ _____ mean the same thing.

Owners' Equity

5-95 If a person bought $1,000 of the firm's stock, his purchase would affect the Net Worth account whose balance represents the amount of assets invested in the business by the owners. This is the _____ _____ and _____-_____ _____ account.

Capital Stock
[and] Paid-in
Surplus

5-96 The balance of the Net Worth account called Capital Stock and Paid-in Surplus represents the amount of _____ invested in the business by the _____ .

assets

owners

5-97 You can see that Total Net Worth is the sum of the amount of owners' investment in the Capital Stock and Paid-in Surplus account and the balance in the _____ _____ account.

Retained Earnings

5-98 The two accounts whose balances represent the owners' share of the total assets are the _____ _____ and Paid-in Surplus and the _____ _____ accounts.

Capital Stock

Retained Earnings

5-99 The amount reflecting the portion of Total Assets remaining after considering creditors' claims is shown under the caption _____ _____ _____ .

Total Net Worth

5-100 The two kinds of claims included under equities are creditors' equities, or Total Liabilities, and Owners' Equity, or Total Net Worth. Current Liabilities and Long-term Debt are subtotaled as _____ _____ on the Balance Sheet.

Total

Liabilities

5-101 Owners' Equity, the amount of Total Assets which the owners have provided, is subtotaled as _____ _____ _____ on the Balance Sheet.

Total Net Worth

5-102 You can see now why this output is called the Balance Sheet. Since the Total Equities represent nothing more or less than the claims against, or sources of, the Total Assets, the two amounts must necessarily _____ .

balance (equal)

5-103 Remember the comparison between the two sides of a Balance Sheet and the two sides of a coin. Although there is no item-for-item matching between asset and equity accounts, Total Assets will *always* equal _____ _____ .

Total Equities

5-104 Whether you think of equities as claims against assets or as sources of assets, it is clear that the total of the
equity accounts must equal the total of the asset accounts.
The Balance Sheet, therefore, follows a necessary equation:

Net Worth

        Assets = Equities
or   Assets = Liabilities + _____ _____

5-105 This is the fundamental accounting equation, and like
all equations, it can be rearranged as long as the equality
is maintained. If you know that Assets equal Equities, you
also know that_____ equal _____ plus Net
Worth.

Assets

Liabilities

5-106 You see on Panel C that Total Assets ($_____)
equal Total Liabilities ($_____) plus Total Net Worth
($_____).

$100,000

$64,000

$36,000

5-107 You can also rearrange the fundamental equation to
emphasize Net Worth. Since Assets equal Equities,

Liabilities

        Net Worth = Assets − _____

5-108 A net asset figure does not appear as such on the
Balance Sheet, but it is important for an understanding of
Net Worth to know the meaning of net assets. The amount of
total assets remaining after deducting the total liabilities is
what accountants call _____ _____.

net assets

5-109 Since net assets will necessarily equal Owners'
Equity, or Net Worth, you can find the amount of net assets
using the same form of the fundamental equation which em-
phazises Net Worth:

Assets

Liabilities

    Net Assets = Total _____ − Total _____

5-110 The Total Assets ($_____) minus the Total
Liabilities ($_____), shown on Panel C, leave net
assets of $_____.

$100,000

$64,000

$36,000

5-111 You can now better understand what the Retained Earnings account represents. The amount of net assets originally contributed by the owners is reflected by the balance of the Capital Stock and Paid-in Surplus account. Net assets in excess of this contribution is reflected by the _____ _____ account.

Retained Earnings

5-112 Net assets, then, is the amount of total assets remaining after deducting all liabilities. The net asset figure would be reflected by the _____ _____ , or Owners' Equity, figure.

Net Worth

5-113 Consider entries in the light of what you know about the Balance Sheet. The reason for entries, of course, is that transactions occur which change account balances. Remembering the fundamental equation, you can see that if the result of an entry is an increase in total assets, there must also be an _____ in total equities.

increase

5-114 Refer now to Panel D. Here in a simplified form is a Balance Sheet showing the result of a firm's first transaction. The owners have invested $15,000 cash in the business in return for stock. The Cash account therefore shows a balance of $_____ .

$15,000

5-115 Since Total Assets equal Total Equities, an equity account also reflects the same transaction. On Panel D you see that the accountant has opened an equity account to reflect the owners' investment. This is the _____ _____ and Paid-in Surplus account.

Capital Stock

5-116 You can see how the accountant prepared this Balance Sheet to reflect the single transaction. The $15,000 cash is an asset in the firm's possession; the source of this asset is the owners' original investment, $_____ .

$15,000

5-117 Refer now to Panel E, a Balance Sheet for the same firm, which reflects one additional transaction. The firm bought $_____ worth of equipment and paid for it with _____ .

$6,000

cash

5-118 Notice that, while the entry increased the Equipment account and decreased the Cash account by an equal amount, it did not change an equity account. Total Assets still equal Total Equities. The $15,000 in the Capital Stock and Paid-in Surplus account reflects the total amount in the two asset accounts,_____ and _____.

Cash

Equipment

5-119 Now refer to Panel F. Here the accountant has altered asset account balances to reflect an additional transaction. The firm bought $_____worth of _____ and paid for it with_____.

$6,000

inventory

cash

5-120 The equity account Capital Stock and Paid-in Surplus remains the same. The firm now has three kinds of assets in its possession:_____ ,_____ , and _____.

cash

inventory

equipment

5-121 Refer now to Panel G. This Balance Sheet shows that the firm has purchased $_____worth of additional inventory on credit.

$15,000

5-122 Notice how the accountant has recorded this transaction. His entry has increased the balance in Inventory, an asset account, by $15,000. Since a creditor has provided this additional inventory, the accountant has introduced a new equity account, _____ _____ , to show the amount of the creditor's claim.

Accounts Payable

5-123 Panel G shows two types of equity accounts. The stockholders or owners still have $15,000 invested, and the _____ has a claim of $_____since he provided the firm with an equivalent value of inventory on credit.

creditor

$15,000

5-124 Notice that, even though the amount of Total Assets has increased to $30,000, the fundamental equation is unchanged. Total_____ still equal Total _____.

Assets

Equities

5-125 Refer now to Panel H, which reflects still another transaction. In order to increase the Cash balance, the firm has signed a promissory note with the bank for $_____.

$9,000

5-126 The transaction reflected on Panel H has increased Cash, an asset account, by $9,000. In order to show the claim against this increase in assets, the accountant has introduced a new account under Equities,_____ _____.

Notes Payable

5-127 The Balance Sheet shows that the firm now has assets worth $39,000. Of this amount, $_____ is claimed legally by the creditors and is a liability reflected in two equity accounts, _____ _____ and _____ _____.

$24,000

Accounts Payable

Notes Payable

5-128 The remainder of the assets have been provided by the stockholders. Total Assets of $_____ less Liabilities of $_____ equal Net Assets of $_____ which are reflected by the Owners' Equity, or Net Worth, of $15,000.

$39,000

$24,000

$15,000

5-129 Suppose that an entry *increases* an asset account. In this case the entry will also_____ an equity account or_____ another asset account.

increase

reduce

5-130 For example, an increase in Inventory (an asset) may be accompanied either by an _____ in Accounts Payable (an equity) or a_____ in Cash (another asset).

increase

reduction

5-131 Here is another example: If an entry *reduces* an asset account, it must either_____ another asset account or_____ an equity account.

increase

reduce

5-132 You can see that every entry will change at least two account balances. The effect of any such "double entry" is to keep intact the fundamental accounting equation: Total _____ equal Total _____.

Assets

Equities

End of Part 5. Turn to the next page for the Review Quiz only when you are ready to complete Part 6.

After each of the following descriptions place the letter or letters corresponding to the appropriate account titles.

A Cash	H Wages and Salaries Payable
B Accounts Receivable	I Notes Payable (due within one year)
C Inventory	J Taxes Payable
D Land	K Mortgage Payable
E Buildings	L Capital Stock and Paid-in Surplus
F Equipment	M Retained Earnings
G Accounts Payable	

1. Cost of merchandise and materials on hand: _____
2. Amount of assets originally contributed by owners: _____
3. Existing financial obligations to employees: _____
4. Land at cost: _____
5. Amounts of taxes owed to governments: _____
6. Amounts of total assets claimed by creditors holding short-term promissory notes: _____
7. Original cost of buildings: _____
8. Original cost of equipment: _____
9. Amount of net assets not accounted for by owners' original contributions: _____
10. Amount owed on mortgages: _____
11. Amounts owed to firm by customers: _____
12. Amounts of total assets claimed by suppliers not holding promissory notes: _____
13. Balance of cash on hand and in banks: _____
14. All considered Current Liabilities: _____ , _____ , _____ , _____
15. All considered Fixed Assets: _____ , _____ , _____
16. All considered Current Assets: _____ , _____ , _____
17. All considered Owners' Equity: _____ , _____
18. Considered Long-term Debt: _____
19. All are equity accounts: _____ , _____ , _____ , _____ , _____ , _____ , _____

After each of the following descriptions place the letter corresponding to the appropriate Balance Sheet classification.

A Current Assets
B Fixed or Other Assets
C Current Liabilities
D Long-term Debt
E Owners' Equity

20. Represents residual claim against, or source of, net assets: _____
21. Includes all assets which, in the normal course of business, are not expected to be converted into cash within one year: _____

22. Represents claims against assets which must be settled or paid within a year: _____
23. Includes cash and those other assets normally convertible to cash within one year: _____
24. Represents liabilities not due and payable within one year: _____

Complete the following sentences.

25. Both the Balance Sheet and the Income Statement report in the same common unit of measurement, _____.
26. Properties owned by the firm are known as _____; claims against, or sources of, these _____ are called _____.
27. Those equities representing the legal claims of creditors are called _____.
28. Complete the following variations on the fundamental accounting equation:
    (*a*) Assets = _____
    (*b*) Assets = Liabilities + _____ _____
    (*c*) Assets = Current Liabilities + _____ − _____ _____ +
    _____ _____
    (*d*) Net Worth = _____ − Liabilities
    (*e*) Net Assets = _____ − Liabilities
29. Net Worth is another term for _____ _____, and they both reflect net assets.
30. Specific equity accounts [do/do not] _____ represent claims against specific assets or asset accounts.
31. The file containing the data for each separate account is called the _____.
32. The temporary storage file for accumulating the effects of transactions for later posting to the Ledger is called the _____.
33. After analyzing a transaction to determine its effects, the accountant makes an _____ to record these effects.
34. The act of analyzing a transaction and recording the resulting entry in the Journal is known as _____.
35. The act of transferring entries accumulated in the Journal to the proper accounts in the Ledger is known as _____.
36. A posting to an account changes the _____ in that account.
37. An investment in a firm through the purchase from the firm of its capital stock would result in an increase in some asset account and be reflected by an _____ in the Capital Stock and Paid-in Surplus account.
38. The purchase of a machine for cash would result in an increase in the _____ account and a _____ in the Cash account.
39. The purchase of merchandise for cash would _____ the _____ account and decrease the _____ account.
40. The purchase of merchandise on credit would _____ the Inventory account and _____ the _____ _____ account.
41. The payment of a Materials Invoice would _____ the Cash account and _____ the Accounts Payable account.

PART 6
recording transactions

6-1 Having learned about the nature of accounts, you can now learn the methods accountants use in posting the amounts of _____ to the various _____ that the accounting system maintains.

entries

accounts

6-2 Accountants, of course, do not post each entry directly to the Balance Sheet. The figures listed after each account on the Panel C Balance Sheet are the account _____ as of the Balance Sheet date.

balances

6-3 Remember that accountants record transactions as they occur in a temporary file called the Journal. Periodically the accountant will post the journalized entries to the _____.

Ledger

6-4 An account in the Ledger looks something like this:

debits

credits

	Account Name
Debits	*Credits*

You can see that the page is divided into two columns for posting. On the left is the column for _____ ; on the right is the column for _____.

6-5 If you have any preconceptions about what the nouns *debit* and *credit* mean, put them out of your mind right now. Accountants use these terms in a simple technical sense. To the accountant, the term *debit* (dr) basically means the _____ side and *credit* (cr) basically the _____ side of the Ledger sheet.

left

right

78

6-6 *Debit* and *credit* are verbs also. If you post an entry to the left column of an account, you _____ the account. If you post an entry to the right column, you_____ the account.

debit

credit

6-7 You also hear that accounts have a *debit* or *credit balance*. If the total debits to an account exceed the total credits, this means that the account has a _____balance.

debit

6-8 On the other hand, if the total of the credits is greater than the total of the debits, this means that the account has a credit _____.

balance

6-9 Traditionally, asset accounts have debit balances and equity accounts have credit balances. Since assets equal equities, total debit balances will equal total _____ balances.

credit

6-10 Refer to the top half of Panel I. Here are represented the accounts whose balances are listed on the partial Balance Sheet below them. Notice first that the Equipment account under Assets has a _____ balance of $_____.

debit

$6,000

6-11 Directly above, you see the Inventory account, which has a_____ balance of $6,000 plus $_____ , or $_____.

debit

$15,000

$21,000

6-12 The Inventory account shows the effect of two transactions which increased the value of inventory. Since this is an asset account, it has a _____ balance. In order to show an increase, the accountant _____the account.

debit

debited

6-13 No matter what accounts we deal with, a debit is always left and a credit is always right. But the effect of a debit or credit depends on the kind of account. A debit will always_____ the balance of an asset account, and a credit will always _____ it.

increase

reduce

6-14 Directly above the Inventory account on Panel I is the Cash account. Since this is an asset account, it will have a debit balance. In order to determine the balance, subtract credits from debits. The account has a_____ balance of $_____.

debit

$12,000

6-15 The Cash account represented on Panel I shows two entries which increased the account balance. In other words the account was debited with entries of $_____ and $_____.

$15,000

$9,000

6-16 The Cash account also shows two entries which reduced the account balance. In other words, the account was _____with two entries, both in the amount of $6,000.

credited

6-17 You can see that in order to increase an asset account, the accountant makes a_____ entry. In order to reduce it, he makes a_____entry.

debit

credit

6-18 Now find the three accounts under Equities. You can see from these that equity accounts have_____ balances.

credit

6-19 It follows from this that in order to increase the balance of an equity account, the accountant would_____ the account.

credit

6-20 Conversely, in order to reduce the balance of an equity account, the accountant would_____the account.

debit

6-21 Recall our hypothetical case which led to Panel D. The initial transaction was the investment in the firm's capital stock amounting to $_____.

$15,000

6-22 To record this transaction, the accountant posted $15,000 to the Cash account to reflect the new asset. Since the $15,000 represented an increase to the balance in Cash, an asset account, he_____the account.

debited

6-23 Simultaneous with the new asset is a new claim against, or source of, assets. In this case the source is represented by capital stock in the hands of the owners. To increase the balance of Capital Stock and Paid-in Surplus, an equity account, the accountant _____ the account.

credited

6-24 Perhaps by now you have learned the logic of debits and credits. In order to keep the fundamental equation intact, each entry is both a _____ to one account and a _____ to another.

debit

credit

6-25 In this first example, shown on Panel D, the accountant increased both an asset and an equity account. He did so by_____ the Cash account and _____ the Capital Stock and Paid-in Surplus account.

debiting

crediting

6-26 Remember that, to maintain the fundamental equation, when you increase (debit) an asset account, you must either increase (credit) an equity account or decrease another asset account by_____ it.

crediting

6-27 Any entry, then, is "double," because if a transaction leads to a credit to one account, it will necessarily lead to a _____ to another account for the same amount. Thus in any entry the amount of _____ will always equal the amount of _____.

debit

debits

credits

6-28 The second transaction, recorded on the Panel E Balance Sheet, was the purchase of $6,000 worth of equipment for cash. The accountant recorded this transaction by _____ the Equipment account and crediting the _____ account, both by $6,000.

debiting

Cash

6-29 Then when the firm bought $6,000 worth of inventory, the accountant debited the_____ account and credited the _____ account, both by $_____.

Inventory

Cash

$6,000

6-30 The firm then acquired $15,000 worth of inventory on credit. Referring to Panel I, you can see that the accountant debited the _____ account and _____ the Accounts Payable account by that amount.

Inventory
credited

6-31 Suppose that after the date of this particular Balance Sheet the firm paid $1,000 on one of its Accounts Payable. If you were the accountant, you would _____ the Cash account with $1,000 and _____ the Accounts Payable account with a like amount.

credit
debit

6-32 Any entry in double-entry bookkeeping consists of both a debit and a credit in order to maintain the fundamental equation. If you increase an asset account balance, you debit that account and _____ either an equity account or another _____ account.

credit
asset

6-33 Similarly, if you reduce an asset account balance, you credit that account and debit either an _____ account or another _____ account.

equity
asset

6-34 The reverse is also true. If you increase an equity account balance, you _____ that account and _____ either an asset account or another equity account.

credit
debit

6-35 If you reduce an equity account balance you _____ that account and _____ either an asset account or another equity account.

debit
credit

6-36 In the last transaction shown on Panel I, the firm increased an asset, Cash, by increasing a liability, Notes Payable. One way to increase assets without increasing liabilities is to sell capital stock, or "shares," representing ownership. Referring back to Panel D, you can see that such an increase in ownership, or Net Worth, is recorded in the specific account called _____ _____ and _____ - _____ _____ .

Capital Stock
[and] Paid-in
Surplus

6-37 An increase of the Capital Stock and Paid-in Surplus account represents an increase in ownership, or _____ _____.

Net Worth (Owners' Equity)

6-38 Net Worth will also increase when the firm earns a profit. This, of course, is management's primary objective. Suppose that you compared two successive Balance Sheets and discovered that Net Worth increased while the Capital Stock and Paid-in Surplus account balance remained constant. You would know that the firm made a _____ during the period.

profit

6-39 In comparing two successive Balance Sheets to find out if the firm made a profit (assuming that no capital stock had been sold or dividends paid), a reduction in Net Worth would indicate a _____ , and an increase would indicate a _____ for the period.

loss

profit

6-40 If, during the period, no capital stock had been sold and no dividends paid, an increase in Net Worth would be reflected in the Retained Earnings account, while the _____ _____ and _____ - _____ _____ would remain unchanged.

Capital Stock [and] Paid-in Surplus

6-41 Recall that the Net Worth figure is equivalent to net assets, a caption ordinarily not shown on the Balance Sheet. If no capital stock is sold, an increase in net assets is reflected by a corresponding increase in the account called _____ _____.

Retained Earnings

6-42 Remember that you can arrange the fundamental equation in this way:

    Net Worth = Total Assets − Total Liabilities

You can also arrange it to show net assets:

    Net Assets = Total _____ − Total _____

Assets

Liabilities

6-43 Thus if no capital stock has been sold and the Retained Earnings account balance has increased, you know that this reflects an increase in _____ assets and that the firm has made a _____ .

net

profit

6-44 Suppose that two successive Balance Sheets showed that while no capital stock was sold, Total Assets increased by $10,000 and Total Liabilities increased by $5,000. You know that net assets have increased by $ _____ , resulting in a like increase in the section called _____

_____ .

$5,000

Net Worth

6-45 Suppose that the firm sold a product to a customer for $1,000 on credit. You know first of all that one of the effects of this transaction is to increase assets. Since this product was sold on credit, you would _____ the Accounts Receivable account with $ _____ .

debit

$1,000

6-46 You know, in addition, that this increase in assets is claimed by someone. Therefore, some equity account must reflect the increase. Now obviously creditors' claims do not increase and hence _____ do not increase.

liabilities

6-47 Since liabilities do not increase and since capital stock is not involved, the only equity account which can reflect this increase in assets is the _____ _____ account.

Retained Earnings

6-48 Since you have debited Accounts Receivable with $1,000 to show the increase in assets, the matching increase in equities would ultimately be reflected by a _____ to Retained Earnings of $ _____ .

credit

$1,000

6-49 Wait a minute. You have accounted for the inflow of assets resulting from the sale, but you have not accounted for the related outflow of assets which occurred when the firm shipped the product to the customer out of inventory. You know that this transaction must have affected the balance of another asset account, _____ .

Inventory

6-50 Assume that the cost of the product is $900. You would account for this decrease in assets by _____ the Inventory account with $ _____ .

crediting

$900

6-51 How, then, is this decrease in assets reflected by a consequent decrease in equities? Obviously the decrease does not reduce creditors' claims, and therefore _____ do not decrease.

liabilities

6-52 Also, the firm's capital stock is not involved. Thus, the only equity account which can reflect this reduction in assets is the _____ _____ account.

Retained Earnings

6-53 Since you have credited Inventory with $900 to show the reduction in assets, the corresponding reduction in equities would be reflected by a _____ to the Retained Earnings account of $ _____ .

debit

$900

6-54 This one transaction has had two effects on Retained Earnings. The debit of $1,000 to Accounts Receivable, an asset, was reflected by a _____ of $1,000 to Retained Earnings. Also, the $900 reduction of Inventory, another asset, was balanced with a _____ to Retained Earnings of a like amount.

credit

debit

6-55 Considering the Retained Earnings account separately for a moment, you can see that the net result of a $1,000 credit and a $900 debit to this account is a $ _____ credit.

$100

6-56 If Retained Earnings is increased by $100 as a result of posting the foregoing entries, you know that the firm has made a _____ of $ _____ .

profit

$100

6-57 What the comparison of two Balance Sheets can tell management about profit and loss is only the net effect on Retained Earnings. If this account balance increases, management knows that the firm made a_____.

profit

6-58 When dividends, which are distributions of assets to   loss
owners, are paid, the Retained Earnings account balance is
reduced. Therefore, if a comparison of two Balance Sheets
reveals a reduction in Retained Earnings, management knows
either that dividends paid exceeded current profits or that
the firm has suffered a _____ .

6-59 Knowing only that the firm made a profit or suffered   Income Statement
a loss is not enough for management to direct the firm. It
is necessary for it to know the factors which cause the
changes from one Balance Sheet to the next. To provide the
major share of this information, the accounting system prepares the _____ _____ , which records the details of revenues and expenses.

6-60 The Income Statement provides management with a   Net Worth
detailed record of revenues and expenses affecting net assets as reflected by changes in _____ _____
between Balance Sheet dates.

6-61 First, it is necessary to see how the Income Statement   Net Worth
relates to the Balance Sheet. As you have seen, equities are
of two kinds: the creditors' equity, recorded as Total Liabilities, and the owners' equity, recorded as Total _____

_____ .

6-62 Within the Net Worth section of equities are two sources Capital Stock
of capital, both from the owners. One source is the exchange   [and] Paid-in
of the firm's capital stock for cash, represented by the ac-   Surplus
count called _____ _____ and _____ -

_____ _____ .

6-63 The other source of assets is the accumulation of   Retained Earnings
profits over and above any dividends paid; this is represented
by the account called _____ _____ .

6-64 If the Capital Stock and Paid-in Surplus account bal-   Retained Earnings
ance remains constant, any change in Net Worth will be reflected entirely by a corresponding change in the balance of
the _____ _____ account.

6-65 As you can see, however, a comparison of two successive Balance Sheets would reveal only the net change in Retained Earnings and therefore only that the firm made a
_____ or possibly suffered a _____ .

profit

loss

6-66 Recall that one of the results of a sales transaction is
to increase assets. The inflow of assets resulting from a sale
are called *revenue.* They are reflected by a corresponding
[debit/credit] _____ to Retained Earnings.

credit

6-67 Inflows of assets, such as cash from a sale, are recorded in part as credits ultimately affecting the balance in
the Retained Earnings account. Such inflows of assets are
called _____ .

revenues

6-68 Similarly, a sales transaction includes an outflow of
inventory. The outflow of assets involved in the normal operations of the firm is called *expense* and is reflected by a
corresponding [debit/credit] _____ to Retained
Earnings.

debit

6-69 Revenues, therefore, are reflected by _____ to
Retained Earnings, and expenses are reflected by
_____ .

credits

debits

6-70 In order to understand the details of revenues and expenses which brought about the net change in the Retained
Earnings account, management refers to the_____
_____ .

Income Statement

6-71 The Income Statement is related to the Balance Sheet
in that it shows the details of revenues and expenses affecting the _____ _____ account.

Retained Earnings

6-72 To accumulate the details of revenues and expenses in meaningful groups in order to facilitate Income Statement preparation, the accountant does not credit and debit revenues and expenses directly to Retained Earnings. Instead, he sets up a group of temporary holding accounts to receive the credits and debits ultimately affecting the _____ _____ account balance.

Retained Earnings

6-73 These temporary holding accounts, also called *nominal* accounts, are ultimately consolidated into Retained Earnings, one of the permanent, or *real*, accounts appearing on the _____ _____ .

Balance Sheet

6-74 All accounts represented on the Balance Sheet are permanent, or _____ , accounts. Those represented on the Income Statement are temporary holding, or _____ , accounts related to Retained Earnings.

real

nominal

6-75 The Income Statement includes temporary holding accounts that the accountant sets up in order to record the details of entries affecting Retained Earnings. Revenues and expenses, therefore, are shown in meaningful detail by the _____ _____ accounts appearing on the Income Statement.

temporary holding

6-76 Refer now to Panel J. The balance of the first of these temporary holding accounts represents total revenues from customers, which ultimately is a credit to Retained Earnings. This is the _____ account, which is a revenue account.

Sales

6-77 Cost of Goods Sold represents the total cost of inventory delivered to customers. It is an expense account, and ultimately its balance is a [debit/credit] _____ to Retained Earnings.

debit

6-78 Gross Profit is not an account but a subtotal reflecting the difference between two temporary holding accounts, _____ and _____ of _____ _____ .

Sales

Cost [of] Goods Sold

6-79 Other Expenses is an expense account reflecting those expenses of doing business other than the _____ of inventory shipped to customers.

cost

6-80 Paying a utility bill is a transaction which would, in part, be reflected by a debit to an expense account, _____ _____.

Other Expenses

6-81 Net Profit Before Taxes is not an account but a sub-total reflecting the difference between Gross Profit and a temporary holding account, _____ _____.

Other Expenses

6-82 You know that all income taxes to be paid to govern-ments also must come out of profits and consequently affect Retained Earnings. The amount of income taxes payable is therefore shown in the expense account _____ _____.

Income Taxes

6-83 Net Profit After Taxes is not an account but another subtotal representing the remainder after subtracting _____ _____ from pretax profits.

income taxes

6-84 Since earnings before dividends are posted to Retained Earnings, the net figure posted or closed to this account is listed under _____ _____ _____ _____.

Net Profit
   After Taxes

6-85 Since dividends were paid, the ultimate net increase in Retained Earnings for the year would be $ _____.

$21,000

6-86 Since the nominal accounts called revenue and ex-pense accounts all relate to Retained Earnings, you can eas-ily derive debit-credit rules for them. Revenue accounts re-flect increases in assets and therefore in Retained Earnings. To increase Retained Earnings, you credit the account. To record revenues, therefore, you must_____the rev-enue accounts.

credit

6-87 Another way to remember this rule is to think of
_____ accounts as temporary holding accounts for
credits to Retained Earnings.

revenue

6-88 Conversely, expense accounts reflect outflows of assets resulting in reductions of Retained Earnings. To reduce
Retained Earnings, you debit this equity account. Therefore,
to record expenses, you_____ an expense account.

debit

6-89 To review, revenue accounts temporarily store
_____ to Retained Earnings, and expense accounts
temporarily store _____ .

credits

debits

6-90 Recall the transaction in which the firm shipped $900
worth of inventory to a customer. In posting the entry, you
would not post the $900 directly to Retained Earnings. In-
stead, after crediting Inventory you would _____ the
_____ of _____ _____ account with $900.

debit

Cost [of] Goods
Sold

6-91 In this same transaction the firm received from the
customer $1,000 worth of assets. This amount would not
directly affect the Retained Earnings account either. Instead, after debiting Accounts Receivable, you would
[debit/credit]_____ the_____account with
$1,000.

credit

Sales

6-92 Of course, if management did not have to know the
factors affecting Net Worth, the temporary holding accounts
would be unnecessary. Remember that all the temporary
holding accounts are simply a breakdown of a single permanent, or _____ , account, the _____ _____
account.

real

Retained Earnings

6-93 The temporary holding accounts are consolidated, or
closed, first to a special account known as Income Summary
as part of the period-end process of closing the books and
preparing financial statements. To close revenue accounts,
you make an entry debiting those accounts by an amount required to leave a zero balance and _____ Income Summary for the same amount.

crediting

6-94 Refer to Panel J. The entry closing the one revenue account shown would be:

	Dr	*Cr*
Sales	$ _____	$ _____
Income Summary	$ _____	$ _____

	Dr	*Cr*
Sales	$600,000	
Income Summary		$600,000

6-95 Similarly, crediting all expense accounts to zero and debiting Income Summary would _____ these accounts.

close

6-96 The closing entry for expense accounts shown on Panel J would be the compound entry (more than two accounts):

	Dr	*Cr*
Income Summary	$ _____	$ _____
Cost of Goods Sold	$ _____	$ _____
Other Expenses	$ _____	$ _____

	Dr	*Cr*
Income Summary	$560,000	
Cost of Goods Sold		$450,000
Other Expenses		110,000

6-97 Although all the temporary holding accounts, when closed, have zero balances, the total debits transferred to Income Summary from these accounts will seldom if ever equal total credits. If they did, the firm made neither a _____ nor a _____ for the period.

profit

loss

6-98 The Income Summary account, after it is adjusted for income taxes due, is closed to Retained Earnings. If, after tax adjustment, Income Summary had a credit balance of $25,000, the entry closing this balance to Retained Earnings would be:

	Dr	*Cr*
_____	$ _____	$ _____
_____	$ _____	$ _____

	Dr	*Cr*
Income Summary	$25,000	
Retained Earnings		$25,000

6-99 Note that the $25,000 credit to Retained Earnings re-
flects a corresponding increase in net assets, which represents a net _____ after taxes.

profit

6-100 Now review the closing sequence. You debited Income
Summary with $560,000 of expenses and credited it with
$600,000 revenue. At this point there would be a_____
balance of $_____ representing the excess of reve-
nues over expenses, or the net _____ before taxes.

credit

$40,000

profit

6-101 If income taxes due were $15,000, the entry recording
this liability and the corresponding charge to Income Summary would be:

	Dr	Cr
_____	$ _____	$ _____
Taxes Payable	$ _____	$ _____

	Dr	Cr
Income Summary	$15,000	
Taxes Payable		$15,000

6-102 The balance in Income Summary after the entry providing for taxes due had been posted would be a _____
balance of $_____ representing profit after taxes.

credit

$25,000

6-103 Recall that as part of the closing process you made
the entry closing the Income Summary balance to_____
_____.

Retained Earnings

6-104 The Income Summary account is set up and then
closed to Retained Earnings only as part of the closing process. One purpose is to accumulate all revenues and expenses
before taxes so that the difference between them, representing _____ or _____ before taxes, may be obtained.

profit [or] loss

6-105 Whether revenues and expenses are closed first to Income Summary and then to Retained Earnings or closed directly to Retained Earnings, the net effect is the same. Hereafter, we will refer to this effect by saying that revenue and expense accounts are "ultimately closed to Retained Earnings." However, remember that the accountant will always close to Retained Earnings via the _____ _____ account.

Income Summary

6-106 From Panel J you know that the after-tax profit ultimately closed to Retained Earnings was $25,000. Dividends paid throughout the year of $_____ are charged directly to Retained Earnings by the following entry:

$4,000

	Dr	Cr
_____	$4,000	
_____		$4,000

	Dr	Cr
Retained Earnings	$4,000	
Cash		$4,000

6-107 This $21,000 net credit to Retained Earnings reflects a $21,000 increase in net assets, or profit after paying dividends. Note that on Panel J this same amount, $_____, is shown as the increase in _____ _____.

$21,000

Retained Earnings

6-108 Now refer to Panels I and C. Note that the amount of increase in Net Worth, reflected entirely in the _____ _____ account over the year 196B, amounts to $_____.

Retained Earnings

$21,000

6-109 Refer again to Panel J and note that the temporary holding accounts on the Income Statement are listed in meaningful order. By comparing successive Income Statements, management can see not only changes in earnings, but also changes in the factors affecting earnings. Thus both the _____ _____ and the statement of financial position—the_____ _____ —are outputs providing information for managing the enterprise.

Income Statement

Balance Sheet

6-110 The Income Statement matches the revenues of the
period with the expenses of obtaining those revenues. Any
balance, or *residual*, is closed to Net Worth via the Retained
Earnings account. The new balance in Retained Earnings,
then, reflects a _____ resulting from the process of
deducting expenses from revenues. In this way income is
determined.

residual (differ-
ence)

6-111 Refer again to Panel C and consider the nature of the
Net Worth section of the Balance Sheet. If all equities are
thought of as claims against assets, then the Owners' Equity
is a residual remaining after deducting Total Liabilities
from Total Assets. In other words, Net Worth can be thought
of as a _____ claim against Total

residual

6-112 You have seen that bookkeeping rules are quite logical and are easily derived from the fundamental accounting
equation. To review briefly, the so-called permanent, or
real, accounts appear on the _____ _____,
which tells management the _____ position of the firm
as of the _____ of the statement.

Balance Sheet

financial

date

6-113 Revenue and expense accounts are sometimes called
temporary, or nominal, accounts because they are
_____ at the end of the accounting period. These accounts are shown on the output called the _____
_____.

closed

Income Statement

6-114 To review, the fundamental accounting equation in
its simplest form is:

Total _____ = Total _____

Assets

Equities

6-115 This fundamental equation can be expressed another
way in order to derive Net Worth:

_____ _____ = _____ − _____

Net Worth

Assets

Liabilities

6-116 Debit-credit rules follow logically from this equation. You know that to increase asset and expense account balances, you _____ these accounts. To reduce their balances, you _____ them.

debit

credit

6-117 You also know that to increase the balance of equity and revenue accounts, you _____ them. To reduce the balances of these accounts, you _____ them.

credit

debit

6-118 In summary, you can see that accounting has a logical framework which provides the rules for double-entry book-keeping. These rules are important, but only because they permit accountants to prepare meaningful and timely reports, the_____ _____ and the _____ _____ , which aid the firm's management in making crucial decisions.

Balance Sheet

Income Statement

End of Part 6. Turn to the next page for the Review Quiz only when you are ready to complete Part 7.

Complete the following sentences.

1. Debit simply means the _____ side of an account, and credit means the _____ side.

2. If the total of the amounts posted to the left side of an account exceeds the total of those posted to the right, the account has a _____ _____ . If the total of the amounts posted to the right exceeds the total of those posted to the left, the account has a _____ _____ .

3. Asset and expense accounts normally have _____ balances. Equity and revenue accounts normally have _____ balances.

4. To increase an equity or revenue account, you _____ it. To increase an asset or expense account you _____ it.

5. In any entry and in all Journals and Ledgers, total _____ must always equal total _____ .

6. If an entry involves a debit to an asset account, it may also involve a _____ to at least one of the following types of accounts:
   (a) _____
   (b) _____
   (c) _____

7. An increase in the Retained Earnings account from one Balance Sheet to the next reflects an increase in _____ assets and indicates that the firm made a _____ .

8. Inflows of assets from customers are called _____ .

9. Outflows of assets not accompanied by a reduction in liabilities and increases in liabilities not matched by a corresponding increase in assets are classified as _____ .

10. The output that provides management with details of revenues and expenses and resultant profit or loss for a period is called the _____ _____ .

11. All revenue and expense accounts eventually affect the _____ _____ account on the Balance Sheet.

12. Revenue and expense accounts are known as _____ _____ , or nominal, accounts, in contrast to asset and equity accounts, which are considered _____ , or real, accounts.

13. As part of the closing process, accountants first close all revenue and expense accounts to a temporary holding account called _____ _____ .

14. After the accountant calculates and posts income taxes owed, he closes this temporary holding account to the permanent account, _____ _____ .

Journalize the following transactions. Even though only one space is provided for account titles, remember that many have titles consisting of more than one word.

15. The owners invest $1,000 cash in the firm.

	Dr	Cr
_____	$ _____	$ _____
_____	$ _____	$ _____

16. The firm buys some equipment for $500 cash.

	Dr	Cr
_____	$ _____	$ _____
_____	$ _____	$ _____

17. The firm buys inventory costing $400 on credit.

	Dr	Cr
_____	$ _____	$ _____
_____	$ _____	$ _____

18. The firm receives an invoice from the telephone company for a $50 monthly charge.

	Dr	Cr
_____	$ _____	$ _____
_____	$ _____	$ _____

19. The firm later pays the $50 telephone invoice.

	Dr	Cr
_____	$ _____	$ _____
_____	$ _____	$ _____

20. The firm sells merchandise costing $120 for $200 on credit.

	Dr	Cr
_____	$ _____	$ _____
_____	$ _____	$ _____
_____	$ _____	$ _____
_____	$ _____	$ _____

21. The firm had total sales of $9,000 for the year. Prepare the entry closing the revenue account.

	Dr	Cr
_____	$ _____	$ _____
_____	$ _____	$ _____

22. Expenses for the year were as follows: Cost of Goods Sold, $5,400; Other Expenses, $1,600; Taxes, $1,000. Prepare the entry closing the expense accounts.

	Dr	Cr
_____	$ _____	$ _____
_____	$ _____	$ _____
_____	$ _____	$ _____
_____	$ _____	$ _____

23. Profit after taxes for the firm (questions 21 and 22) amounted to $ _____ .

24. The entry closing the Income Summary account for this firm is:

	Dr	Cr
_____	$ _____	$ _____
_____	$ _____	$ _____

25. Suppose this same firm paid out $600 in dividends. The net increase in the Retained Earnings account at the end of the year would be $ _____ .

PART 7
specific accounting procedures

7-1 You now know the methods accountants use in categorizing and storing input data. With this knowledge you
can better understand how the accounting system fulfills the
three major responsibilities leading to the preparation of

_____ .

outputs

7-2 Recall that the first major responsibility of the
accounting system is to process and record all "events"
affecting the status of the firm's assets and equities. These
"events" are called _____ .

transactions

7-3 Refer again to Panel B. You see there that this first
responsibility includes five specific activities. The first
activity is the processing and recording of payroll informa-
tion--the _____ _____ .

payroll activity

7-4 The first step in the payroll activity is to determine
each employee's gross earnings. For instance, you would
multiply the number of hours worked by an hourly paid
employee by his rate of pay to determine his _____

_____ .

gross earnings

7-5 An employee's take-home pay is gross earnings less
deductions. After computing an employee's gross earnings,
you would next subtract his individual deductions in order to
determine his _____ - _____ pay.

take-home

7-6 You would compute an hourly paid employee's pay in
the following way. First, you would multiply the number of
_____ worked by his individual _____ of
_____ to determine his gross earnings.

hours

rate [of] pay

7-7 You would then subtract from his gross earnings all his individual _____ ; the net would be his_____ _____ _____ , the amount of his Payroll Check.

deductions

take-home pay

7-8 All deductions withheld are liabilities, since the firm owes the amounts deducted to others. For example, the firm owes any withheld taxes to the government. After computing an employee's pay, you would record all his deductions as _____.

liabilities

7-9 In addition to the liabilities, you would also record the employee's gross earnings as a payroll expense. As you processed payroll information leading to the Payroll Check, you would record total earnings as a _____ _____ and deductions as _____ .

payroll expense

liabilities

7-10 The Payroll Master File provides the accounting system with information about each employee's payroll status. For example, you would find an employee's rate of pay listed with his name and payroll number in the _____ _____ _____ .

Payroll Master
   File

7-11 Since the number of dependents may affect the rate of tax, the Payroll Master File contains the number of each employee's _____ .

dependents

7-12 In addition, the Payroll Master File lists all other authorized deductions, such as bonds, health insurance, and union dues, for each employee. You can find the number of an employee's dependents and his other authorized deductions in the _____ _____ _____ .

Payroll Master
   File

7-13 Listed with each employee's name and payroll number in the Payroll Master File are the following items of information:

1. _____ of _____
2. _____ of _____
3. Other _____ _____

1. rate [of] pay

2. number [of]
   dependents

3. authorized
   deductions

7-14 Now that you know the steps in the payroll activity, you can use your knowledge to complete a sample problem. Suppose that Mike Jones worked forty-two hours in one week and that his rate of pay is $2 an hour. Figuring the hours over forty at time and a half, you would compute his gross earnings in this way:

$(40 \times \$2) + (2 \times \$3) = \$86$

(_____ × $ ____) + (_____ × $ ____) = $ _____

7-15 Referring to the Payroll Master File again, you find that Mike has a wife and two children, or three dependents. For the present example, assume that the firm withholds 20 per cent of his wages as Federal income tax. You would then compute his withholding tax deductions this way:

$86

0.20

$17.20

$_____ × _____ = $ _____

7-16 In addition, you know that Mike has authorized a weekly deduction of $1 for union dues. His deductions figured to this point are $ _____ + $ ____ .

$17.20

$1

7-17 Like most employees in the United States, Mike pays Social Security tax. If you computed this at 4 per cent of his gross earnings, this would amount to $_____ × _____ , or $ _____ .

$86

0.04

$3.44

7-18 You can compute Mike's take-home pay by subtracting his total _____ from his _____ earnings: $86 − ($ _____ + $ _____ + $ ____) = $ _____ .

deductions

gross

($17.20 + $3.44 + $1) = $64.36

7-19 You would then prepare a _____ _____ for Mike Jones in the amount of $64.36.

Payroll Check

7-20 However, this completes only part of the payroll operation. Remember that the accounting system must, in addition, record Mike's _____ earnings, which represent to the firm a payroll _____ , and also his deductions, which represent new _____ .

gross

expense

liabilities

7-21 Of course, if you processed payroll information for all employees of the firm for a particular pay period, you would separately total the _____ of all employees, as well as the various kinds of _____ representing new liabilities.

earnings

deductions

7-22 Keeping such totals simplifies journalizing, a part of the bookkeeping activity. But for illustration, consider only the steps necessary for recording Mike Jones' payroll expense. When computing payroll expense in this case, you know that _____ _____ , rather than take-home pay, is the portion of the payroll expense for Mike's work.

gross earnings

7-23 In addition, employers are required by law to match the amount employees pay for Social Security. This means that Mike's firm also pays 4 per cent on Mike's total earnings:

$$\$86 \times \underline{\hspace{2cm}} = \$ \underline{\hspace{2cm}}$$

[$86 ×] 0.04
   $3.44

7-24 Payroll expense for Mike's work, then, is not $86, but $86 plus the firm's Social Security payment of $_____ , which totals $_____ .

$3.44

$89.44

7-25 Also note that the total Social Security liability consists of Mike's deduction plus the employer's matching contribution. This amount, then, would be $3.44 plus $_____ , or $_____ .

$3.44

$6.88

7-26 Mike's two other deductions, withholding taxes and union dues, must also be recorded as _____ .

liabilities

7-27 After you computed these figures, you would set them aside to be journalized as part of another activity, the bookkeeping activity. Remember that all transactions processed and recorded by the first four activities of this responsibility are journalized in the fifth, the _____ _____ .

bookkeeping
activity

7-28 The payroll activity is similar for salaried employees. The Salary List provides the names of those authorized to receive salaries for the period, and you would find the fixed salary rate, number of dependents, and authorized deductions listed with the name and payroll number of each salaried employee in the _____ Master File.

Payroll

7-29 Another activity by which the accounting system fulfills the processing and recording responsibility is the one leading to the preparation of Checks to Creditors. This is the _____ activity.

payables

7-30 The first step in processing and recording purchase information is to verify that Incoming Invoices are correct. Obviously, the firm cannot prudently issue a Check to Creditor without first examining the charges on the _____ _____ to see if they are correct.

Incoming Invoice

7-31 Recall that there are two kinds of Incoming Invoices: _____ Invoices, which cover the receipt of inventory items, and _____ _____ Invoices, which cover purchases not involving inventory.

Materials

Other Incoming

7-32 Verification is necessarily different for each kind of Incoming Invoice. The Materials Invoice, since it covers materials purchased and received into inventory, has two matching inputs, the _____ _____ _____ and the _____ _____ .

Purchase Order Copy

Receiving Record

7-33 In order to verify the legitimacy of the Materials Invoice, you would accumulate the three inputs involving each separate purchase transaction for "matching." This means that you would first check the Materials Invoice against the _____ _____ _____ to see if the quantity had been authorized for purchase and if the charges were correct.

Purchase Order Copy

7-34 To complete the matching process, you would check the Materials Invoice against the _____ _____ to see if the quantity of items invoiced had been received in good condition from the supplier.

Receiving Record

7-35 This "matching" process permits verification of quantity and price figures on Materials Invoices and verification of the receipt of the material covered. However, because inventory items are not involved, you do not have these matching inputs for _____ _____ Invoices, such as phone bills.

Other Incoming

7-36 Although different firms have different policies, all require some kind of positive verification of Other Incoming Invoices. The first step in the _____ activity, then, is to verify the legitimacy of all Incoming Invoices, either by the matching process for _____ Invoices or by some other approved method for _____ Incoming Invoices.

payables

Materials

Other

7-37 The next step in the payables activity is to record the new assets received or the new expenses incurred. Inventory covered by a Materials Invoice is obviously a new _____. A typewriter is another kind of _____, and the charge for the phone is an example of an _____, both of which would be covered by Other Incoming Invoices.

asset

asset

expense

7-38 At the same time that you record the new asset or expense, you must record for ultimate posting to Accounts Payable the new_____, which is the amount owed to the supplier.

liability

7-39 Materials Invoices always represent new assets received. Other Incoming Invoices may represent either new _____ received or new _____ incurred.

assets

expenses

7-40 However, all Incoming Invoices represent increases in amounts owed to creditors. At the same time that you record the new assets or new expenses, you must also record the amounts of all Incoming Invoices as new_____ for later posting to Accounts Payable.

liabilities

7-41 The first step in the payables activity, then, is to verify the legitimacy of all _____ _____. The second step is to record the new _____ or expenses and the new _____.

Incoming Invoices

assets

liabilities

7-42 The third step is to settle the liability, i.e., pay the bill. To do this, you would issue a _____ to _____ for the amount owed.

Check [to]
Creditor

7-43 Some firms settle liabilities the same day that Incoming Invoices are approved, while others follow a practice know as "batching." Many modern business firms have a policy of paying approved invoices on hand on the tenth and twenty-fifth of each month. These firms follow a practice called _____.

"batching"

7-44 After the verification of Incoming Invoices and the recording of the new assets or expenses and liabilities represented, the third step is to settle the _____.

liability

7-45 This payment, then, involves a fourth step, that of recording the amount of the liability settled and the consequent decrease in cash represented by the amount of the _____ to _____ issued.

Check [to]
Creditor

7-46 On issuing the Check to Creditor, you would record the amount of the _____ settled and the consequent [increase/reduction] _____ in Cash that the payment represented.

liability

reduction

7-47 The first step in the payables activity is to _____ the legitimacy of all _____ _____.

verify

Incoming Invoices

7-48 The second step is to record the new _____ or expense plus the new _____ .

asset

liability

7-49 The third step is to settle the _____ by issuing a _____ to _____ in the amount owed.

liability

Check [to] Creditor

7-50 The fourth step in the payables activity is to record the amount of the _____ settled and the reduction in _____ represented by the Check to Creditor.

liabilities

Cash

7-51 Another activity by which the accounting system fulfills its responsibility of processing and recording transactions is the one leading to the preparation of the Customer Invoice. This is the _____ _____ .

billing activity

7-52 Your first step in the billing activity is to determine the total list price for all items shipped to a customer. You then compute the appropriate trade discounts based upon the _____ _____ of the items shipped.

list price

7-53 After determining trade discounts, you would apply these to list prices to determine selling price as follows:

trade discount

selling price

List price − _____ _____ = _____ _____

7-54 On the basis of selling price, you would determine the amounts of appropriate taxes. After determining taxes, you would then prepare a _____ _____ .

Customer Invoice

7-55 The Customer Invoice, then, "bills" the customer for a net invoice amount equal to the list price of the shipment minus the appropriate _____ _____ and plus the appropriate _____ .

trade discounts

taxes

7-56 The selling price, tax, and net invoice figures are recorded for later inclusion in accounting records, which are maintained by another processing and recording activity called the _____ activity.

bookkeeping

7-57 The billing activity requires the use of two master files—the Parts Master File and the Customer Master File. After receiving a Shipping Notice covering a shipment of a certain number of items, you would find the list price of each item with its part number and exact description in the _____ _____ File.

Parts Master

7-58 The Parts Master File contains a list of part numbers and the exact descriptions of all items sold by the firm. In performing the billing activity, your first step would be to find in this file the _____ _____ of each item shipped.

list price

7-59 The Customer Master File carries the correct *customer name* and *shipping address*, along with the correct *billing address*. Firms often order materials shipped to branches and request that billing be made at some other location. For this reason the Customer Master File carries both the correct _____ address and the correct _____ address for each of the firm's customers.

shipping

billing

7-60 Individual customers will generally have trade discounts and payment terms applicable to their purchases. You would find this information also in the _____ _____ _____.

Customer Master File

7-61 The Customer Master File also carries any taxes applicable to a particular customer's purchase. This is in addition to the customer's name, correct _____ and _____ addresses, and any _____ discounts and _____ terms.

shipping

billing

trade

payment

7-62 You would find the tax rate applicable to a particular customer's purchases in the _____ _____ _____.

Customer Master File

7-63 Suppose you received a Shipping Notice covering a shipment to the Ace Dingbat Company of 300 dingbats. You would first look up the _____ number and description of dingbats in the Parts Master File, where you would find the _____ _____ of dingbats.

part

list price

7-64 If the shipping notice carried only one line item

Part no. 1001 . . . . Dingbat . . . . 300 shipped

the Customer Invoice you prepare would also have only one _____ _____ .

line item

7-65 After you ascertained that dingbats sell for $1, you would *extend* the line item by multiplying this price by 300, the quantity shipped. This would give you the shipment's extended _____ price, $300.

list

7-66 You would then refer to the Customer Master File for the correct shipping and billing address of the Ace Dingbat Company. Here you would also find the trade_____ , the payment_____ , and any _____ applicable to Ace Company's purchases.

discount

terms

taxes

7-67 Suppose that the Ace Dingbat Company was a whole-saler entitled to a 40 per cent trade discount. In order to compute this discount, you would multiply $300 by_____. The result is a discount of $_____.

0.40

$120

7-68 You would then subtract this discount from the ex-tended _____ price of $300. This would give you the net selling price for the invoice, $_____.

list

$180

7-69 In addition, suppose that there was a 3 per cent sales tax applied to the selling price of purchases by Ace. The sales tax would be computed on the _____ price as follows: $180 times_____ equals a total sales tax on the shipment of $_____ .

selling

0.03

$5.40

7-70 Net invoice price, the amount for which the customer is billed, equals the extended selling price plus applicable taxes. If the extended selling price was $180 and the total applicable taxes were $5.40, the _____ _____ price would be $185.40.

net invoice

7-71 After completing the Customer Invoice, you would record the selling price, tax, and net invoice figures from the invoice for inclusion in the accounting records. This would be performed by another activity of processing and recording, the _____ activity.

bookkeeping

7-72 A fourth activity of processing and recording involves Checks from Customers, Canceled Checks, and Bank Statements. This is the _____ _____ and _____ activity.

cash receipt [and] reconciliation

7-73 The cash receipt and reconciliation activity includes recording the receipt of Checks from Customers for later journalizing. The checks are then deposited in the _____.

bank

7-74 The accounting system does not prepare any major output as part of the cash receipt and reconciliation activity. However, it is necessary to record the settlement of the customer's account when the firm receives _____ from _____ .

Checks [from] Customers

7-75 When the firm receives its Canceled Checks, along with a Bank Statement, the accounting system must reconcile the firm's records with the bank's. This is also part of the _____ _____ and _____ activity.

cash receipt [and] reconciliation

7-76 As part of the cash receipt and reconciliation activity, the accounting system must _____ the receipt of _____ from Customers and provide for their _____ in the bank.

record

Checks

deposit

7-77 When the firm receives Canceled Checks, along with its Bank Statement, the accounting system must_____ the firm's records with those of the_____ .

reconcile

bank

7-78 As you know by now, each of the four activities involves keeping records of all the transactions processed. It is the function of the fifth activity, the_____ _____ , to *categorize* and *store* this information in the cumulative accounting records that the accounting system maintains.

bookkeeping
   activity

7-79 The bookkeeping activity, then, includes the_____ and _____of the effects on the firm's financial position of transactions also processed by the other four activities.

categorizing

storing

7-80 Recall the payroll activity that processed Mike Jones' Timecard and issued a Payroll Check to him. Mike's total earnings amounted to $86; however, you learned that the firm pays an additional 4 per cent for Mike's Social Security. Therefore, the payroll expense for Mike's week of employment was not $86, but $_____ plus $_____ , or $_____ .

$86

$3.44

$89.44

7-81 For this example, consider Mike a shipping clerk whose total time is part of shipping expenses. The firm would have established a temporary holding account for such payroll expenses, which will ultimately affect Retained Earnings. Thus you would journalize the $89.44 as a [debit/credit] _____ to this expense account.

debit

7-82 Now since Taxes Payable is a Current Liability account, the total of the two taxes--withholding ($17.20) and Social Security ($6.88)--would be _____ to Taxes Payable.

credited

7-83 Union Dues Payable is another Current Liability account that many firms maintain for the convenience of their employees. Mike's $1 deduction would be a_____ to that account.

credit

7-84 Finally, Mike's Payroll Check in the amount of his take-home pay depletes the balance of the Cash account by that amount. The $64.36 would be a _____ to the Cash account.

credit

7-85 Review the last four frames. On the simulated journal page below, place all the figures in the correct columns.

	Dr	Cr
Payroll Expense	$ _____	$ _____
Taxes Payable	$ _____	$ _____
Union Dues Payable	$ _____	$ _____
Cash	$ _____	$ _____

Check to see if total debits equal total credits.

	Dr	Cr
Payroll Expense	$89.44	
Taxes Payable		$24.08
Union Dues Payable		1.00
Cash		64.36

7-86 Suppose Joe Smith, Mike's fellow employee, earned a total of $100; his dependents and tax rates are the same as Mike's. The total payroll expense of $104 would be a _____ to Payroll Expense. The total of the two taxes ($20 plus $8) would be a _____ to Taxes Payable. His $1 union dues would be a _____ to Union Dues Payable. Finally, his take-home pay of $75 would be a _____ to Cash.

debit

credit

credit

credit

7-87 In journalizing this transaction you know that total debits must equal total credits. Review the last frame and total them here.

Debits: _____   Credits: _____

$104

$104

7-88 Suppose now that in the payables activity you recorded the receipt of 300 widgets at $1 each; to journalize this transaction, you would enter $_____ in the Journal as a _____ to Inventory.

$300

debit

7-89 This, of course, is only half the entry. You would also enter $_____ as a _____ to Accounts Payable.

$300

credit

7-90 Remember, however, that there are two kinds of Incoming Invoices. The preceding example obviously can only
apply to one kind—the _____ Invoice.

Materials

7-91 How, then, would you journalize a transaction
recorded on an Other Incoming Invoice? Suppose that you
had before you an invoice for $50 worth of stationery sup-
plies. Such supplies are usually not part of inventory and
consequently do not affect the _____ account.

Inventory

7-92 The cost of stationery supplies is usually accounted
for as an operating expense. One of the temporary holding
accounts closed into Retained Earnings is the Other
Expenses account, maintained to include such expenses.
You would therefore journalize the cost of the stationery
supplies first as a _____ to this account.

debit

7-93 Assuming that the transaction was on credit, you
would then enter a like amount as a _____ to
Accounts Payable.

credit

7-94 Later, when a Check to Creditor is issued to settle
the liability represented by an Incoming Invoice, you would
journalize the amount of the check as a _____ to the
Cash account.

credit

7-95 Since this check would settle a liability represented
as part of the Accounts Payable balance, you would also
enter the amount as a _____ to Accounts Payable.

debit

7-96 Journalizing the information generated as part of the
billing activity involves the use of the same simple principles. When the firm shipped 300 dingbats at $1 each, the
extended figure of $300 represented the_____
shipped times the _____ price.

quantity

list

7-97 Remember that you subtracted a trade discount of 40
per cent and added a tax of 3 per cent. The net invoice
amount owed by the customer is $_____.

$185.40

7-98 You would journalize the net invoice amount as a _____ to Accounts Receivable.

debit

7-99 The selling price, which is list price less trade discount, must be accounted for as revenue. This means that you would enter the $180 figure as a_____to Sales, another temporary holding account ultimately affecting _____ Earnings.

credit

Retained

7-100 Finally, you would have to account for the taxes charged. You would do this by entering the tax of $5.40 as a _____ to Taxes Payable.

credit

7-101 However, this completes only part of the necessary recording. Remember that these dingbats were shipped from the firm's stock and that the shipment therefore affected the _____ account.

Inventory

7-102 Suppose the 300 dingbats cost the firm 50 cents each. You would make an additional journal entry first by entering the $150 as a _____ to Cost of Goods Sold, another expense account affecting Retained Earnings.

debit

7-103 Finally, you would enter the same amount as a _____ to Inventory.

credit

7-104 Review the last seven frames and journalize these entries, using the form below.

	Dr	Cr
Accounts Receivable	$ _____	$ _____
Sales	$ _____	$ _____
Taxes Payable	$ _____	$ _____
Cost of Goods Sold	$ _____	$ _____
Inventory	$ _____	$ _____

	Dr	Cr
Accounts Receivable	$185.40	
Sales		$180.00
Taxes Payable		5.40
Cost of Goods Sold	150.00	
Inventory		150.00

7-105 Refer to the answer to the preceding frame. The first of the two entries is a *compound* entry, that is, one affecting more than two accounts. You can check both entries by seeing if total _____ equal total _____ .

debits

credits

7-106 When a customer sends a check in settlement, another activity is involved. This is the _____ _____ and _____ activity.

cash receipt [and]
reconciliation

7-107 Since a Check from Customer increases the Cash account balance, you enter the amount as a _____ to Cash.

debit

7-108 Simultaneously, the check reduces the balance which the customer owes the firm. To complete the entry, you enter the amount of the check as a _____ to Accounts Receivable.

credit

7-109 Firms frequently offer customers a discount for prompt payment; this is called a cash discount. Sometimes a discount of 2 per cent is allowed if payment is made within 10 days. If, then, a customer sent a check for $98 within 10 days in settlement of a $100 invoice, you would know he was taking a _____ _____ of $____ .

cash discount
[of] $2

7-110 As a first step in journalizing this transaction, you would _____ Cash by $____ , the amount received.

debit

$98

7-111 Since the customer had settled his account, you would _____ Accounts Receivable by $_____ , the amount of the original invoice.

credit

$100

7-112 The $2 discount granted represents a reduction in revenue and is treated as an expense; it is charged to an account called Discounts and Allowances. The complete entry recording the transaction would be:

	Dr	Cr
Cash	$_____	$_____
_____ and _____	$_____	$_____
Accounts Receivable	$_____	$_____

	Dr	Cr
Cash	$98	
Discounts and Allowances	2	
Accounts Receivable		$100

7-113 The bookkeeping activity, then, involves abstracting and summarizing all information regarding the transactions processed in the four activities. The five activities discussed comprise the accounting system's first major responsibility, that of _____ and _____ transactions.

processing

recording

End of Part 7. Turn to the next page for the Review Quiz only when you are ready to complete Part 8.

Complete the following sentences.

1. Two inputs and one reference file are used in the payroll activity. They are the _____ , the _____ _____ , and the _____ Master File.
2. This master file, in addition to names and payroll numbers, carries each employee's _____ of _____ , number of _____ , and all authorized _____ .
3. The extension of hours worked times rate of pay (including overtime premium where applicable) gives the employee's _____ _____ .
4. The amount determined by the procedure in question 3 less the applicable deduction equals net earnings, more popularly known as _____ - _____ _____ .
5. Assume that an employee worked forty-five hours during a given week and that this included five hours overtime at time and a half. His straight-time pay was $2 per hour; he was in a 20 per cent tax bracket; his Social Security amounted to 5 per cent; and his authorized union dues amounted to $2 per week. His net earnings for this week would be $ _____ .
6. To journalize all expenses incurred as a result of this employee's work week, the following four accounts would be involved:
   (*a*) _____ _____
   (*b*) _____
   (*c*) _____ _____ (including Social Security)
   (*d*) Union Dues Payable
7. From data given in question 5, complete the entry referred to in question 6, including the employer's matching contribution for Social Security:

	Dr	*Cr*
_____	$ _____	$ _____
_____	$ _____	$ _____
_____	$ _____	$ _____
_____	$ _____	$ _____

8. The employer's payroll expense exceeds gross earnings by the amount of the _____ contribution to employment taxes.
9. The Materials Invoice is checked against two other inputs for verification. These two inputs are the _____ _____ Copy and the _____ _____ .
10. This matching process is part of the _____ activity.
11. The billing activity uses a single input and two reference files. These are:
   (*a*) The _____ _____
   (*b*) The _____ Master File
   (*c*) The _____ Master File
12. The Parts Master File contains, for each item, its _____ number, description, and _____ price.
13. The Customer Master File usually contains at least seven pieces of information for each customer, as follows:
   (*a*) Customer name
   (*b*) _____ address
   (*c*) _____ address
   (*d*) Trade _____

(e) _____ _____
(f) Applicable _____
(g) Customer number

14. Assume that a Shipping Notice recorded a shipment of four gadgets costing $15 apiece to Gadget Supply, a wholesaler entitled to a 40 per cent trade discount. His purchases were subject to a 4 per cent sales tax. The list price of a gadget is $35. The net invoice amount for this sale would be $ _____ .

15. The entries recording this sale and this shipment would involve five accounts:
    (a) _____ _____
    (b) _____
    (c) Taxes Payable
    (d) _____ of _____ _____
    (e) _____

16. With data from question 14, complete the entries referred to in question 15:

	Dr	Cr
_____	$ _____	$ _____
_____	$ _____	$ _____
_____	$ _____	$ _____
_____	$ _____	$ _____
_____	$ _____	$ _____

17. Gross profit on the sale to Gadget Supply (assuming no Sales Discounts and Allowances) would be $_____ .

18. Processing Checks from Customers and the firm's Canceled Checks received from the bank, together with Bank Statements, is the _____ _____ and _____ activity.

19. Suppose that Mike Smith, a customer, had been invoiced for $400 and that no sales tax was involved. He was entitled to a 2 per cent discount for prompt payment. Assume that he sent his check in settlement within the discount period and took advantage of the terms. The entry recording this transaction would be:

	Dr	Cr
_____	$ _____	$ _____
_____	$ _____	$ _____
_____	$ _____	$ _____

specific accounting procedures (continued)

8-1 Remember that one major responsibility of the accounting system involves preparation of the Balance Sheet and the Income Statement. This responsibility is that of _____ reporting.

financial

8-2 The financial reporting responsibility involves the periodic preparation of two outputs, the _____ _____ and the _____ _____.

Balance Sheet

Income Statement

8-3 The first step in preparing the Balance Sheet is to make sure that all entries reflecting the period's transactions have been journalized and posted to the proper accounts in the _____.

Ledger

8-4 Next, all the Ledger account balances are summarized to verify that the "books are in balance," or in other words, that total debit balances equal total _____ _____. This step is called taking a *trial balance*.

credit balances

8-5 After making sure that all entries have been journalized and _____ to the Ledger, the accountant takes a _____ _____.

posted

trial balance

8-6 The trial balance involves summarizing all Ledger account balances to see if total _____ balances equal total _____ balances.

debit

credit

8-7 Next, the accountant makes special adjusting entries, which will be described later. After this, the accountant makes his closing entries, which eventually consolidate such temporary holding accounts as the revenue and expense accounts into the permanent account _____ _____.

Retained
Earnings

8-8 After making special adjusting entries, the accountant consolidates temporary holding accounts into the permanent, or real, accounts by making appropriate_____ _____.

closing entries

8-9 The final step in preparing the Balance Sheet is to list all the _____ account balances on the conventional Balance Sheet form.

permanent (real)

8-10 To review, the first step in preparing the Balance Sheet is to _____ _____
(Answer in your own words.)

Make sure that
all entries have
been journalized
and posted to
the Ledger.

8-11 The second step is to take the_____ _____.

trial balance

8-12 The third step is to make special adjusting entries. The fourth is to make the _____ entries, which consolidate all temporary holding accounts into the_____ accounts.

closing

permanent (real)

8-13 The final step is to list all the _____ account balances on the conventional _____ _____ form.

permanent

Balance Sheet

8-14 Preparation of the Income Statement involves recording the temporary holding account balances. It is important to remember that revenue and expense accounts,
after adjustments, are closed to the Income Summary account, which in turn is closed to the _____ _____
account.

Retained
Earnings

8-15 As part of the overall closing process, the accountant prepares the Income Statement by listing in meaningful
order all the _____ and _____ account bal-
ances.

revenue

expense

8-16 To review briefly, recall that the Income Statement,
in showing these account balances, reveals the revenue and
expense factors changing the _____ _____ of
the firm between the dates of two successive _____
_____.

financial
position

Balance Sheets

8-17 The Income Statement supplements the Balance
Sheet, since it shows the revenue and expense account balances that contributed to the change in the_____
_____account from the preceding Balance Sheet
date.

Retained
Earnings

8-18 The accounting system prepares the Balance Sheet
and the Income Statement to fulfill a major responsibility
called _____ _____.

financial
reporting

8-19 A third major responsibility relates to the preparation of five specific outputs which permit close management
control of the firm. This is the _____ _____
responsibility.

control
reporting

8-20 Recall that the first kind of output maintained to provide control reporting informs management constantly of
quantities of all inventory items on hand, on order, and
required. These are unit _____ _____
_____.

Inventory Control
Records

8-21 In modern business, inventory control is crucial. Carrying too much inventory is extremely costly; yet if the firm cannot fill its customers' demands within a reasonable time, it will lose business. Recall that inventory information is reported on the _____ _____ in total dollars.

Balance Sheet

8-22 An overly high Inventory account balance may reveal an oversupply; business lost owing to items being out of stock will reveal an _____.

undersupply

8-23 However, to take corrective action, management must also know which items are overstocked or in short supply. Inventory control must therefore be exercised by item, and to provide this information the accounting system maintains unit _____ _____ _____.

Inventory Control Records

8-24 Unit Inventory Control Records, in addition to carrying quantities on hand by item, also usually carry quantities on _____, i.e., those purchased but not yet received. They may also carry units required for forecasted customer orders.

order

8-25 Since the basic problem of inventory control is to ensure that the firm maintains inventory stocks which are neither too large nor too small, Inventory Control Records may carry *maximum* and *minimum* figures, which represent allowable limits. If the stock figures dropped below the _____ figure, the firm would reorder the particular item immediately.

minimum

8-26 The firm would attempt to delay, or even possibly cancel, any existing orders it had placed with suppliers for a particular item if the quantity appeared to be above the _____ figure.

maximum

8-27 The following is a simplified unit Inventory Control
Record for lawnmower handles:

42

Handles (*max. 200, min. 50*)

Date	On hand	On order
1/20	142	0

If 100 were withdrawn from stock, the on-hand balance
would be reduced to _____ .

8-28 After the withdrawal of 100 handles, the record
would be:

order

minimum

Handles (*max. 200, min. 50*)

Date	On hand	On order
1/21	42	0

The record would now indicate that a new _____
should be placed since stock has fallen below the _____
figure.

8-29 Where lead time (the time it takes to replace stock)
is long and management wishes to minimize the danger of
stockouts, forecasted requirements may also be shown on
the _____ _____ _____ .

Inventory Control
Record

8-30 The following table represents the Inventory Control
Record for steel tubing:

Correct answer
included in next
frame

Steel tubing, feet (*coverage: max. 200, min. 50*)

Date	Required	On order	On hand	Total	Coverage
2/1	500	100	450	550	50
2/2	___	___	___	___	___

The coverage figure represents the difference between estimated current production requirements and the total on
hand and on order. It is set at 50 because of the lead time
required. Suppose that on February 2 production estimates
that it will require 700 feet. Update the above record accordingly.

8-31

Date	Required	On order	On hand	Total	Coverage
2/1	500	100	450	550	50
2/2	700	100	450	550	−150
2/2	___	___	___	___	___
2/15	___	___	___	___	___

Correct answer
included in next
frame

The minus figure for coverage is the signal for a reorder
of tubing. Since the minimum coverage is 50, the minimum
reorder for steel tubing is 200 feet. On February 2 the
firm placed the order, and on February 15 the first 100
feet was received from the supplier. Update the above record for both dates.

8-32

Date	Required	On order	On hand	Total	Coverage
2/2	700	300	450	750	50
2/15	700	200	550	750	50
2/20	___	___	___	___	___
2/21	___	___	___	___	___

Correct answer
included in next
frame

On February 20 production withdrew 400 feet and at the
same time made a new estimate—600 feet—of their current
requirements. The next day purchasing placed an order to
maintain the minimum coverage figure of 50 feet. Update
the above record accordingly.

8-33

Date	Required	On order	On hand	Total	Coverage
2/20	600	200	150	350	−250
2/21	600	500	150	650	50
2/23	___	___	___	___	___
2/25	___	___	___	___	___

Correct answer
included in
next frame

On February 23, all tubing orders placed prior to the order
of February 21 were received. On February 25, production
requisitioned 100 feet. Purchasing took advantage of a good
price by placing an order which raised the coverage to the
maximum 200 feet. Update the record.

8-34

Date	Required	On order	On hand	Total	Coverage
2/23	600	300	350	650	50
2/25	600	550	250	800	200

100

part

If, on February 30, the current production requirements
were dropped to 500 feet, the coverage in excess of the
maximum would be_____ feet. Purchasing might therefore consider canceling [all/part] _____ of the outstanding order for 550 feet of tubing.

8-35 The following is a similar Inventory Control Record, this one for finished goods:

Answer is in next frame

Model Q lawnmowers (coverage: max. 100, min. 10)

Date	Required	Production scheduled	Finished stock	Total	Coverage
2/1	300	100	220	320	20
2/6	___	___	___	___	___

The "required" figure is based on the current customer demand for this lawnmower, as estimated by the sales department. Shipping Notices for the week ending February 6 indicated fifty lawnmowers shipped. If 300 were currently required, update the above record, reducing stock and increasing production to maintain minimum coverage.

8-36

240

Date	Required	Production scheduled	Finished stock	Total	Coverage
2/1	300	100	220	320	20
2/6	300	140	170	310	10

If, on February 6, the sales department had notified you that their revised current sales estimate was 400, you would have increased the production schedule to_____ lawnmowers.

8-37 You should by now be familiar with the inputs which provide the information for maintaining Inventory Control Records. When the firm received the 100 feet of tubing from the supplier, you would find this information on the

_____ _____ .

Receiving Record

8-38 When the firm shipped fifty lawnmowers to the customer, you would record the shipment from information provided by the_____ _____ recording the shipments.

Shipping Notices

8-39 Internal transactions, such as the transfer of steel tubing to the production department and of lawnmowers to finished goods, are recorded on one of the two inputs providing internal transfer information. This input is the

_____ _____ .

Stores
Requisition

8-40 Suppose that a lawnmower was found defective and had to be scrapped. The input information would be provided by the _____ _____ , and you would alter the _____ - _____ balance and the _____ balance of the proper Inventory Control Record accordingly.

Scrap Notice

on-hand

coverage

8-41 To fulfill a second function in control reporting, the accounting system abstracts and summarizes sales information and prepares outputs called _____ _____ _____.

Sales
Performance
Analyses

8-42 Sales Performance Analyses provide detailed information on the firm's sales results which is not available from revenue accounts whose balances appear on the _____ _____.

Income Statement

8-43 Sales Performance Analyses can be prepared to show sales in terms of dollars, quantities, or both. If these reports are prepared on the basis of orders received, the accounting system would abstract and summarize the information provided by inputs called _____ _____.

Customer Orders

8-44 If it is more meaningful, the accounting system can instead abstract and summarize the dollar amounts or quantities of sales on the basis of orders shipped to customers. In this case the inputs used would be _____ _____.

Shipping Notices

8-45 Whether the accounting system uses Customer Orders, Shipping Notices, or both, its prime responsibility in sales reporting is to _____ and _____ sales data into meaningful classifications for Sales Performance Analyses.

abstract

summarize

8-46 Sales management might desire sales information classified according to each of the firm's products. For instance, if the firm sold electrical appliances, managers would be able to spot weaknesses in the sales effort regarding specific items if they had before them periodic _____ _____ _____ on which sales were classified by type of product.

Sales Performance Analyses

8-47 Some large modern firms employ large sales staffs. In order to know how well each of the salesmen was doing his job, sales managers would require a Sales Performance Analysis on which sales were classified according to the total turned in by each _____ during the period.

salesman

8-48 If total sales reported on the Income Statement were falling off, management would need to know if the loss came about because certain customers were not buying as much of the firm's products as before. In order to know the particular customers for whom the firm should increase its sales efforts, management would need a Sales Performance Analysis summarized according to the firm's individual

_____.

customers

8-49 However sales information is reported, the purpose is management control of sales efforts. The accounting system therefore provides Sales Performance Analyses as a part of a third major responsibility, that of _____

_____.

control reporting

8-50 The third output prepared as part of control reporting also relates to the Income Statement but in this case gives the details affecting another group of temporary holding accounts, the expense accounts. This output is the

_____ _____ _____.

Cost Analysis Report

8-51 The total of all expense accounts provides management with a total cost figure for the firm as a whole during
the particular period. But if costs were high, management
would not be able to tell what particular cost problems
needed attention merely by studying the _____
_____.

Income Statement

8-52 For instance, management would be able to examine
labor costs in detail only if it had a detailed Cost Analysis
Report that listed the actual cost of _____ separately.

labor

8-53 Labor costs, material costs, sales costs, and _____
shipping costs are among the many kinds of costs requiring
management's close attention. In order to control related
cost problems successfully, management needs _____
_____ Reports which list these costs separately.

Cost Analysis

8-54 In order to study the profitability of particular products, management needs Cost Analysis Reports which
categorize actual costs that affect each of the firm's
_____.

products

8-55 Suppose management discovered that the firm was
selling more lawnmowers at the same prices but making
less profit on each. It would refer to the Cost Analysis Report that recorded the costs related to the product in an
effort to increase the _____ on lawnmowers by reducing the_____ involved in their manufacture and
handling.

profit

costs

8-56 The obvious usefulness of Cost Analysis Reports is
that they provide management with a means of controlling
cost problems affecting the firm's operations. For this
reason the accounting system prepares Cost Analysis Reports as part of its third major responsibility, that of
_____ _____.

control reporting

8-57 The fourth output that the accounting system prepares as part of control reporting is the Budget. You already know that the accounting system is responsible for
summarizing input data called _____ _____
and publishing the Budget.

Budget
Information

8-58 Budget Information consists of the planned revenues
and expenses for the firm as a whole and for each_____
_____ within the firm.

profit center

8-59 Budget Information is one of the inputs leading to the
fifth output prepared in control reporting, the _____
_____ _____.

Budget
Performance
Analysis

8-60 The Budget Performance Analysis provides management with a comparison of _____ and _____
revenues and expenses for the budget period.

anticipated
(planned)

actual

8-61 Planned revenue and expense figures for both the
Budget and the Budget Performance Analysis are provided
by input data called _____ _____.

Budget
Information

8-62 Actual revenue and expense figures for the Budget
Performance Analysis come from the revenue and expense
accounts, the temporary holding accounts that are ultimately closed to the _____ _____ account
when the Balance Sheet is prepared.

Retained
Earnings

8-63 These total figures appear on the Budget Performance Analysis concerning the firm as a whole. However,
since the accounting system prepares Budget Performance
Analyses for each _____ _____ within the
firm, revenue and expense figures must, in addition, be abstracted for each.

profit center

8-64 You would not show shipping costs as part of the purchasing department's expense. Logically you would show
such costs as an expense on the _____ _____
_____ prepared for the shipping department.

Budget
Performance
Analysis

8-65 If Budgets are prepared in advance for each month, then the matching Budget Performance Analyses would be prepared every _____ to cover the prior budget period.

month

8-66 In addition to anticipated and actual revenue and expense figures, Budget Performance Analyses carry the variances—the differences between anticipated and actual figures—for the month and also often for the year to date. These _____ , usually expressed both in dollars and percentages, highlight significant deviations for management's attention.

variances

8-67 The current month's variance and the cumulative variance between planned and actual _____ and _____ may be expressed in both dollars and _____ on the Budget Performance Analysis.

revenues

expenses

percentages

8-68 The Budget Performance Analysis, then, is the last of five outputs which the accounting system prepares to fulfill its third major responsibility, that of _____ _____ .

control

reporting

8-69 Two additional activities help the accountant fulfill the accounting system's three major responsibilities. The first of these involves processing and recording special input data related to the maintenance of the master files. Recall that three of these files are maintained, one for the payroll activity and two for the billing activity. These are the_____ Master File, the _____ Master File, and the _____ Master File.

Payroll

Customer

Parts

8-70 Because of their importance in the activities involving their use, the accounting system must be prepared to modify these three _____ files constantly in order to keep the information they contain accurate and up-to-date.

master

8-71 Information on a new employee, a change in the pay rate or number of dependents of an employee, and an additional payroll deduction authorized by an employee are examples of special input data which would affect the information contained in the _____ Master File.

Payroll

8-72 A change in a customer's address, a new trade discount given a customer, and a change in a customer's payment terms are examples of special input data affecting the _____ Master File.

Customer

8-73 A change in a product's price and the addition of a new product to the firm's line are examples of input data affecting the _____ Master File.

Parts

8-74 It is clear that the accounting system must record changes in the information contained in these files as soon as such changes become effective. Unless the files are current, the outputs prepared by the _____ and _____ activities are subject to serious errors.

payroll

billing

8-75 There is, of course, no such thing as an error-proof accounting system; nor is there such a thing as an error-proof accountant. To allow for human failure, accountants have devised a systematic method for _____ correction.

error

8-76 Double-entry bookkeeping allows accountants to maintain a constant check on their work. For instance, an accountant can check himself when journalizing entries simply by testing the entry to see if _____ equal _____ . This is a simple way of checking for balance.

debits

credits

8-77 However, errors will inevitably occur—hopefully not often. Accountants avoid the possibility of backtracking through a large volume of work by first inspecting at frequent intervals all the work they have done since the last inspection. The simple way to do this is the same as for checking individual entries: The accountant simply _____ for _____ .

checks [for]
balance

8-78 This method of testing, however, cannot pinpoint the
particular error. Accountants therefore maintain what they
call an audit trail, which is a record of all entries made
since the last inspection. In locating an error, accountants
follow the _____ _____ back through the work
they have completed since the previous inspection.

audit trail

8-79 Accountants avoid lengthy searches for errors by
_____ for _____ at frequently scheduled intervals. If they discover during an inspection that an error
has appeared, they can locate the specific error without
difficulty by following the _____ _____ back
through their recent work.

checking [for]
balance

audit trail

8-80 Accountants maintain an audit trail by cross refer-
encing all the documents involved. First, the accountant
dates the Journal entry to match the date on the input from
which he abstracted the entry. If an error should occur, he
can find the original input easily by locating the input
carrying the same _____ as the _____

_____.

date

Journal entry

8-81 Later, when he posts the entry to the Ledger, the accountant dates the entry in the Ledger as an index to the
original input and the Journal entry date. He also notes
the Ledger record number in the Journal. Thus, if he found
an incorrect entry in the Journal, he could trace that entry
to the Ledger accounts affected by referring to the Ledger

_____ _____.

record number

8-82 If he found what seemed an incorrect posting in the
Ledger, he could find the original entry in the Journal by
referring to the _____ of the posting, which serves
as an index to the Journal.

date

8-83 The original input, the Journal entry, and the corresponding posting to the Ledger are cross indexed by
_____ or by Ledger _____ _____.

date

record number

8-84 By cross-referencing his work in this way, the accountant maintains what is called an _____ _____
in his work.

audit trail

8-85 To review, accountants avoid difficult error-correction problems by _____ for _____ at fre-
quently scheduled intervals. If they should discover an in-
balance, they can follow the _____ _____ back
through their work to locate the specific erroneous entry.

checking [for]
balance

audit trail

8-86 Once they locate the error, correcting it is simply a
matter of reversing the erroneous entry and then making
the correct one. Since a further error might be involved,
and since all records, even erroneous ones, must be pre-
served to maintain the audit trail, accountants never erase
or obliterate an incorrect entry. Instead they correct the
error by _____ the incorrect entry and by making
the _____ entry.

reversing

correct

8-87 Reversing an entry simply involves making the incorrect entry backwards, that is, with the original debit and
credit amounts reversed. For example, suppose an out-of-
balance condition revealed that a zero had been omitted in
journalizing the receipt of inventory costing $500, which was
purchased on credit. The incorrect entry was found to be:

	Dr	Cr
Inventory	$500	
Accounts Payable		$50

Following the above principle, complete the reversing en--
try:

	Dr	Cr
_____	$_____	$_____
_____	$_____	$_____

	Dr	Cr
Accounts Payable	$50	
Inventory		$500

8-88 You can see how this works. The erroneous entry involved a debit of $500 to Inventory, which [increased/reduced] _____ the Inventory account balance by that amount.

increased

8-89 Reversing this part of the entry involves a credit of $500 to the Inventory account. The original incorrect debit increased this account. The reversing credit cancels this increase by _____ the account by an equal amount.

reducing

8-90 The same is true of the Accounts Payable account, although in an opposite way. The erroneous entry involved a _____ of $50 to this account, which [increased/reduced] _____ the balance. The reversing entry involves a _____ to the account, which _____ the balance by the same amount, thus canceling the effect of the error.

credit

increased

debit

reduced

8-91 How you would make another entry, the correct one that should have been made originally. Add the figures to the proper columns.

	Dr	Cr
Inventory	$ _____	$ _____
Accounts Payable	$ _____	$ _____

	Dr	Cr
Inventory	$500	
Accounts Payable		$500

8-92 Let's look at one more example. Suppose that land costing $10,000, which was paid for in cash, had been incorrectly recorded as equipment. The incorrect entry was:

	Dr	Cr
Equipment	$10,000	
Cash		$10,000

Journalize the reversing entry.

	Dr	Cr
_____	$ _____	$ _____
_____	$ _____	$ _____

	Dr	Cr
Cash	$10,000	
Equipment		$10,000

8-93 Now complete the correction procedure by journalizing the correcting entry.

	Dr	Cr
_____	$ _____	$ _____
_____	$ _____	$ _____

	Dr	Cr
Land	$10,000	
Cash		$10,000

8-94 Error correction, then, involves two entries: The accountant makes a _____ entry to "wipe out" the effect of the incorrect entry; he then makes the _____ entry.

reversing

correct

8-95 Accountants do not erase or remove any entry, even though erroneous, because they must maintain the_____ trail.

audit

End of Part 8. Turn to the next page for the Review Quiz only when you are ready to complete Part 9.

review quiz on part 8

1. Before making adjusting and closing entries, the accountant usually checks the Ledgers by taking a _____ _____ .

2. Suppose that an Inventory Control Record with a maximum of 100 and a minimum of 20 for coverage shows a coverage of 40. If a Stores Requisition for 10 is received, a re-order [would/would not]_____ be indicated.

3. After the requisition for 10 was entered, a reorder would be made when additional requisitions totaling _____or more were received.

4. Assume that the initial coverage is 40 and that later requisitions total 50. If the maximum coverage is 100, what is the maximum reorder quantity? _____

5. A shipment is received in the quantity ordered. Indicate by an X which of the following balances on the Inventory Control Record would be changed:
   (a) Required _____
   (b) On order _____
   (c) On hand _____
   (d) Total _____
   (e) Coverage _____

After each event described below, indicate its effect on coverage by the appropriate letter.

   A   coverage reduced
   B   coverage increased
   C   coverage unchanged

6. A present requirement is increased: _____
7. A present requirement is reduced: _____
8. An order is received for the original order quantity: _____
9. On an order for 100 items, 98 are received, and the order is closed out: _____
10. An item in stock is found defective and scrapped: _____
11. Quantities in excess of existing orders are received from suppliers and placed in inventory: _____

Complete the following sentences.

12. In addition to planned and actual figures, a _____ figure is often calculated and shown on the Budget Performance Analysis.

13. A variance is often reported in both dollars and _____ to assist in the evaluation of its significance.

14. To minimize the amount of backtracking required, the accounting records should be checked at frequent intervals to see if they are in _____ .

15. Accountants also minimize backtracking by maintaining an _____ trail through the accounting records.

16. When an error is discovered and located, the accountant makes two entries a
    _____ entry and the _____ entry.

17. When recording the purchase of supplies costing $70 *cash*, an accountant made the fol-
    lowing incorrect entry:

	Dr	Cr
Supplies Expense	$700	
Accounts Payable		$70

    The proper entries to correct this error would be:

	Dr	Cr
_____	$ _____	$ _____
_____	$ _____	$ _____
_____	$ _____	$ _____
_____	$ _____	$ _____

PART 9
cost accounting

9-1 The reason that management gives so much attention to costs is this: Costs are extremely important in determining profitability, yet it is difficult to compute _____ figures exactly.

cost

9-2 Moreover, the term "cost" has no meaning without careful qualification. In dealing with a particular cost figure, you must know precisely what cost data it represents in order to understand its significance. As you will see, the cost figures for a particular product determined one way may be _____ from the cost figures for the same product determined another way.

different

9-3 You learned earlier that, in general, all asset account balances reflect the *original cost* of the particular assets. This section will deal with the problems involved in computing _____ _____ figures with meaningful accuracy.

original cost

9-4 To illustrate the problems facing accountants, suppose that a firm purchased a turret lathe from a supplier in Chicago and installed it in its Los Angeles plant. What two factors can you see which might make the original cost of the lathe higher than the net invoice cost?

1. _____ charges
2. _____ charges

1. freight (These
are called
freight-in
costs.)

2. installation

9-5 The firm might have purchased the lathe at a net invoice price that included freight-in costs and installation costs. If this were the case, the original cost of this fixed asset is the _____ _____ cost.

net invoice

9-6 If the net invoice cost covered only the lathe, however, you would have to compute its original cost by adding the _____ - _____ costs, along with the _____ costs, to the net invoice cost.

freight-in

installation

9-7 The original cost of all fixed assets includes any freight-in and installation costs, in addition to the _____ _____ cost.

net invoice

9-8 Obviously, merchandise or materials inventory does not require installation. But in computing inventory costs, you would have to add any_____ - _____ costs to the _____ _____ _____ .

freight-in

net invoice cost

9-9 If all cost factors remained constant from year to year, it would be relatively easy to determine costs. But they don't. Prices, freight rates, and installation charges are a few cost factors subject to constant change, and the accountant must consider these when computing meaningful _____ figures.

cost

9-10 For instance, the mythical Jones Company, which manufactures power lawnmowers, might have in its materials inventory two identical lots of steel tubing purchased at different times. The chances are that the costs of the two lots were entered into the Materials Inventory account at [the same/different] _____ figures.

different

9-11 The total cost figure represented by the balance in the Materials Inventory account may be accurate but deceptive. Two identical lots of steel tubing may have been purchased at different times, and therefore both the _____ _____ costs and the_____ - _____ costs on each lot may have been different.

net invoice

freight-in

9-12 Since materials are added to the Materials Inventory account at actual cost, even when different lots have different costs, the Jones Company accountant has no problem recording the receipt of inventory. However, he does have a problem in determining a proper cost figure when recording withdrawals from the _____ _____ account.

Materials
Inventory

9-13 Accountants generally use one of four standard methods to "price" or "cost" inventories and hence transfers out of Materials Inventory. Refer to Panel K. As you can see, there was no beginning inventory. During the period covered, four lots of identical steel tubing were received. The first two lots, totaling 1,000 feet, cost 10 cents per foot, and the second two lots, totaling 3,000 feet, cost 12 cents per foot. The total charge to Materials Inventory was $_____.

$460

9-14 If withdrawals of steel tubing from inventory can be related to specific lots, the withdrawals can be costed out by the price paid for the particular tubing. By this *specific identification method,* if 500 feet of the lot purchased on January 2, and 500 feet of the lot purchased on September 1, were withdrawn, the total credits to Materials Inventory would be $_____ ; the balance in the account would be $_____.

$110

$350

9-15 If materials are held in inventory in such a way that they can be related to specific acquisition costs, accountants can use the inventory valuation method called

_____ _____.

specific
identification

9-16 Most firms find that keeping the various lots separate is not feasible; they will use other methods of materials inventory valuation. One of these is called average cost. When accountants relieve, or credit, Materials Inventory for materials withdrawn at an *average* of all acquisition costs at which the various lots of materials were entered, they are using the _____ _____ method.

average cost

9-17 Normally a simple average will not be adequate be-cause the size of the various lots purchased at different prices will vary. Accountants therefore use a *weighted average*, determined by dividing the total cost by the total quantity. Refer to Panel K. The weighted average would be computed by dividing $ _____ by _____ feet. The average cost per foot would be _____ cents.

$460

4,000

$11\frac{1}{2}$

9-18 If 1,000 feet were relieved by the average cost method, the balance in the Materials Inventory account for steel tubing would be $460 minus $ _____ , or $ _____ .

$115

$345

9-19 So far you have seen two methods used for materials inventory valuation. One of these relates withdrawals and ending balances to specific acquisition costs; it is known as the _____ _____ method. The other uses a weighted average of acquisition unit prices; this is called the _____ _____ method.

specific
  identification

average cost

9-20 A third method of materials inventory valuation as-sumes that costs are transferred out of Materials Inventory in the same order that they are transferred in. This method is called first-in, first-out, or FIFO. Refer to Panel K. If the accountant uses FIFO, the first two withdraw-als totaling 1,000 feet would result in a credit of $ _____ to Materials Inventory.

$100

9-21 Since the withdrawal of 1,000 feet resulted in re-lieving Materials Inventory of the total acquisition cost of the first two lots, the withdrawal of another 500 feet would be credited at _____ cents per foot.

12

9-22 The accountant using FIFO assumes that the first costs debited to Materials Inventory are the _____ costs credited to this account.

first

9-23 On the other hand, the accountant may assume the
exact opposite—that costs flow through inventory in reverse
order from that in which they were entered. If he assumes
this, he will use the LIFO method of materials inventory
valuation. LIFO stands for _____ - _____,
_____ - _____.

last-in,
first-out

9-24 The last acquisition of tubing reported on Panel K is
2,000 feet at 12 cents per foot. To record the withdrawal of
2,000 feet during the period, the accountant using LIFO
would credit Materials Inventory with $_____ .

$240

9-25 To see how these methods differ, look again at Panel
K. Only 2,000 feet were withdrawn during the period. The
ending balance of Materials Inventory is:

1. Under FIFO: $460 – $_____ = $_____
2. Under LIFO: $460 – $_____ = $_____

1. $460 – $220 =
   $240

2. $460 – $240 =
   $220

9-26 If we assume that the firm sold withdrawn tubing
directly to its customers, you see that the Cost of Goods
Sold, reported on the Income Statement, is:

1. Under FIFO: $_____
2. Under LIFO: $_____

1. $220

2. $240

9-27 The result of charging the more recent acquisition
costs to Cost of Goods Sold by using LIFO increases expenses over the FIFO method by $20. Consequently, the
profit reported under LIFO would be $20 [less/more]
_____than under FIFO.

less

9-28 Conversely, you can see that under FIFO the more
recent costs are held in inventory. The Materials Inventory
account on the Balance Sheet would be $20 [less/more]
_____under FIFO than under LIFO.

more

9-29 Average cost, FIFO, and LIFO consider the cost flows through Materials Inventory as independent of the physical movement of materials. Even though the physical flow is generally FIFO, the accountant would use the _____ method to attach a more recent cost to outflows of materials.

LIFO

9-30 On the other hand, if the accountant preferred to price the inventories on the Balance Sheet at the most recent acquisition costs, he would use the _____ method.

FIFO

9-31 Many managers, when forecasting expenses and the resulting profits, think in terms of what it will cost to replace inventory sold. These managers would find that the inventory method charging to Cost of Goods Sold the more nearly current costs, the _____ method, was most meaningful.

LIFO

9-32 Under the condition of unchanging inventory acquisition costs, all methods would yield the same results. In times when acquisition costs are rising, the method yielding the highest Cost of Goods Sold figure and the lowest inventory valuation is _____ . The method yielding the highest inventory valuation and the lowest Cost of Goods Sold is _____ .

LIFO

FIFO

9-33 Four methods of materials inventory valuation are:

1. _____ _____
2. _____ _____
3. _____
4. _____

1. specific identification

2. average cost

3. FIFO

4. LIFO

9-34 Any of these methods can be used for determining income taxes payable. While it is beyond the scope of this text to deal with taxation problems, this shows you that in times of rising costs a firm will report lower profits and pay less income tax by using the _____ method.

LIFO

9-35 Refer to the withdrawal figures on Panel K. Suppose that on December 31 the accountant computed all the credits for each of the withdrawals listed. He would proceed differently under these two methods:

	FIFO	LIFO
	$ 50	$ 60
	50	60
	120	120
	220	240

	FIFO	LIFO
500 ft on 3/10	$ _____	$ _____
500 ft on 6/10	$ _____	$ _____
1,000 ft on 12/15	$ _____	$ _____
Total	$ _____	$ _____

9-36 Under FIFO, the costs remaining in inventory are $_____ and represent the costs for the December 1 purchase. Under LIFO, the costs remaining in inventory are $_____ and represent the costs of the purchases made on _____ , _____ , and _____ .

$240

$220

January 2

June 1

December 1

9-37 Now if an additional 1,000 feet had been withdrawn on December 15, the credit for this additional withdrawal would be:

1. Under FIFO: $ _____
2. Under LIFO: $ _____

1. $120

2. $120

9-38 So far we have concerned ourselves solely with a manufacturer's *material costs*. These consist of the _____ _____ cost plus any _____- _____ costs involved.

net invoice

freight-in

9-39 In addition to material costs, a manufacturer will incur labor and overhead costs in converting raw materials to finished products. Three costs are therefore involved in a manufacturer's cost accounting:

1. _____ costs
2. _____ costs
3. _____ costs

1. material

2. labor

3. overhead

9-40 Since a manufacturer usually has an inventory of items in production, a separate inventory account entitled Work in Process is maintained to carry the costs of material, _____ , and _____ already expended on such items.

9-41 Also, a stock of finished products is usually on hand. A third inventory account titled Finished Goods is maintained to carry the product costs, which include all material, labor, and overhead _____ of the completed products.

9-42 The three manufacturing inventory accounts—Materials, Work in Process, Finished Goods—may appear separately, or they may be summarized on the Balance Sheet after the caption _____.

9-43 If you saw a manufacturer's Balance Sheet with only one inventory figure listed, you would know that this amount was the summary of at least three separate inventory account balances:

1. _____ Inventory
2. _____ _____ _____ Inventory
3. _____ _____ Inventory.

9-44 The balance in the Materials account reflects the _____ of materials in the firm's possession that have not yet entered production.

9-45 A Stores Requisition initiates the transfer of raw materials—the steel tubing, for instance—from the storeroom to the production department. When the accountant receives the Stores Requisition, he [debits/credits] _____ Materials Inventory and _____ Work in Process Inventory, each with the cost of materials determined by one of the four methods of valuation.

9-46 Suppose that an accountant received a Stores Requisition recording the transfer of 100 feet of steel tubing from the raw material storeroom to the production department. He would debit _____ _____ _____ and credit _____ with the _____ of the steel tubing.

Work in
Process

Materials

cost

9-47 As labor and overhead costs accumulate, the accountant adds them to the Work in Process account. For example, if $1,500 of labor and overhead costs had accumulated, the accountant would [debit/credit]_____ the _____ _____ _____ account with $1,500.

debit

Work in
Process

9-48 When the accountant receives the Stores Requisition advising him of the transfer of a finished product into the finished goods storeroom, he adjusts the inventory accounts according to the product cost. He [debits/credits] _____Work in Process and_____Finished Goods, each with the _____ _____ .

credits

debits

product cost

9-49 Before considering labor and overhead costs in detail, let's complete the cost cycle. Recall that when an item is sold, its product cost, originally carried in inventory, is transferred to the expense account _____ of _____ _____ , which appears on the Income Statement.

Cost [of]
Goods Sold

9-50 When the accountant receives a Shipping Notice advising him that a product has been shipped to a customer, he [debits/credits]_____ Finished Goods Inventory and_____the Cost of Goods Sold account. The latter account is ultimately closed into the_____ _____ account at the end of the accounting period.

credits

debits

Retained
Earnings

9-51 Recall in passing that accountants close revenue and
expense accounts first to an interim account called Income
Summary, which they in turn close to Retained Earnings.
However, revenue and expense accounts ultimately affect
the _____ _____ account.

Retained
Earnings

9-52 Remember that you can determine the material cost
component of product costs quite easily. It consists of the
_____ _____ costs recorded on the Materials
Invoice and any additional_____ - _____ costs
involved.

net invoice

freight-in

9-53 These costs are assigned to material used in production by one of four methods:

1. _____ _____
2. _____ _____
3. _____
4. _____

1. average cost

2. specific
identification

3. FIFO

4. LIFO

9-54 The two additional kinds of costs, _____ costs
and _____ costs, are added to a product's cost while
it is carried in the _____ _____ _____
account.

labor

overhead

Work in Process

9-55 Accountants distinguish two kinds of factory labor
costs—*direct* and *indirect*. The cost of man-hours of work
specifically involved in the manufacture of a product is obviously a _____ labor cost of that product.

direct

9-56 A factory also employs maintenance men, janitors,
truckers, and others, who are necessary to the factory's
operation but who do not work in production. The cost of
the man-hours they work must be classified as_____
labor costs.

indirect

9-57 The distinction between direct and indirect labor costs arises from necessity. Take the example of two workers, one an assembler putting lawnmowers together, the other a janitor responsible for cleaning the assembly department. The assembly worker's wages are clearly chargeable as _____ labor.

direct

9-58 Like material costs, direct labor costs are readily identifiable and assignable to a product. The time the assembly worker spends putting lawnmowers together is directly and exclusively part of the product cost, and therefore the_____ _____ cost his wages represent can be directly assigned to the lawnmowers produced.

direct labor

9-59 Overhead is a cost category which includes all the costs and expenses not readily identifiable with specific products but which must be considered product costs. Indirect labor, since it cannot be identified with the production of a particular product, falls into the cost category of

_____.

overhead

9-60 Even though necessary for efficient production, the janitor's services cannot be accurately identified either with the assembly of lawnmowers or with any other products also going through the assembly department. Therefore, the _____ _____ costs represented by the janitor's wages are necessarily included in factory

_____.

indirect labor

overhead

9-61 The distinction between direct and indirect labor is by *job performed*, not always by *worker*. If a man spends four hours in the morning operating a turret lathe and four hours in the afternoon on maintenance, his morning hours would be classified as _____ _____ and his afternoon hours as_____ _____.

direct labor

indirect labor

9-62 If you were reviewing a group of Timecards to determine how many hours were chargeable to direct labor and how many to indirect labor, you would base your distinctions on the _____ _____ rather than on the _____.

job performed

worker

9-63 However, certain workers obviously spend their total time in indirect labor. While the accountant is obliged to divide the turret lathe operator's time into direct and indirect labor, a janitor's total time is quite clearly _____ _____.

indirect labor

9-64 The accountant adds direct labor costs incurred in each accounting period to the _____ _____ _____ account. In other words, he [debits/credits] _____ that account by the appropriate amount. Indirect labor costs, on the other hand, become part of overhead costs. This will be discussed below.

Work in Process

debits

9-65 Remember that indirect labor costs [are/are not] _____ part of overhead costs.

are

9-66 Another important distinction accountants make is between *product costs* and *period costs.* In a manufacturing firm, product costs are those directly related to the production of inventory. Obviously, costs of materials and direct labor costs are _____ _____.

product costs

9-67 During an accounting period a manufacturer incurs expenses not chargeable to the cost of producing any product. General office expenses, selling expenses, and administrative expenses are examples of _____ costs.

period

9-68 In a manufacturing firm the sales manager's salary is considered a _____ cost and a machinist's wages a _____ cost.

period

product

9-69 The distinction between product and period costs is important. Product costs [are/are not] _____ added to the Inventory (Work in Process) account, and period costs [are/are not]_____.

are

are not

9-70 Period costs are considered expenses. It is generally assumed, for instance, that the firm benefitted completely from the sales manager's efforts during a particular accounting period. Therefore, it is logical that his salary, a _____ cost, is charged as an expense of the current _____ _____ .

period

accounting
  period

9-71 On the other hand, the firm may not benefit from the efforts of a machinist during a particular period because the products he worked on may not be sold. His wages, a _____ cost, are debited to Inventory (Work in Process), an asset account.

product

9-72 The machinist's wages, debited to the _____ _____ _____ Inventory account, are later transferred as part of a completed product's cost to the _____ _____ Inventory account, where they remain until the product is sold.

Work in Process

Finished Goods

9-73 Let's review what you have already learned and trace direct labor costs through the various inventory accounts. Recall first that a machinist's labor costs are debited to the _____ _____ _____ Inventory account on the basis of work performed.

Work in Process

9-74 When a product is completed and transferred to the finished goods storeroom, the transfer is recorded at product cost, which includes _____, _____, and _____ costs.

material, labor,
  [and] overhead

9-75 The accountant records this transfer by [debiting/crediting_____ Work in Process and _____ Finished Goods with the product _____.

crediting

debiting

cost

9-76 The costs represented by the machinist's wages would therefore have been transferred from the _____ _____ _____ account to the _____ _____ account as part of product costs.

Work in Process

Finished Goods

9-77 If a product is not sold by the end of a particular period, the normal assumption is that it will be sold and thus produce revenue in a future period. The product, therefore, has future value, and its cost is carried as an asset on the Balance Sheet in the _____ _____ Inventory account.

Finished Goods

9-78 Turn now to Panel L, an Income Statement of a manufacturing firm. Notice that it lists all product costs under the general heading _____ of _____ _____ and all period costs under _____ _____.

Cost [of] Goods
  Sold

Operating
  Expenses

9-79 The financial vice president's salary, a _____ cost, [would/would not] _____ always appear at the end of an accounting period as part of _____ _____ Expenses.

period

would

General
  Administrative

9-80 If the product that included the machinist's wages as part of its _____ _____ has been sold by period end, this cost [would/would not] _____ be reflected under Cost of Goods Sold.

product cost

would

9-81 Suppose that the product, a power lawnmower, had a product cost of $50 and a selling price of $75. When it is sold, and if there are no sales taxes or discounts, the two entries recording the sale and shipment are as follows:

	Dr	Cr
Accounts Receivable	$ _____	$ _____
Sales	$ _____	$ _____
Cost of Goods Sold	$ _____	$ _____
Finished Goods	$ _____	$ _____

	Dr	Cr
Accounts Receivable	$75	
Sales		$75
Cost of Goods Sold	50	
Finished Goods Inventory		50

9-82 The machinist's wages, a _____ cost, are thus finally reflected in _____ of _____ _____, an expense account.

product

Cost [of] Goods Sold

9-83 Note that this accounting practice matches the expense incurred for the machinist's labor with the benefit, or revenue, received in the same accounting_____.

period

9-84 We have skipped over the subject of overhead costs, but now that you understand the flow of material and labor costs, we can consider overhead in detail. Recall that the accountant adds three kinds of costs to the Work in Process account:_____ , _____ _____, and _____ costs.

material

direct labor

overhead

9-85 Direct labor and overhead costs, then, along with material costs, are part of _____ _____.

product cost

9-86 Recall also that labor costs are of two kinds, _____ and _____ , and that _____ labor costs are considered part of factory overhead costs.

direct

indirect

indirect

9-87 Three kinds of factory costs, called _____ costs since they are added to Inventory rather than to a period's expenses, are:

1. Material costs
2. Direct labor costs
3. _____ costs, including _____ labor costs

product

overhead

indirect

9-88 Besides indirect labor costs, overhead includes all costs of operating a factory that cannot be identified as material or direct labor costs. The salaries of foremen and factory managers, factory utilities (electricity, heat, and the like), and depreciation on plant and equipment are examples of _____ costs.

overhead

9-89 Overhead costs, like material and direct labor costs, are product costs; they are therefore also added to the value of the _____ _____ _____ Inventory account.

Work in Process

9-90 The example of the janitor's wages illustrates the basic problem of assigning overhead costs to a product. As you can see, overhead is a catch-all title including all factory costs not specifically identifiable as either_____ costs or _____ _____ costs.

material

direct labor

9-91 How then can the accountant assign a meaningful overhead figure to a product? Certainly the accountant cannot determine how much of the_____ costs represented by the janitor's wages is assignable to a particular product assembled in the department he services.

overhead

9-92 Many firms solve this problem by establishing an overhead rate, which they use to allocate overhead to inventory on the basis of direct labor dollars involved. In such a case, the accountant assigns overhead costs to inventory by multiplying the amount of direct labor dollars incurred by the _____ _____.

overhead rate

9-93 Overhead rates are usually established for the forth-coming year as a ratio of total expected overhead costs to total expected direct labor dollars. To set the overhead rate, the accountant requires an estimate of total _____costs and total expected_____ _____ _____ for the coming year.

overhead

direct labor
  dollars

9-94 The allocation of overhead by the use of a constant rate also tends to level the otherwise variable patterns of actual overhead costs. Thus, although an overhead cost such as that for heating fuel would vary with the seasons, the application of a constant overhead rate results in a [constant/varying] _____overhead charge per direct labor dollar throughout the year.

constant

9-95 If, in a given period, there were $4,000 of direct labor and the overhead rate was $2.50, the_____ _____ _____ Inventory account would absorb $_____of overhead expense.

Work in Process

$10,000

9-96 Accountants can determine an overhead rate because they can estimate with reasonable accuracy for a coming year both the amount of total_____ costs and the number of _____ _____ dollars to be ex-pended.

overhead

direct labor

9-97 However, there is invariably a difference between the actual amount of overhead incurred during a period and the amount of overhead absorbed into the _____ _____ _____ Inventory account.

Work in Process

9-98 If some overhead remains, it is called *underabsorbed overhead.* For instance, if Work in Process Inventory ab-sorbed $10,000 of overhead during a month in which actual overhead costs were $12,000, the difference of $_____ would be considered _____ _____ .

$2,000

underabsorbed
  overhead

9-99 Using a single overhead rate can also lead to *overab-sorbed overhead*. If $10,000 of overhead were absorbed into Work in Process Inventory and overhead costs were actually $9,000 for the month, the difference of $_____ would be considered _____ _____.

$1,000

overabsorbed
overhead

9-100 With an accurate overhead rate, amounts of overhead *variances* (underabsorbed and overabsorbed) from month to month will tend to cancel out over the year. The accountant therefore usually accumulates these variances separately. At year end he closed the net difference to _____ of _____ _____, the expense account recording product costs.

Cost [of] Goods
Sold

9-101 Like material costs and direct labor costs, overhead is charged (debited) to the _____ _____ _____ Inventory account; it is then transferred to _____ _____ when the product is completed; finally it is transferred to the _____ of _____ _____ account when the product is_____.

Work in Process

Finished Goods

Cost [of] Goods
Sold

sold

9-102 If, at the Balance Sheet date, the firm considers that all or part of a product cost will benefit the firm in some future period, then all or some portion will remain in the appropriate inventory account and be reported on the _____ _____ as an_____.

Balance Sheet

asset

9-103 On the other hand, all or part of the cost may be considered to have been used up, or expired, in gaining revenues for the current period. Then all or a portion of that cost has become an _____ of doing business, and it is reported on the _____ _____ for the current period.

expense

Income
Statement

9-104 Thus the cost of acquiring goods or services will be reported either as an _____ on the Balance Sheet or as an _____ on the Income Statement.

asset

expense

9-105 Expense means simply that the benefit of a particular cost has been realized as revenue. If the benefit has
not been realized, but will be in a future period, the cost
is recorded as an _____ on the _____.

asset

Balance Sheet

**End of Part 9. Turn to the next page for the Review Quiz only when you
are ready to complete Part 10.**

review quiz on part 9

Complete the following sentences.

1. The word *cost* [does/does not] _____ have a precise meaning.
2. What is included in a given cost figure as reported to management [may/maynot] _____ vary both by the purpose for which it is intended and by specific company practice.
3. The original cost of a new piece of equipment as debited to the appropriate fixed asset account would include, in addition to the purchase price, any _____ - _____ and _____ costs incurred.
4. Materials Inventory in a manufacturing concern, and Merchandise Inventory for a non-manufacturer, includes costs of the material or merchandise itself plus _____ - _____ costs.
5. Four different methods of materials inventory valuation are:
    (*a*) _____ _____
    (*b*) _____ _____
    (*c*) _____
    (*d*) _____
6. If specific identification were the method of inventory valuation adopted in a given firm and if all material was taken out of inventory in the same order as it was received, the _____ method would result in the same dollar valuation.
7. Regardless of which of the four methods is adopted, material [is/is not] _____ debited into inventory at the total purchase cost including freight-in.
8. In times of changing prices, the _____ method of inventory valuation provides most recent costs in the Cost of Goods Sold account.
9. In times of changing prices, the _____ method most closely records inventory on the Balance Sheet in terms of most nearly recent costs.
10. Product costs of a completed manufactured product include three kinds of costs:
    (*a*) _____ cost
    (*b*) _____ _____ cost
    (*c*) _____ cost
11. A manufacturing concern generally has at least three separate inventory accounts:
    (*a*) _____
    (*b*) _____ _____ _____
    (*c*) _____ _____
12. All factory labor is considered either _____ labor or _____ labor.
13. It is assumed that the firm receives the full benefits of period costs during the accounting _____ in which they are incurred.
14. The benefits from product costs occur when the products are _____ ; such benefits [are/are not] _____ always realized during the same period in which the costs are incurred.
15. Period costs [are/are not] _____ included as part of Cost of Goods Sold on the Income Statement.

Identify the following costs as direct labor (L), overhead (O), or period cost (P).

16. Financial vice president's salary ____
17. Sales manager's salary ____
18. Janitor's salary (works in factory) ____
19. Janitor's salary (works in executive office) ____
20. Labor hours spent on product assembly ____
21. Labor hours spent on repairing equipment ____
22. Property taxes on factory ____
23. Property taxes on a regional sales office ____
24. Sales commissions earned ____

Complete the following sentences.

25. All product costs not identifiable as materials cost or direct labor are included in

    _____ .

26. When overhead is applied to Work in Process Inventory, it is said to be _____ into inventory.

27. Overhead is frequently applied to inventory at a predetermined rate based on

    _____ _____ _____ .

28. If less overhead is absorbed than was actually incurred during a period, the excess, or variance, is known as _____ overhead.

29. If more overhead is absorbed than was actually incurred, the variance is known as _____ overhead.

30. As a unit of material moves progressively through a manufacturing firm on a perpetual inventory system from a supplier to a customer, its cost is debited and credited to the various accounts as follows:

    Step 1: _____ Materials Inventory, _____ Accounts Payable
    Step 2: _____ Materials Inventory, _____ Work in Process Inventory
    Step 3: _____ Finished Goods Inventory, _____ Work in Process Inventory
    Step 4: _____ Finished Goods Inventory, _____ Cost of Goods Sold

cost accounting (continued)

10-1 Let's review briefly the cost flow through the manufacturing inventory accounts. First, on the basis of approved Incoming Invoices covering the cost of raw material and the freight-in charges, you [debit/credit] _____ the _____ Inventory account and _____ Accounts Payable.

debit

Materials

credit

10-2 When you receive a Stores Requisition covering the transfer of raw materials into the production department, you _____ Materials Inventory and _____ Work in Process Inventory.

credit

debit

10-3 Recall that labor costs, which consist of gross earnings and employer's taxes, are originally [debit/credit] _____ to the Factory Payroll Expense account and concurrently _____ to Cash or Wages and Salaries Payable and to Taxes Payable.

debited

credited

10-4 Direct labor costs are computed as part of the payroll activity. During, or at the end of, each accounting period, they are charged to inventory by a _____ to the _____ _____ _____ Inventory account and a _____ to Factory Payroll Expense.

debit

Work in Process

credit

10-5 The remaining labor costs in the Factory Payroll Expense account would represent _____ labor, which must be included as part of _____.

indirect

overhead

157

10-6 Following the same pattern as that established for the Factory Payroll Expense account, overhead expenditures other than indirect labor are accumulated throughout the period as [debits/credits] _____ to the Factory Overhead account and as _____ to Cash or Accounts Payable.

debits

credits

10-7 The accountant transfers indirect labor to overhead by [debiting/crediting] _____ Factory Overhead and _____ Factory Payroll Expense.

debiting

crediting

10-8 After any necessary adjustments (covered in Part 11), overhead is charged to inventory by _____ Work in Process Inventory and _____ Factory Overhead with the amount calculated by multiplying the amount of _____ _____ dollars by the standard overhead _____.

debiting

crediting

direct labor

rate

10-9 The residual, or variance, remaining in the Factory Overhead account would be ultimately closed to _____ of _____ _____ via appropriate debits and credits to the two accounts.

Cost [of] Goods
Sold

10-10 A Stores Requisition records the transfer of completed products to the finished goods storeroom. The accountant then credits _____ in _____ Inventory and debits _____ _____ Inventory for the _____ costs.

Work [in] Process

Finished Goods

product

10-11 The product cost in Finished Goods Inventory is composed of three distinct kinds of costs:

1. _____ costs
2. _____ _____ costs
3. _____ costs

1. material

2. direct labor

3. overhead

10-12 When the accountant receives a Shipping Notice advising him that a product has been shipped, he [debits/credits] _____ Finished Goods and _____ Cost of Goods Sold with the product _____.

credits

debits

cost

10-13 Cost of Goods Sold, then, represents the product costs for products sold during the period. The operating expense accounts, on the other hand, represent the period costs. These accounts and the Sales, or_____, account are closed to the Income Summary account and hence ultimately affect the _____ Earnings account.

revenue

Retained

10-14 Whenever costs are matched with revenues to determine profit or loss, the costs by convention are called expenses. One expense account carries the cost of the products sold; this is the _____ of _____ _____ account. The operating expense accounts carry the type of cost referred to as a _____ cost.

Cost [of] Goods
Sold

period

10-15 You have learned that under one method of costing, usually referred to as "actual costing," one of the cost elements is absorbed into inventory at a predetermined rate. This cost element is_____.

overhead

10-16 In another cost system, the overhead rate is looked upon as a "should be" cost. Any under- or overabsorbed overhead is called the overhead variance; it represents the difference between the "should be" and the _____ overhead costs.

actual

10-17 In other words, the predetermined rate is looked upon as a standard. A cost system designed to use predetermined or standard rates for all three cost elements is therefore called a _____ cost system.

standard

10-18 In standard costing, all cost elements are absorbed into inventory at a predetermined, or _____, rate based on the anticipated, or "should be," costs for these elements under normal operating conditions.

standard

10-19 The difference between the overhead absorbed by means of a predetermined rate and the actual overhead for the period is known as a _____.

variance

10-20 In standard costing, there are three variances, one for each cost element. These are:

1. _____ cost
2. _____ _____ cost
3. _____ cost

1. material

2. direct labor

3. overhead

10-21 You have seen that one method of closing over- or underabsorbed overhead—the overhead variance--is to close such costs to the _____ of _____ _____ account. Under standard costing, this same procedure may be followed for all variances.

Cost [of] Goods
   Sold

10-22 Some standard cost systems put raw materials into inventory at the predetermined, or standard, cost. If $103,000 is paid for materials during the year, even though the standard cost or price is $100,000, there would be a(n) [favorable/unfavorable]_____materials cost _____ of $3,000.

unfavorable

variance

10-23 Assume that all entries made during the year were to be combined into one "summary" entry. The entry for the figures in frame 10-22 would be:

	Dr	Cr
_____	$ _____	$ _____
Cost of Goods Sold	$ _____	$ _____
_____	$ _____	$ _____

	Dr	Cr
Materials Inventory	$100,000	
Cost of Goods Sold	3,000	
Accounts Payable		$103,000

10-24 In practice, accountants use temporary variance accounts. When these are closed to Cost of Goods Sold, the ultimate effect is identical to closing directly to Cost of Goods Sold. We may therefore assume here, for convenience, that variances are closed directly. Now if all Stores Requisitions total $19,000 for a period, and if the total for material usage at a standard rate was $20,000, the summary entry would be:

	Dr	Cr
Work in Process	$ _____	$ _____
_____	$ _____	$ _____
_____	$ _____	$ _____

	Dr	Cr
Work in Process	$20,000	
Cost of Goods Sold		$ 1,000
Materials Inventory		19,000

10-25 Production therefore completed work with $1,000 less materials at their standard cost than the standard usage rate called for. This means that the materials usage variance, for which Cost of Goods Sold is credited, is [favorable/unfavorable]_____ .

favorable

10-26 Variances for all cost elements can be separated into at least two kinds, such as materials price and usage variance, in a_____ _____ system. For convenience, however, we shall hereafter consider only the total variances, or accounting variances, for each of the three cost elements.

standard cost

10-27 Let's consider an example. The total charges of $12,000 to Factory Payroll Expense included charges of $2,500 for indirect labor. Make the entry transferring indirect labor to the Factory Overhead account.

	Dr	Cr
_____	$ _____	$ _____
_____	$ _____	$ _____

	Dr	Cr
Factory Overhead	$2,500	
Factory Payroll Expense		$2,500

10-28 The remaining balance of $9,500 in Factory Payroll
Expense represents direct labor. If the standard direct
labor allowed for the period was $10,000, the variance would
be a(n) [favorable/unfavorable]_____ labor variance.
Complete the summary entry.

	Dr	Cr
Work in Process Inventory	$_____	$_____
Cost of Goods Sold	$_____	$_____
Factory Payroll Expense	$_____	$_____

favorable

	Dr	Cr
Work in Process Inventory	$10,000	
Cost of Goods Sold		$ 500
Factory Payroll Expenses		9,500

10-29 If a period's direct labor, calculated at the standard
rate, is $9,250, and the actual direct labor is $9,500, the
variance is [favorable/unfavorable]_____. Make the
summary entry.

	Dr	Cr
_____	$_____	$_____
_____	$_____	$_____
_____	$_____	$_____

unfavorable

	Dr	Cr
Work in Process	$9,250	
Cost of Goods Sold	250	
Factory Payroll Expense		$9,500

10-30 Assume that the debit balance in Factory Overhead is $22,000, which includes all overhead costs; you are told that the standard overhead rate is $2 for each standard direct labor dollar (SDLD). If the total SDLD in the period's production is $10,000, complete the summary entry closing Factory Overhead.

	Dr	Cr
Work in Process Inventory	$_____	$_____
_____	$_____	$_____
_____	$_____	$_____

	Dr	Cr
Work in Process Inventory	$20,000	
Cost of Goods Sold	2,000	
Factory Overhead		$22,000

10-31 Suppose that you are responsible to materials usage and are given this report:

less

> This month:
> Materials used $50,000
> Materials allowed at standard rate 49,000
> Last Month:
> Materials used 52,000
> Materials allowed at standard rate 53,000

You would know that this month's production was [more/less] _____ efficient with respect to material usage.

10-32 Note that the totals ($50,000 and $49,000; $52,000 and $53,000) are important only in determining the _____ figures for materials usage.

variance

10-33 Following this report, you would concentrate on finding and correcting the cause of the change from last month's [favorable/unfavorable] _____ variance of $1,000 to this month's _____ variance of $1,000.

favorable

unfavorable

10-34 Now suppose that you were responsible for labor management and received this report:

This month:
Standard direct labor dollars $30,000
Actual direct labor dollars 30,000

Then if neither the labor rates nor the methods had changed, you [would/would not]_____concentrate on labor efficiency.

would not

10-35 In short, you would concentrate on the exceptions to, or variances from, the "should be" or _____costs. You would be following the principle of "management by exception."

standard

10-36 Under standard costing, completed products are inventoried at standard cost. Suppose that during the month 1,000 power lawnmowers at a standard cost of $50 each were received by the finished goods warehouse. If the total actual costs on these lawnmowers were $55,000, the summary entry would be:

	Dr	Cr
Finished Goods	$ _____	$ _____
_____	$ _____	$ _____

	Dr	Cr
Finished Goods	$50,000	
Work in Process		$50,000

10-37 During this same month, Shipping Notices recorded the shipment of 800 of these lawnmowers to customers. Complete the summary entry.

	Dr	Cr
Cost of Goods Sold	$ _____	$ _____
_____	$ _____	$ _____

	Dr	Cr
Cost of Goods Sold	$40,000	
Finished Goods		$40,000

10-38 Remember that under actual cost systems, under- or overabsorbed overhead cost figures are easily obtainable. On the other hand, a standard cost system automatically produces variance figures for all three cost elements:

1. _____
2. _____ _____
3. _____

1. material

2. direct labor

3. overhead

10-39 A total variance figure, however, seldom gives sufficient information for management control. For example, if there was a $1,000 favorable variance for material price and a $1,000 unfavorable variance for materials usage, the total variance would be $_____ .

$0 (zero)

10-40 For this reason, total variances are broken down into variances relating to materials price and usage, labor rates and usage, etc. A detailed analysis of the causes for each variance would be given on the output which lists costs analyzed, the _____ _____ _____ .

Cost Analysis Report

10-41 Although variances arise under both standard costing and budgeting, these are complementary, not competing, control devices. Standard costing produces variances within the accounts. Budget variances are determined outside the cost account and are reported on the _____ _____ Analysis.

Budget Performance

10-42 If the firm has accurate standard cost figures, it could budget, say, material costs for the budget period by multiplying the quantities of products budgeted for production by their _____ material cost figures.

standard

10-43 If a material shortage caused production to suspend, there would be less actually spent on materials than planned. This _____ between planned and actual expenditure would appear on the _____ _____ _____ .

variance

Budget Performance Analysis

10-44 If during this same budget period materials were purchased at standard and, for any production achieved, were used at the standard usage rate, then a standard cost system [would/would not]_____ produce a variance.

would not

10-45 Standard costs are applied to activities other than manufacturing that can be objectively measured. However, some activities, such as those of the president's office, have to be budgeted because they do not lend themselves to such measurement. Control, therefore, would be exercised through a _____.

Budget

10-46 Whether or not budgeting or standard costs are used, detailed cost analysis will be found in the _____ _____ Report.

Cost Analysis

10-47 Period costs, you will remember, are costs which management does not relate to some readily measurable activity. These costs, then, are set forth on the_____, and the variances are set forth on the_____ _____ _____.

Budget

Budget Perform-
ance Analysis

10-48 So far we have assumed that firms maintain per-petual inventory records both in units and dollars. Units of inventory appear on the _____ _____ Records, and dollars appear as balances in the _____ accounts.

Inventory Control

inventory

10-49 For many firms the expense of accounting for all in-ventory transactions as they occur would be too expensive relative to the advantages gained. These firms, therefore, maintain inventory records on a periodic rather than a _____ basis.

perpetual

10-50 Frequently, when periodic inventories are used, a separate temporary holding account is established for each cost element:

1._____
2._____ _____
3._____

1. material

2. direct labor

3. overhead

10-51 As costs occur, they are charged, or [debited/credited]_____ , to these accounts throughout the accounting period.

debited

10-52 At the end of each period, a physical inventory—an actual physical count—is made of all goods on hand: raw materials, goods in production, and _____ _____ .

finished goods

10-53 This physical inventory is then "priced," or valued, on a cost basis. The accountant then has three significant account figures:

1. Ending _____ Inventory
2. Ending _____ in _____ Inventory
3. Ending _____ _____ Inventory

1. Materials

2. Work [in] Process

3. Finished Goods

10-54 Refer now to Panel M, a schedule of Cost of Goods Manufactured. Note that with regard to materials, Beginning Inventory plus purchases less _____ Inventory equals the cost of materials used.

Ending

10-55 Think of the logic underlying this basic inventory equation. The amount you start with plus the amount you add gives you the total available for use. The difference between the total cost of the materials available and the cost of the amount remaining must be the _____ _____ for the period.

Material Cost

10-56 Note that this same equation is applied again to determine Cost of Goods Manufactured. Total Manufacturing Costs plus _____ Work in Process Inventory less _____ Work in Process Inventory equals Cost of Goods Manufactured.

Beginning

Ending

10-57 On Panel L, you can see the basic formula applied once again. You know that the Cost of Goods Manufactured figure includes all product costs of goods completed during the period. This is added to the _____ Finished Goods Inventory figure.

Beginning

10-58 Beginning Inventory plus Cost of Goods Manufactured equals _____ _____ for _____ .

Goods Available [for] Sale

10-59 Goods Available for Sale minus Ending Inventory— the same figure that would appear on the Balance Sheet— equals the _____ of _____ _____ figure.

Cost [of] Goods Sold

10-60 The actual closing entries made by the accountant to reflect the effect of this basic equation in the Ledger are equally straightforward. Recall that under a periodic inventory system the accountant at the end of the period would have debit balances in six accounts—three inventory accounts and three accounts for the cost elements:

1. Materials

2. Work [in] Process

3. Finished Goods

4. Material

5. Direct Labor

6. Overhead

1. _____ Inventory
2. _____ in _____ Inventory
3. _____ _____ Inventory
4. _____ Costs
5. _____ _____ Costs
6. _____ Costs

10-61 Each of the three inventory account balances would reflect the [beginning/ending]_____ balance for the prior period. This figure would be the same as the _____ balance for the current period.

ending

beginning

10-62 The accountant could then establish a temporary account for closing, called Cost of Goods Sold. Refer now to Panel N. As a first step, he would close Materials Purchases ($140,000) and Beginning Materials Inventory ($10,000) to _____ of _____ _____ .

Cost [of] Goods Sold

10-63 At this point, Cost of Goods Sold would have a [debit/credit] _____ balance of $_____ representing the cost of materials available for use.

debit

$150,000

10-64 The accountant then [debits/credits]_____ Cost of Goods Sold and _____ Materials Inventory with the $5,000 of ending physical inventory.

credits

debits

10-65 The debit balance of $145,000 remaining in Cost of Goods Sold would represent the _____ of _____ used.

cost [of] materials

10-66 Next, Direct Labor of $_____ and Overhead Costs of $_____ are closed to Cost of Goods Sold.

$100,000

$200,000

10-67 Also, the beginning Work in Process Inventory of $_____ would be similarly closed. The new Cost of Goods Sold balance of $460,000 represents the cost of goods either completed or still in _____.

$15,000

process (produc-
tion)

10-68 Ending Work in Process Inventory of $_____ is now recorded by [debiting/crediting]_____Cost of Goods Sold and _____Work in Process Inventory for this amount.

$20,000

crediting

debiting

10-69 The debit balance of $440,000 now remaining in the Cost of Goods Sold account represents the _____ of _____ _____.

cost [of] goods
manufactured

10-70 Beginning Finished Goods Inventory of $_____ is closed to Cost of Goods Sold. This gives a debit balance of $_____, which represents the cost of goods _____ for_____.

$25,000

$465,000

available [for]
sale

10-71 Finally, the Ending Finished Goods physical inventory of $_____ is recorded. This leaves a balance of $_____ representing the cost of goods actually sold.

$15,000

$450,000

10-72 In addition, overhead variance under actual costing and all cost variances under standard costing may also be appropriately closed to the _____ of _____ _____ account.

Cost [of] Goods
Sold

10-73 For a wholesaler or merchandising firm having no labor or production overhead costs, the formula is basically the same, but simpler: Beginning Inventory [plus/minus] _____ cost of merchandise purchased _____ Ending Inventory equals _____ of _____ _____ .

plus

minus

Cost [of] Goods
Sold

10-74 A retailer, such as a department store, cannot afford to keep detailed cost records for each item, many of which have a low profitability. Such retailers use what is called the retail inventory method, based on the fact that the retail price for each item is readily available. However, to arrive at the Cost of Goods Sold figure, the selling-price figure must be converted to a _____ figure.

cost

10-75 Ordinarily retailers mark up incoming merchandise to a selling price. Assume that a particular incoming item costing 60 cents is marked up to $1. The gross profit is 40 cents, and the gross profit ratio stated in terms of the percentage is ____ per cent.

40

10-76 If this mark-up is maintained, the retailer can take a physical inventory at the selling price of all such items and deduct ____ per cent from the selling price to determine the cost.

40

10-77 Beginning inventories and the purchases made during the period are already carried at cost. These two constitute Goods Available for Sale. By subtracting the Ending Inventory converted from selling price to cost, the accountant readily obtains the _____ of _____ _____.

Cost [of] Goods
Sold

10-78 The retail method of inventory valuation, which adjusts to cost via a ratio or percentage, is the simplest and least costly system. You probably wonder why all firms, including manufacturers, do not use the _____ method.

retail

10-79 The answer is that it is less accurate than actual or standard cost methods; it is used by retailers, because the other methods would be prohibitively _____ .

expensive (costly)

10-80 Reporting Inventory and Cost of Goods Sold as accurately as possible is a prime responsibility of the accounting system. Remember that Cost of Goods Sold is a major expense item on the Income Statement. If this item is substantially in error, the reported _____ figure on the Income Statement will also be in error.

income (profit)

10-81 It is vital to understand the relationship over time between the Inventory and Cost of Goods Sold accounts. Assuming correct data for Goods Available for Sale, if Ending Inventory is overstated, Cost of Goods Sold will be

_____.

understated

10-82 If Costs of Goods Sold is understates, income or profit will be _____, resulting in Retained Earnings being _____ to match the original overstatement of Inventory.

overstated

overstated

10-83 Conversely, if, for a given period, Ending Inventory is understated, then:

1. Cost of Goods Sold will be _____.
2. Income or profit will be _____.
3. Retained Earnings will be _____.

1. overstated

2. understated

3. understated

10-84 Such errors not only distort a firm's financial position in the current year or period, but will inevitably distort at least one future year. For example, if Inventory, income, and Retained Earnings are overstated this year and the error is corrected next year, the "loss" will be borne next year, with the result that reported income will be_____ than the "true" figure.

lower (less)

10-85 Thus an error in Inventory and Cost of Goods Sold figures will distort reported_____ over at least _____ periods.

income (profit)

two

10-86 Not only will errors in inventory valuation distort reported income over more than one period, but so will arbitrary changes in methods of inventory valuation. Recall that the four methods of materials inventory valuation, in addition to the retail method, are:

1. _____ _____
2. _____ _____
3. _____
4. _____

1. average cost
2. specific identification
3. FIFO
4. LIFO

10-87 Remember that in times of changing prices each of the four methods could yield a _____ dollar valuation for the same inventory.

different

10-88 Therefore, if, from one period to another, a firm changed its method, modifications *not* reflecting any transactions would necessarily find their way into the Cost of Goods Sold account and thus distort reported _____.

income

10-89 To avoid such "bookkeeping" distortions, accountants follow the *principle of consistency*; that is, they follow a given adopted method _____ from period to period.

consistently

10-90 The principle of _____ does not rule out the possibility of changing from one method to another.

consistency

10-91 It does mean, however, that the reason for the change and its effects must be given in the annual report sent to the owners or stockholders. The annual report will always include the two outputs prepared as part of the financial reporting responsibility, the _____ _____ and the _____ _____.

Balance Sheet

Income Statement

10-92 When the accountant hesitates to switch accounting methods without justification, he is not necessarily being obstinate; he may be simply following the principle of _____ in order to minimize distortions of reported _____.

consistency

income

10-93 Since reported income and the change in it from period to period is the most important measurement of management performance, accountants are vitally concerned with its _____ .

accuracy (fairness)

10-94 To ensure the most accurate reporting of income, accountants concentrate a major share of their efforts on ensuring the accuracy of the expense account having the greatest impact on income and the highest probability of error—the _____ of _____ _____ account.

Cost [of] Goods Sold

10-95 Note that we have used the phrase "most accurate reporting." No report for a single period can be completely accurate since some judgment is involved in the determination of many figures. For example, it may be desirable to consider part of the company president's salary as a _____ , rather than as a period, cost.

product

10-96 The allocation of a portion of the president's salary to factory overhead involves judgment as to how much to _____ , a decision which cannot be made precisely or "accurately."

allocate

10-97 In addition to problems of proper allocation of expenses, it is unrealistic to attempt to apportion accurately such insignificant items as costs of paper cups between the factory and the general office. Many similar costs are too small to affect _____ reporting materially.

financial

10-98 To achieve a balance between precise accuracy and economical accounting, accountants follow the *principle of materiality*. This basic principle is simply that accounting efforts to achieve accuracy will be concentrated on those items which are _____ .

significant (material)

174   the accounting process

10-99 In review, the principle of materiality and the desire for accuracy in Inventory and Cost of Goods Sold valuation indicate that firms whose products have high unit value— automobile manufacturers, for example—would use a [periodic/perpetual] _____ inventory system.

perpetual

10-100 On the other hand, a manufacturer of small hand tools would probably adopt a _____ system.

periodic

10-101 Finally, a retailer or wholesaler with many low-profit items would necessarily follow the _____ _____ of inventory valuation.

retail method

10-102 Throughout this text we have touched upon the relationship between costs and profits. As you will now learn, costs and volume are crucial determiners of a firm's _____.

profits

10-103 Remember that overhead costs include the factory manager's salary, depreciation on plant and equipment, and property taxes on the factory. Since these costs relate to production, they are considered _____ costs.

product

10-104 A parallel group of costs are administorators' salaries, and both depreciation and taxes on office buildings and equipment. These costs are_____costs.

period

10-105 You will notice that the specific costs mentioned have this in common: They are relatively *fixed* regardless of the volume of sales and production. Although they may be segregated as either product or period costs for inventory valuation, they are both called _____ costs for other purposes.

fixed

10-106 Fixed costs, then, include all _____ and _____ costs which remain relatively fixed regardless of the _____ of sales and production.

product

period

volume

10-107 Other costs, such as material costs, direct labor costs, and salesmen's commissions, vary with the volume of sales and production. In contrast to fixed costs, these are considered _____ costs.

variable

10-108 All costs, whether product or period costs, can be generally divided into two groups when considered from the standpoint of volume: _____ costs and _____ costs.

fixed

variable

10-109 Although the distinction is sometimes arbitrary, costs are considered either fixed or variable on the basis of the effect that the _____ of production and sales has on them.

volume

10-110 If a firm sells for $10 a particular product that has a variable cost of $6, this product's contribution to fixed costs and profit is $____ .

$4

10-111 The difference between an item's variable cost and selling price is known as its _____ to fixed costs and profit.

contribution

10-112 Suppose the firm's annual fixed costs total $200,000. If the firm sold 50,000 units (variable cost $6, selling price $10), the year's revenues would be $_____ and the year's expenses would be $_____.

$500,000

$500,000

10-113 In other words, the firm would *break even*. Hence businessmen call this zero profit position the _____ - _____ point.

break-even

10-114 Refer now to Panel O. Here you see a chart of break-even information for a firm selling a product for $10. The firm's fixed costs are $_____.

$300,000

10-115 For this product the break-even volume is _____ units.

50,000

10-116 If total costs at the break-even point are $500,000 and fixed costs are $300,000, then variable costs are $_____.

$200,000

10-117 If variable costs are $200,000 at a volume of 50,000 units, each unit has a variable cost of $____. This leaves a contribution of $____ per unit to fixed costs and profit.

$4

$6

10-118 Let's complete the circle. With $300,000 of fixed costs, to which each unit contributes $6, the firm would have to sell _____ units to break even.

50,000

10-119 When 50,000 units are sold, fixed costs are covered. Therefore, if volume does not exceed the point where fixed costs will rise, profits expand rapidly above the break-even point at a rate of $____ per unit.

$6

10-120 Below the break-even point losses expand at the same rate, since _____ _____ are not covered until 50,000 units have been sold.

fixed costs

10-121 Knowledge of the cost-volume-profit relationship and the break-even point is extremely valuable to management. Break-even analysis provides information for forecasting costs and profits at different levels of _____.

volume

10-122 Suppose a firm were contemplating the purchase of new, more efficient equipment for its factory. Higher depreciation and property taxes on such new equipment would raise total _____ _____ for each subsequent period.

fixed costs

10-123 The efficiency of the new equipment might reduce variable costs in the long run. However, additional fixed costs [raise/lower] _____ the break-even point.

raise

10-124 Thus, in determining the long-run value of such equipment, management must know exactly the extent that the purchase would raise the _____ - _____ _____.

break-even point

10-125 As you can see, control of costs is one way by which
management increases profits. In a competitive economy the
market itself determines the price for which a firm sells a
product. Since prices cannot be easily raised, management
can increase the profitability of its product by_____
its _____.

reducing [its]
costs

10-126 Remember that an additional dollar of sales above
the break-even point is *not* an additional dollar of profit
since _____ costs are still deductible.

variable

10-127 However, costs saved are pure _____, assuming adequate sales volume.

profit

10-128 Thus you can see how accurate cost accounting can
aid management's cost-control efforts by supplying vital
information on cost factors. To rephrase an old saying, a
cost dollar saved is a _____ _____.

dollar earned

End of Part 10. Turn to the next page for the Review Quiz only when
you are ready to complete Part 11.

review quiz on part 10

Complete the following sentences.

1. When material, labor, and overhead are all entered into Inventory at a predetermined rate, the company is using a _____ cost system, as opposed to an _____ cost system.

2. Overhead variances under either actual or standard costing, together with material and labor variances under standard costing, may be debited or credited directly to the _____ _____ _____ _____ account during the period in which they are incurred.

3. A standard cost system provides management automatically with _____ figures for cost and budget analysis.

4. A firm may use a _____ inventory accounting system instead of a perpetual one, especially if its products have a _____ unit cost.

5. A manufacturing firm using periodic inventory accounting determines Cost of Goods Sold with the following formula: _____ Inventory plus _____ of Goods _____ less _____ Inventory equals _____ _____ _____ _____ .

6. A merchandising firm using periodic inventory accounting determines Cost of Goods Sold with the following formula: _____ Inventory plus _____ of Goods _____ less _____ Inventory equals _____ _____ _____ _____ .

7. When a firm on periodic inventory ''prices'' its ending physical inventory at selling price and then determines cost by applying an overall gross-profit ratio, it is following the _____ _____ of inventory valuation.

8. The accountant attempts to be as accurate as possible in the valuation of Inventory and Cost of Goods Sold since errors could significantly affect _____ reported on the _____ _____ .

9. If Ending Inventory is understated in a given accounting period, Cost of Goods Sold will be _____, and both reported _____ and _____ _____ will be understated.

10. An error in inventory valuation will distort reported income in at least _____ accounting periods.

11. When an accountant concentrates his efforts on important cost factors and slights small miscellaneous ones, he is following the principle of _____ .

12. A firm using periodic inventory [does/does not] _____ credit Finished Goods Inventory for the cost of each item at the time shipment is reported by the input called the _____ _____ .

13. Regardless of a particular firm's methods of determining costs, it is important that the methods be _____ from year to year.

14. Costs which do *not* vary with the volume of production and sales are known as _____ costs.

15. Costs which do vary directly with volume are known as _____ costs.

16. When a firm sells just enough to have a zero profit, it is at the _____ - _____ point.

17. The difference between the selling price of an item and its variable cost is known as its _____ to fixed costs and profit.

18. If a firm sold its product at $5 each and had variable costs of $2 apiece and fixed costs of $30,000, its break-even volume would be _____ units, or $ _____ of sales revenue.

19. Above break-even volume, a firm is operating at a _____ ; below break-even, at a _____ .

20. Break-even analysis is valuable to management as a tool for forecasting _____ and _____ at different levels of _____ .

PART 11
adjustments

11-1 The earlier parts introduced you to the three major accounting responsibilities. These are:

1. _____ and _____
2. _____ reporting
3. _____ reporting

11-2 You have also become familiar with the journalizing and later posting of _____ that record transactions.

entries

11-3 Part 11 will introduce some additional accounting concepts and activities to complete the general picture of the accounting system's functions. So far, most of the postings to the firm's accounts have resulted from _____ determined by analyzing the effects of specific inputs.

entries

11-4 Not all entries originate with specific inputs. For instance, the closing entries do not. Prior to closing, as you shall see, some accounts may require adjusting, and the entries for this are called adjusting _____.

entries

11-5 You have already learned about two kinds of adjusting entries—those used in the error-correction procedure. Remember that to correct an erroneous entry, you journalize two additional entries. The first, called a _____ entry, wipes out the effect of the original error; the second correct entry completes the procedure.

reversing

11-6 Note that neither the reversing entry nor the correct entry was based on any new specific_____. Rather, both are the result of the accountant's decision to modify the books so that they reflect more accurately transactions that have already occurred.

input

11-7 Suppose your firm purchased a new truck for $4,000 cash at the beginning of the year. The original entry would be a [debits/credits]_____of $4,000 to the Equipment account and a _____ of $_____ to the _____ account.

debit

credit

$4,000

Cash

11-8 Because the firm had acquired a truck, a property with continuing usefulness, you recorded the $4,000 expenditure, not as an increase in expense, but rather as an increase in_____.

assets

11-9 Assume that the truck had a useful life of only four years. At the end of four years, if you had made no prior adjustments, you would be forced to [debit/credit] _____ the Equipment account for the full $4,000 to reflect the expiration of this asset.

credit

11-10 You know further that this would be only half such an entry. The $4,000 thus used up is an expense over the four years, and therefore the balancing debit of $4,000 will ultimately affect the _____ _____account.

Retained Earnings

11-11 Recall that debits ultimately reflecting a reduction of Retained Earnings usually represent the _____ of doing business during a period.

expense (cost)

11-12 Therefore, by writing off the entire cost of the truck at the end of the fourth year, you would be charging the full _____of the truck as an expense against one year's revenues.

cost

11-13 Since the firm used the truck during all four years
of its life, the charging of the total cost to the fourth year
would not be equitable or realistic. At the end of the first
year part of the truck's useful life had been used up, an
event which accountants call depreciation. The disappear-
ance, or expiration, of future usefulness is therefore
called _____.

depreciation

11-14 Remember that depreciation refers to expiration of
future usefulness, not to loss of market value. In the case
of the truck, one way of apportioning the total depreciation
over four years might be to assign one- _____ of the
original cost to each year's expense.

fourth (quarter)

11-15 Apportioning total depreciation of a fixed asset in
equal amounts over the expected life of the asset is called
straight-line depreciation. If you were using the straight-
line method with the firm's $4,000 truck over four years,
the firm would "take," or charge, $_____ each year as
_____ expense on the truck.

$1,000

depreciation

11-16 There are other, more complicated methods of depreciation accounting, some of which may have significant
income tax advantages. However, _____-_____
depreciation adequately illustrates the basic concept.

straight-line

11-17 Regardless of the method used by the accountant to
determine the actual amount, the fact remains that the
_____ of fixed assets should be reflected in the related accounts at the end of each accounting period.

depreciation

11-18 To review, depreciation is the expiration of future
_____ of a fixed asset. Straight-line depreciation is
a method of apportioning the total depreciation of a
_____ asset in _____ amounts over its expected
useful _____.

usefulness (*not
market value*)

fixed

equal

life

11-19 Since depreciation is a normal expense of doing business, the entry for depreciation has on one side a charge, or [debit/credit] _____ , to an _____ account called Depreciation Expense.

debit

expense

11-20 It would seem logical that the corresponding credit would be to the fixed asset account—in this case Equipment—to reflect the _____ of future usefulness.

expiration (reduc-
tion)

11-21 However, for clarity of financial reporting on the conventional Balance Sheet, the fixed asset accounts often show the full amount of the original cost of assets still in the firm's possession. The accountant consequently sets up a separate account called Accumulated Depreciation to receive the amounts of [debits/credits] _____ from the depreciation entries.

credits

11-22 The Accumulated Depreciation account, therefore, will have a _____ balance, reflecting accumulated depreciation taken on those assets still in the firm's possession.

credit

11-23 The adjusting entry for the amount taken for depreciation would be a _____ to the Depreciation Expense account and a _____ of the same amount to the Accumulated Depreciation account.

debit

credit

11-24 Refer to Panel P, a conventional Balance Sheet format. The Accumulated Depreciation account is listed on the Balance Sheet along with the fixed asset accounts to which it relates. Since it has a _____ balance, accountants call it an asset-credit, or contra-asset, account.

credit

11-25 Note that the use of the contra-asset account enables the accountant to show both the original cost of the fixed assets and, by subtracting the accumulated depreciation, their current book value, or depreciated value. To clarify this point, first total the account balances showing the original cost of all fixed assets still in the firm's possession: $ _____ .

$30,000

11-26 Depreciation accumulated to date on these fixed assets, except on land, which does not depreciate, amounts to $_____. This is the balance in the _____ _____ account.

$6,000

Accumulated Depreciation

11-27 Therefore, the net amount that fixed assets contribute to total assets, known as their "book" or depreciated value, is $_____ minus $_____, or $24,000.

$30,000

$6,000

11-28 Note that a depreciation entry reflects a transaction but does *not* involve a flow of money. It reflects only the _____ of the future usefulness of certain fixed _____.

expiration

assets

11-29 A depreciation entry leads to a reduction in the depreciated, or book, value of a fixed asset and a corresponding charge to an _____ account, Depreciation Expense, which ultimately reduces the _____ Earnings account.

expense

Retained

11-30 Such an entry, since it does not reflect a transaction recorded as a result of a specific input received, is called an _____ entry.

adjusting

11-31 The use of the phrase "assets still in the firm's possession" is deliberate. In practice, both the original cost and the related accumulated depreciation are carried in the accounts until the _____ _____ is disposed of.

fixed asset

11-32 If the firm had only one asset, such as the $4,000 truck depreciated at $1,000 per year, the accounts at the end of three years would show:

$4,000

$3,000

Equipment $_____(Dr balance)
       Accumulated Depreciation $_____(Cr balance)

At this point the book value is $_____.

$1,000

11-33 If the firm still had the truck at the end of four years, $4,000

the accounts would show: $4,000

    Equipment $_____(Dr balance)

        Accumulated Depreciation $_____ (Cr balance)

                                                       0

At this point the truck is fully depreciated. Its book value is

$____.

11-34 If the firm continued to use the truck during the fifth   fully depreciated

year, the firm would not take any more depreciation on it

because the truck would already be _____ _____.

The resulting "free ride" would reflect an initial error in

the original estimate of the truck's useful life.

11-35 Suppose that the truck was disposed of at the end of   credit

four years and that the firm received nothing for it. The ac-

countant would record this event with a [debit/credit]   debit

_____to Equipment of $4,000 and a _____ to   would not

Accumulated Depreciation of $4,000. This entry [would/

would not]_____ affect total assets.

11-36 Suppose instead that when the fully depreciated truck   1. Cash

was disposed of it brought $100 cash for scrap. The result-

ing compound entry would be: 2. $100 (Dr)

                                        Dr   *Cr*   3. $4,000 (Dr)

1. _____ 2. $_____ $_____

Accumulated Depreciation   3. $ _____ $_____

Equipment $4,000

Gain on Sale of Assets (a revenue account) $ 100

11-37 Suppose instead that the truck was sold for $400 cash
at the end of three years, at which time only $3,000 depre-
ciation had accumulated. The entry would be:

	Dr	Cr
Cash	$_____	$_____
_____	$_____	$_____
Loss on Sale of Equipment	$_____	$_____
_____	$_____	$_____

	Dr	Cr
Cash	$ 400	
Accumulated Depreciation	3,000	
Loss on Sale of Equipment	600	
Equipment		$4,000

11-38 This transaction, then, resulted in a loss of $600.
At the time of the sale, the truck had a book value (amount
of unexpired original cost) of $4,000 minus $3,000, or $1,000.
In the transaction the firm exchanged an asset with a book
value of $ 1,000 for another asset, $400 cash. Therefore,
total assets were [increased/reduced]_____ by
$_____.

reduced

$600

11-39 The $600 reduction in total assets was not matched
by any corresponding reduction in liabilities or capital.
Therefore, the only equity account that can ultimately reflect
the reduction is _____ _____.

Retained Earnings

11-40 Since land is considered permanent, it is never depreciated. Other fixed assets, such as buildings, tools, and
office furniture, are depreciated. Patents and goodwill are
also assets subject to _____ ,which is called *amortization* in reference to these intangible assets.

depreciation

11-41 Another kind of adjusting entry deals with bad debts.
In the normal course of business, a few of a firm's customers will fail to pay their bills, and at the end of an accounting period, the accountant wishes to show as current assets
only the amount of receivables against which collection can
reasonably be expected. Such receivables are reflected in
the current asset account called_____ _____.

Accounts Receiv-
able

11-42 Recall that when a firm makes a sale, one part of the entry is a [debit/credit] _____ for the amount of the sale to Accounts Receivable. The other is a _____ to Sales, a revenue account.

debit

credit

11-43 Now assume that a firm finds it cannot collect $100 owed by a customer. The firm in this case suffers a loss, recorded in an expense account called Bad Debt Expense. Correspondingly, the balance of Accounts Receivable is too high by $100, and this amount must be "written off." The adjusting entry which records this loss and reduces Accounts Receivable would be:

	Dr	*Cr*
Bad Debt Expense	$ _____	$ _____
_____	$ _____	$ _____

	Dr	*Cr*
Bad Debt Expense	$100	
Accounts Receivable		$100

11-44 Let's look at another example. In 196B a firm finds that it cannot collect $1,000 of its Accounts Receivable; this amount was part of the revenue from sales made during the prior year, 196A. Following the procedure just outlined, journalize the adjusting entry:

	Dr	*Cr*
_____	$ _____	$ _____
_____	$ _____	$ _____

	Dr	*Cr*
Bad Debt Expense	$1,000	
Accounts Receivable		$1,000

11-45 The $1,000 expense for bad debts came from 196A sales but was not recorded until 196B; this means that 196A expenses were [overstated/understated] _____ and 196B expenses are _____ .

understated

overstated

11-46 If a firm does a large credit business, this mismatch-ing of revenues and expenses may lead to serious distortions in the financial statements. To reduce these distortions, the accountant uses a contra-account. Refer to Panel P; note that under Accounts Receivable there is a contra-asset ac-count called _____ _____ _____ .

Bad Debt Allow-ance

11-47 The Bad Debt Allowance account is similar to the Accumulated Depreciation account. Both are listed in the asset section. The asset accounts which they offset have _____ balances, and since both these contra-asset accounts act to reduce assets, they have _____ bal-ances.

debit

credit

11-48 Although the accountant does not know which specific customer accounts will be worthless, he can estimate from experience the proportion of all receivables remaining at the end of a period that will be uncollectible. Thus to charge the current period with the estimated bad debt expense, he [debits/credits] _____ Bad Debt Expense and _____ Bad Debt Allowance by the amount of the esti-mate.

debits

credits

11-49 The result of this adjusting entry is to charge the current year with the bad debt expense and to [increase/reduce] _____ the Accounts Receivable amount shown on the Balance Sheet to their estimated realizable value.

reduce

11-50 When a specific customer account is found to be un-collectible, it must be removed from Accounts Receivable. Since the expense for bad debts has already been recorded, the adjusting entry would not affect an expense account. It would be journalized as a _____ to Accounts Receiv-able and a _____ to Bad Debt Allowance.

credit

debit

11-51 To review, the accountant avoids charging future periods with current bad debts by estimating at the and of the
period what proportion of receivables will be uncollectible.
Suppose that his estimate was $500 and that at period end
the Bad Debt Allowance account had only a $100 credit bal-
ance after write-offs. Journalize the adjusting entry:

	Dr	*Cr*
_____	$ _____	$ _____
_____	$ _____	$ _____

	Dr	*Cr*
Bad Debt Expense	$400	
Bad Debt Allowance		$400

11-52 As a result of this entry, Bad Debt Allowance would
have the desired credit balance of $500, an offset to the
balance of Accounts Receivable. Then if a customer's account for $100 proves uncollectible in the following year,
the entry would be:

	Dr	*Cr*
_____	$ _____	$ _____
_____	$ _____	$ _____

	Dr	*Cr*
Bad Debt Allowance	$100	
Accounts Receivable		$100

11-53 Bad Debt Allowance, like Accumulated Depreciation,
is a real, or permanent, account. Bad Debt Expense, like
other expense accounts, is a nominal, or _____ holding, account closed to Income Summary at period end; its
balance is reported on the _____ _____ along
with the other expense accounts.

temporary

Income Statement

11-54 Whether or not a firm's accountant uses a Bad Debt
Allowance account, the Bad Debt Expense account is closed
to the Income Summary account. Hence expenses for bad
debts ultimately affect the permanent account called

_____ _____.

Retained Earnings

11-55 So far you have covered three types of adjusting entries: one involving error correction; one involving _____ ; and one involving the allowance for _____ _____.

depreciation

bad debts

11-56 A fourth type of adjusting entry is the accrual. Like other adjusting entries, it too represents a transaction that may not be based on a specific _____.

input

11-57 The term *accrual* usually refers to the effects of events that have occurred but have not been processed and recorded at the Balance Sheet date. Some inputs leading to normal entries may not be on hand at the end of an accounting period; the accountant then estimates their eventual effect on the accounts involved and makes adjusting entries called _____.

accruals

11-58 The Balance Sheet must reflect all transactions that have occurred during the period, even though all inputs reflecting these transactions have not been received. If a particular input is not on hand, the accountant estimates the amount involved and makes a type of _____ entry called an accrual to the accounts involved.

adjusting

11-59 For example, to reflect properly a utility bill that had not arrived in time for processing, the accountant estimates, or accrues, the amount of the bill and makes an adjusting entry to record the accrual with a _____ to Accounts Payable and a _____ to Utility Expense.

credit

debit

11-60 Or, to record properly any rent owed to the firm but not yet received, the accountant _____ Rents Receivable, an asset account, and _____ Rental Income, a revenue account.

debits

credits

11-61 Accountants follow a similar procedure for wages and salaries. Unless the payroll period happens to end at the close of an accounting period, earned but unpaid wages and salaries are a liability and should be shown on the _____ _____.

Balance Sheet

11-62 To record this liability, the accountant accrues the amount of wages and salaries owed by journalizing a [debit/credit] _____ to Payroll Expense and a _____ to Accrued Wages and Salaries, a liability account.

debit

credit

11-63 Accruals can affect any type of account. For example, if at the Balance Sheet date the firm has an unrecorded interest expense it will pay in a future accounting period, the accrual is made by a _____ to Interest Expense and a _____ to Accrued Interest, a current liability account.

debit

credit

11-64 Similarly, other expenses, such as taxes and rent owed by the firm, may not yet be recorded. To do so, you would _____ the appropriate expense accounts and _____ the appropriate current _____ accounts.

debit

credit

liability

11-65 If a customer owes the firm interest that he will pay in a future accounting period, then the accrual for the current period is made by a _____ to Interest Receivable, a current asset account, and a _____ to Interest Income, a revenue account.

debit

credit

11-66 If the accruals were on the books in the new accounting period, the actual input could lead to a double count when processed and recorded. To avoid this, the accountant "wipes out" the accruals in the same way that he corrects errors, by making a series of adjusting entries called _____ entries at the beginning of the new accounting period.

reversing

11-67 Recall that such reversing entries would merely be reversals of the original accrual entries, thereby negating their effect. In the case of the utility bill, assume the accrual entry was:

	Dr	Cr
Utility Expense	$50	
Accounts Payable		$50

The reversing entry for the same amount would be:

	Dr	Cr
_____	$_____	$_____
_____	$_____	$_____

	Dr	Cr
Accounts Payable	$50	
Utility Expense		$50

11-68 Another type of adjusting entry involves prepaids, which are similar to accruals but have the opposite effect. Suppose that at the end of a period the accountant discovered that the firm had purchased a two-year insurance policy that still had a year of coverage left. At the time of the purchase, the entire policy had been "expensed" by an entry which consisted of a [debit/credit] _____ to Insurance Expense and a _____ to Accounts Payable for the entire cost.

debit

credit

11-69 If the two-year policy had cost $2,000, $1,000 of this would be an asset at the end of one year since the policy had future usefulness or value. To show this, the accountant would make, at the end of the first year, an adjusting entry to record the prepaid asset:

	Dr	Cr
Prepaid Insurance	$1,000	
_____		$1,000

	Dr	Cr
Prepaid Insurance	$1,000	
Insurance Expense		$1,000

11-70 By the foregoing entry the accountant shows the unexpired value of the policy as a _____ asset. The entry correspondingly [increases/reduces] _____ the
amount of the current year's expense to the more correct
figure.

prepaid

reduces

11-71 In order to avoid possible future errors, the accountant may make a reversing entry for prepaids at the beginning of the new period. Such a reversing entry for the prepaid insurance example would be to the following accounts:

	Dr	Cr
_____	$1,000	
_____		$1,000

	Dr	Cr
Insurance Expense	$1,000	
Prepaid Insurance		$1,000

11-72 A reversing entry may also be used for a transaction
that is the opposite of a previous transaction. For example,
suppose the firm returned materials to a supplier *after* the
original Materials Invoice had been recorded. If the amount
involved was $100, you would post the reversing entry to In-
ventory and Accounts Payable:

	Dr	Cr
_____	$ _____	$ _____
_____	$ _____	$ _____

	Dr	Cr
Accounts Payable	$100	
Inventory		$100

11-73 In addition, you would [increase/reduce] _____
the stock-on-hand balance of the appropriate_____
_____ Record.

reduce

Inventory Control

11-74 If a customer returns merchandise, which the firm
replaces in inventory, and the original transaction did not
involve a tax, two reversing entries would be required. One
would offset the sale and the other would record the return
of _____.

merchandise (in-
ventory)

11-75 The reversing entry to cancel or offset the above sale would involve a _____ to Accounts Receivable and a _____ either to Sales or to a special contra-account called Sales Returns and Allowances for an amount equal to the total [selling price/cost] _____.

credit

debit

selling price

11-76 You record the receipt of merchandise returned by a customer with a reversing entry [debiting/crediting] _____ Inventory and _____ Cost of Goods Sold for the [selling price/cost] _____ of the merchandise.

debiting

crediting

cost

11-77 Throughout these examples you have seen that, in all entries for transactions, adjustment, closing, and error correction, debits always equal _____.

credits

11-78 This is not just a meaningless or mechanical rule, but a logical extension of the fundamental accounting equation, which states that for every asset there must be a corresponding claim or source. This logic is expressed in the equation _____ = _____ + _____ _____.

Assest = Liabilities + New Worth (Owners' Equity)

11-79 In learning how to journalize, you should not attempt to memorize rules or entries for every possible transaction. In business there are too many possible types, and a person's memory is too often subject to error. Instead, you should analyze the Balance Sheet effect. If an asset has increased, then either another asset has been _____ or an equity or revenue account has been _____.

reduced

increased

11-80 When one asset is increased and another decreased by an equal amount, no equity, expense, or revenue account is involved. The transaction merely involves an exchange of _____.

assets

11-81 Where an asset is reduced and no other asset is increased by an equal amount, you know that an equity or expense account must be involved. If the asset credit is not matched by a liability debit, then the debit must be either to an _____ account or, if dividends have been distributed, to the _____ _____ account.

expense

Retained Earnings

11-82 When a transaction increases an asset but neither an exchange of assets nor a sale of stock is involved, you know that the original entry must credit either a _____ account or a _____ account.

liability

revenue

11-83 If a liability is increased with no asset acquired and no dividend declaration involved, an _____ account must therefore be [debited/credited] _____.

expense

debited

11-84 Particular account titles will vary by company and industry. But you will usually be able to identify accounts by their type or function. For example, if you saw an account labeled Wages and Salaries Payable, you should know that this is a _____ account serving the same purpose as the account labeled Accrued Wages and Salaries.

liability

11-85 Remember that you do not want to learn that debits equal _____ simply as a meaningless rule. Instead, you should recall that this equality merely shows that for all assets there must be_____, or sources.

credits

claims

11-86 Therefore, this basic equality is maintained when any changes occur. A knowledge of debit-credit equality is also useful for error control. If you total the debits and credits of a series of entries and find them unequal, you know they contain an _____.

error (mistake)

11-87 The rule of equality therefore enables you to check $988
your work frequently and thereby minimize backtracking
when an error is discovered. For example, error control
is exercised over the billing activity by taking daily totals,
known as control totals, of each of the appropriate accounts.
Suppose your control totals revealed the following: Sales,
$1,000 (Cr); Taxes Payable, $38 (Cr); and Discounts Allowed, $50 (Dr). You know that your total debits to Accounts
Receivable should be $_____.

11-88 If your Accounts Receivable additions did not equal   error
$988, you would know an _____ had been made during
that day's billing operation. You would therefore have to go   balanced
back only to the point where previous control totals had

_____.

11-89 Unfortunately, being "in balance" does not guarantee   accounts
absolute accuracy. Two other types of errors could still
exist. One would be that the amounts were correct but entered to the wrong _____.

11-90 Also, a balanced entry to the proper accounts could   amount
still be for the wrong _____.

11-91 Nevertheless, errors of account are rare, and the   errors
chances of using the wrong amounts on *both* sides of an entry
are slim. Therefore, the double-entry system, in addition to
providing more useful information, greatly assists in detect-
ing and minimizing the work necessary to correct_____.

11-92 Your basic knowledge of the accounting system ena-   data-proc-
bles you to understand the application of modern electronic   essing
data-processing (EDP) equipment to accounting activities.
The immense efficiency of this equipment is well known, but
the question facing modern business management is: What
operations are best suited to the application of electronic
_____ - _____ equipment?

11-93 To answer this question, you would first examine the firm's operation to find those functions involving large volume. The reason for this is obvious. If a shipbuilder made and sold only one ship a year on special order, machines for processing this firm's accounts receivable would not be necessary. On the other hand, a department store with 100,000 charge customers might find such machines highly desirable. Logically, those operations involving _____ _____ call for some kind of mechanization.

large volume

11-94 Besides those involving large volume, you would look for operations involving relatively standardized activities. Inventory control for a builder of custom racing cars containing many special parts would not involve the same relatively _____ _____ as those involved in inventory control for a mass producer of passenger automobiles.

standardized activities

11-95 Because of the great number of transactions processed and recorded, many modern accounting activities involve both _____ _____ and relatively _____ _____ .

large volume

standardized activities

11-96 When seeking applications for electronic data-processing (EDP) equipment, large volume and relatively standardized operations are not the only characteristics you would look for. Conventional office equipment, including calculators, billing machines, and punched-card equipment, provides sufficient mechanization for many of these activities; therefore _____ _____ - _____ equipment is not always called for.

electronic data-processing

11-97 However, if these activities also involve the use of master files, the continuous updating of records carrying balances, or the multiple use of input data, EDP equipment may be desirable. The ability of EDP equipment to search a file and abstract information thousands of times faster than a human being makes it efficient for activities involving the use of _____ _____ .

master files

11-98 The high speed with which EDP equipment can locate and update the balance on a record makes it efficient for activities involving the continuous updating of _____ carrying _____ .

records

balances

11-99 To take advantage of EDP, input information must first be translated from man-language to machine-language, usually by means of punched cards. The cost of this translation step is effectively reduced where there is multiple use of _____ data so that the cost of the single translation can be spread over several outputs.

input

11-100 When examining accounting activities, you have five criteria which point toward the possible use of EDP equipment:

1. Large _____
2. _____ activities
3. Use of _____ files
4. _____ _____ of records with balances
5. _____ _____ of input data

1. volume
2. standardized
3. master
4. continuous updating
5. multiple use

11-101 Accounting activities vary by industry, by size of company, and even by companies of the same size, and general rules applicable to all cases are therefore impossible to formulate. These five criteria, however, serve as a starting point for any examination of a firm's operations to find those suitable for application of _____ _____-_____ equipment.

electronic dataprocessing

11-102 To see how EDP equipment can be effectively applied, let's consider an example. Recall that the output providing management with detailed sales information is the

_____ _____ _____ .

Sales Performance Analysis

11-103 Earlier you learned that there were many classifications, or "sorts," of sales data which could be useful to management. A few possible meaningful groupings include reporting by_____ , by_____ , and by_____ .

Any three of these product, salesman customer, sales territory

11-104 However, to produce more than one classification in the Sales Performance Analysis by a manual system can be prohibitively costly. Management would be forced to settle for the one most meaningful _____ and forego the control benefits of others.

classification (sort)

11-105 On the other hand, if the billing activity was handled on EDP equipment, the required data would already have been translated from _____-language to _____-language and would be stored within the computer.

man
machine

11-106 Since the major proportion of the cost of preparing EDP outputs lies in the _____ of data to machine-language, and since the computer can classify data with great speed and efficiency, additional Sales Performance Analyses can be produced economically.

translation (conversion)

11-107 Another example of the ready availability of additional classifications of existing data is the ageing of Accounts Receivable. Classifying Accounts Receivable to show those that are past due is called the _____ of Accounts Receivable.

ageing

11-108 The Accounts Receivable Ledger is usually maintained in alphabetical order by customer for ease in posting. To "age" Accounts Receivable, you merely abstract the data in chronological order by due dates. The resulting list is valuable in distinguishing accounts that are _____ _____, in order to begin special collection efforts.

past due

11-109 When a firm has many customers, a manual procedure for ageing can be quite expensive and time-consuming. Therefore, it is often not economical to provide this information more than a few times a year. However, if Accounts Receivable are already in _____-language, the computer could be programmed to prepare an aged listing at minimal cost.

machine

11-110 An advantage of EDP equipment is the ability to use data stored in the equipment for additional _____ at low _____ .

classifications
(sorts)

cost

11-111 The ready availability of additional data classifications permits the production of additional _____ _____ Analyses and the frequent ageing of_____ _____ .

Sales Performance

Accounts Receivable

11-112 Although not necessarily a criterion, another advantage of mechanization is that of additional data reporting at low cost. Recall that once data has been converted from man-language to _____ - _____ on punched cards and has been stored in the computer, the major _____ of any output derived from this data has already been covered.

machine-language

cost

11-113 Therefore, additional reports of value to management could be machine-prepared at low cost. Management is often deprived of extremely useful reports because the _____ of preparing them manually is prohibitive.

cost

11-114 It is possible to program, or set up, EDP equipment to produce scientific statistical trend analyses of parts usage. If Inventory Control Records are in machine-language, it is possible to produce _____ _____ of parts usage more accurately and at less cost than under manual systems.

trend analyses

11-115 Trend analysis would also be possible as a further sophistication of sales analysis. Instead of reporting past sales only by item or by customer, the computer could be programmed to estimate the _____ of future sales.

trends

11-116 You can therefore consider additional data reporting as another advantage of EDP equipment. Examples of possible supplementary statistical reporting would be _____ _____ , both of parts usage and of sales.

trend analyses

11-117 Finally, an important consideration of any system's outputs is *timely* preparation. Consider how ineffective the sales manager would deem a weekly Sales Analysis Report issued a month later. To be effective for management control, reports or outputs must be _____.

timely

11-118 The high speed of EDP equipment compared with manual operations for large masses of data facilitates _____ reporting, which is essential for good control.

timely

11-119 There are several advantages of EDP equipment when properly employed. Four significant advantages are:

1. Low-_____ processing
2. Ready availability of additional _____ of existing data
3. Additional reports at _____ cost
4. _____ preparation of outputs

1. cost
2. classifications (sorts)
3. low
4. timely

11-120 In order to understand properly how management reaches decisions regarding the use of EDP equipment, you need to know five criteria used in choosing suitable operations for EDP application. These are:

1. Large_____
2. Relatively_____ activities
3. Use of _____ files
4. Continuous _____ of records carrying _____
5. _____ use of input data

1. volume
2. standardized
3. master
4. updating...balances
5. multiple

11-121 One of the most valuable things you have learned in this text is a mental picture of the flows of data from inputs through the various activities to the preparation of

_____.

outputs

11-122 The process of accounting is dynamic and therefore best understood in terms of continuous data flow. Refer to Panel Q. This flow chart shows visually the flows of _____ from _____ through the various activities to the preparation of outputs.

data

inputs

11-123 Reported data is far more meaningful when you can
visualize the source of such data. Moreover, you will find
it easier to understand the application of EDP equipment if
you can visualize the multiple use of _____ data.

input

11-124 For instance, with the help of Panel Q you know that
Timecard inputs affect, either directly or through the Journal,
the following outputs:

1. _____ Checks
2. _____ _____ Reports
3. _____ Sheet
4. _____ Statement
5. _____ _____ Analysis

1. Payroll [Checks]

2. Cost Analysis
   [Reports]

3. Balance [Sheet]

4. Income [State-
   ment]

5. Budget Perform-
   ance [Analysis]

11-125 Because these particular inputs affect so many different outputs, they satisfy one of the requisites of mechanization—multiple use of input data. Payroll involves, in addition, a standard operation and, if a firm has many employees,
large volume. You would therefore consider payroll for
_____ application.

EDP (computer)

11-126 Note on Panel Q that Shipping Notices affect directly
and through the Journal the following outputs:

1. _____ _____ Records
2. Customer _____
3. _____ _____ Analysis
4. _____ _____ Analysis
5. _____ Sheet
6. _____ Statement

1. Inventory Con-
   trol [Records]

2. [Customer] In-
   voices

3. Sales Perform-
   ance [Analysis]

4. Budget Perform-
   ance [Analysis]

5. Balance [Sheet]

6. Income [State-
   ment]

11-127 Therefore, the Shipping Notice is also a strong candidate for_____ application.

EDP (computer)

11-128 Shipping Notices, then, lend themselves to EDP.
Flow charts similar to Panel Q are devices which facilitate
a firm's decision as to which of the inputs are to be put on
EDP. If a flow chart revealed that a particular input had a
low volume and affected only one output, it probably
[would/would not]_____ be considered for EDP application.

would not

11-129 Whether or not they are considering the use of EDP
equipment, most firms prepare flow charts to show the flow
of data through the accounting system. The objective is to
obtain efficient low-cost production of meaningful information, which enables management to make sound business
_____.

decisions

End of Part 11. Take the Review Quiz beginning on the next page now.
Begin Part 12 when you are ready to review the origination of entries.

Complete the following sentences.

1. All entries in some way reflect _____ .
2. Entries reflecting transactions which do *not* arise from input data received at the time are called _____ entries.
3. The five kinds of adjusting entries you have learned about are those for
   (*a*) _____ _____
   (*b*) _____
   (*c*) _____ _____
   (*d*) _____
   (*e*) _____
4. Five examples of adjusting entries other than error corrections involve:
   (*a*) Accumulated _____
   (*b*) Allowance for _____ _____
   (*c*) _____ expenses
   (*d*) _____ revenues
   (*e*) _____ expenses
5. Depreciation as an expense [does/does not] _____ involve an outflow of money or the incurrence of a liability.
6. Depreciation represents the expiration of future _____ of a _____
   _____ .
7. When depreciation is taken in equal increments over the expected life of an asset, the method used is called _____-_____ depreciation.
8. Assume that a piece of equipment costing $5,000 with an estimated life of ten years was being depreciated on a straight-line basis. At the end of the second year, the book value would be $_____ and the asset and contra-asset account balances would be:

   Equipment: $_____ [debit/credit] _____ balance
   Accumulated Depreciation: $_____ [debit/credit] _____ balance

9. The adjusting entry for depreciation covering the third year would be:

	Dr	*Cr*
_____	$_____	$_____
_____	$_____	$_____

10. Suppose this same equipment after seven full years of use was sold for $1,000. The entry recording this transaction would be:

	Dr	*Cr*
Cash	$_____	$_____
Accumulated Depreciation	$_____	$_____
Loss on Sale of Equipment	$_____	$_____
Equipment	$_____	$_____

11. Instead, suppose that, contrary to expectations, this same piece of equipment were still being used twelve years after purchase. The depreciation entry for the twelfth year would debit Depreciation Expense by $_____and credit Accumulated Depreciation by $_____.

The balance in the asset and contra-asset accounts would be: Equipment, $ _____;
Accumulated Depreciation, $ _____ .

12. Now suppose that the equipment were scrapped with no value at the end of the thirteenth
year. The entry to record this event would be:

	Dr	Cr
_____	$ _____	$ _____
_____	$ _____	$ _____

13. One fixed asset, _____ , is never depreciated.

14. Assume that after writing off receivables known specifically to be uncollectible, account
balances showed Accounts Receivable of $100,000 (Dr) and Allowance for Bad Debts of
$1,700 (Cr) from the previous year. If loss experience indicated a reasonably constant
3 per cent rate, the appropriate adjusting entry would be:

	Dr	Cr
Bad Debt Expense	$ _____	$ _____
Allowance for Bad Debts	$ _____	$ _____

15. Suppose that a firm uses a Bad Debt Allowance account. Make the entry to write off a
specific account in the amount of $100.

	Dr	Cr
_____	$ _____	$ _____
Accounts Receivable	$ _____	$ _____

16. Suppose that at year end the accountant knew that a telephone bill for approximately
$200 covering December charges was due but not yet received. He would make an entry
adjusting the books to reflect the _____ as follows:

	Dr	Cr
Telephone Expense	$ _____	$ _____
Accounts Payable	$ _____	$ _____

17. Suppose also at year end the accountant discovered that a three-year insurance policy
costing $600 with two years left to go had been charged to Insurance Expense. He would
make the following adjusting entry:

	Dr	Cr
Prepaid Insurance	$ _____	$ _____
Insurance Expense	$ _____	$ _____

18. At the beginning of the new year, the accountant would _____ those prior year's
adjusting entries for accruals and prepaids. He would not normally _____ adjusting entries for _____ and _____ _____ .

19. When evaluating a system or part of a system for possible EDP application, there are
five criteria which point towards feasible mechanization. These five criteria are:

(a) Large _____
(b) _____ activities or processing
(c) Use of _____ files
(d) Continuous _____ of records carrying balances
(e) _____ use of input data

20. The criterion in part e of question 19 enables the significant cost of translating information from _____ -language to _____ -language to be spread over many out-
puts, thereby reducing the effective cost of each.

21. Where some or all of the foregoing criteria are satisfied, EDP equipment may offer
three major advantages:

(a) _____ - _____ processing
(b) _____ reporting

(c) Additional reports for management at relatively small extra _____

22. In the area of sales analysis, additional Sales Performance Analyses with different _____ to emphasize different aspects of the same raw data would usually be economically feasible with EDP equipment.

23. An advantage from having Accounts Receivable maintained on EDP equipment is that they may economically be frequently analyzed, or _____, to reveal which accounts are past due.

24. If the necessary data is already in machine-language, it would be economical to estimate the _____ in sales demand and parts usage.

review of entries

The problems in this part provide an overall review of basic bookkeeping entries. It is strongly recommended that the student of accounting complete the exercises carefully so that he can correlate and fix in his memory the principles involved. If the student makes an error, he should correct it by lining out the erroneous item and writing the correct answer above or at one side. This will highlight sources of difficulty and types of error for later review. Frames 12-1 to 12-28 deal with general accounting; frames 12-29 to the end deal with cost accounting. *Correct responses, often with explanations, are below all frames in this part.*

12-1 A group of men decide to form a new company. These men invest $50,000 cash, land valued at $10,000, and buildings valued at $40,000; in return they receive capital stock. Journalizing the transaction involves this compound entry:

	Dr	Cr
_____	$_____	$_____
_____	$_____	$_____
_____	$_____	$_____
_____	$_____	$_____

	Dr	Cr
Cash	$50,000	
Land	10,000	
Buildings	40,000	
Capital Stock		$100,000

The receipt of these new assets was recorded as a debit to each of the appropriate asset accounts, which increased their balances. Simultaneously the sources of these same assets were recorded as a credit to the appropriate equity account, which increased its balance by an amount equal to the total investment. Note that here we use a short title for the account you are familiar with as Capital Stock and Paid-in Surplus.

12-2 The firm then purchased equipment costing $20,000.
Freight costs were an additional $1,000 and installation
costs another $3,000. All but $10,000, due on a note payable
in six months, was paid for with cash. Journalize this
transaction.

	Dr	Cr
_____	$ _____	$ _____
_____	$ _____	$ _____
_____	$ _____	$ _____

	Dr	Cr
Equipment	$24,000	
Cash		$14,000
Notes Payable		10,000

The original cost of the new asset, which includes freight-
in and installation costs, is recorded as a debit to the appropriate fixed asset account. Cash paid out is recorded as
a credit or reduction to the Cash account. Finally, the new
claim against the firm's assets arising as part of the
transaction is recorded as a credit increasing the appropriate equity account.

12-3 This firm is a distributor; it buys merchandise for
resale and has no factory costs; it follows a perpetual inventory system. If merchandise costing $28,000 with
$2,000 of additional freight-in costs is received, and
$10,000 of the total cost is paid in cash, the appropriate
compound entry would be:

	Dr	Cr
_____	$ _____	$ _____
_____	$ _____	$ _____
_____	$ _____	$ _____

	Dr	Cr
Inventory	$30,000	
Cash		$10,000
Accounts Payable		20,000

The increase in the asset—Inventory—is recorded at a cost
figure which includes freight-in cost. The reduction in
Cash and the increase in creditors' claims are both recorded as credits.

12-4 The firm purchases during 196A for $3,000 cash an insurance policy which will become effective January 1, 196B, and will cover the next three years. The entry would be:

	Dr	Cr
_____	$ _____	$ _____
_____	$ _____	$ _____

	Dr	Cr
Prepaid Insurance	$3,000	
Cash		$3,000

The policy has three years of future usefulness or value to the firm and is therefore entered as an asset.

12-5 During December, 196A, the New Company incurred $6,000 of organization costs. Such costs include expenditures incurred in organizing the firm—fees for lawyers, accountants, consultants, and the like. These costs were considered to have a future value, and the owners decided to record them in an asset account called Organization Costs, to be written off in equal annual installments over six years beginning in 196B. If all **$6,000** was owed to creditors, make the summary entry for 196A.

	Dr	Cr
_____	$ _____	$ _____
_____	$ _____	$ _____

	Dr	Cr
Organization Costs	$6,000	
Accounts Payable		$6,000

The write-off beginning the next year will be by a debit to the account called Amortization Expense and a credit to Organization Costs. Amortization is a form of depreciation applied to intangible assets such as Organization Costs.

12-6 On Panel R you will find T accounts representing the
asset and equity accounts in the firm's Ledger. Post the
correct entries for frames 12-1 to 12-5 to these accounts.
After you have completed the posting, note that the Cash
account has a [debit/credit]_____ balance of
$_____ , and the Capital Stock account has a_____
balance of $_____ .

Cash: debit balance of $23,000
Capital Stock: credit balance of $100,000

The Cash account balance is the net of a $50,000 debit
(frame 12-1) and credits of $14,000 (frame 12-2), $10,000
(frame 12-3), and $3,000 (frame 12-4). The Capital Stock
account reflects the single initial source of the $100,000 of
assets (frame 12-1).

12-7 On Panel S, complete the Balance Sheet for the New
Company as of December 31, 196A, from the accounts on
Panel R. Total Current Assets are $_____ , Total
Assets are $_____ , and Total Liabilities are
$_____ .

Total Current Assets . . . . $ 56,000
Total Assets   136,000
Total Liabilities   36,000

12-8 The following events occurred during the first year of the New Company's operation. Make the appropriate entry summarizing the effect of the events. In all transactions assume that the company is on a perpetual inventory system. For your reference the following entries carry journal numbers.

The firm purchased additional merchandise on credit at a net invoice cost of $200,000. Freight-in costs amounted to $15,000.

	Dr	Cr
(1) _____	$_____	$_____
_____	$_____	$_____

	Dr	Cr
Inventory	$215,000	
Accounts Payable		$215,000

The original cost of the inventory includes freight-in costs, and therefore the entire amount is an increase in assets accompanied by a corresponding increase in liabilities.

12-9 Total sales to customers on credit amounted to $300,000. A 5 per cent sales tax was applicable to all items sold.

	Dr	Cr
(2) _____	$_____	$_____
_____	$_____	$_____
_____	$_____	$_____

	Dr	Cr
Accounts Receivable	$315,000	
Sales		$300,000
Taxes Payable		15,000

Note that the full amount due from customers—selling price plus applicable taxes—represents an asset. Of the total new assets amounting to $315,000, $300,000 reflects revenue and is credited to the Sales account. The remaining $15,000 is offset by a tax liability of $15,000.

12-10 Merchandise shipped to customers throughout the year had a cost, including freight-in, of $195,000.

	Dr	*Cr*
(3) _____	$ _____	$ _____
_____	$ _____	$ _____

	Dr	*Cr*
Cost of Goods Sold	$195,000	
Inventory		$195,000

The reduction in assets becomes an expense of doing business.

12-11 Throughout the year, customers paid $270,000 on their accounts.

	Dr	*Cr*
(4) _____	$ _____	$ _____
_____	$ _____	$ _____

	Dr	*Cr*
Cash	$270,000	
Accounts Receivable		$270,000

Since no cash discounts are involved, these events represented exchanges of assets, i.e., an increase in one asset offset by a corresponding reduction in another.

12-12 Throughout the year, the firm paid its creditors $195,000, which included settlement of the note payable on equipment.

	Dr	*Cr*
(5) _____	$ _____	$ _____
_____	$ _____	$ _____
_____	$ _____	$ _____

	Dr	*Cr*
Accounts Payable	$185,000	
Notes Payable	10,000	
Cash		$195,000

Recall that the note payable on equipment amounted to $10,000 (frame 12-2). The expenditure of cash is offset by an appropriate reduction in the two liability accounts.

12-13   Covering all but the last few days of the year, the firm had a payroll expense of $40,000. Of this, $30,000 was paid out in cash; the balance represented income taxes withheld and both employees' and employer's shares of Social Security taxes.

		Dr	Cr
(6)	_____	$_____	$_____
	_____	$_____	$_____
	_____	$_____	$_____

	Dr	Cr
Payroll Expense	$40,000	
Cash		$30,000
Taxes Payable		10,000

Both the reduction in cash and the increase in liabilities represent payroll expenses to the firm.

12-14   A customer who had not yet paid his account returned merchandise he had purchased for $5,000. The items returned had a cost of $3,000. They were in good condition when returned and were placed back into inventory.

		Dr	Cr
(7)	_____	$_____	$_____
	_____	$_____	$_____
(8)	_____	$_____	$_____
	_____	$_____	$_____

	Dr	Cr
Sales	$5,000	
Accounts Receivable		$5,000
Inventory	3,000	
Cost of Goods Sold		3,000

Note that two events must be recorded: the cancellation of the sale and the return of stock. As shown, the original entries recording the sale and shipping transactions have been reversed. In practice, the accountant may often debit a special contra-revenue account, such as Sales Returns and Allowances.

12-15 The firm returned to one of its suppliers inventory items costing $1,000 on which it had not yet paid the materials invoice. No freight adjustment or additional expense was involved.

	Dr	Cr
(9) _____	$_____	$_____
_____	$_____	$_____

	Dr	Cr
Accounts Payable	$1,000	
Inventory		$1,000

The reduction in inventory is offset by the corresponding reduction in liabilities.

12-16 During the year, $10,000 total dividends were paid to the owners.

	Dr	Cr
(10) _____	$_____	$_____
_____	$_____	$_____

	Dr	Cr
Retained Earnings	$10,000	
Cash		$10,000

Remember that for dividends the reduction in cash is not considered an expense. Instead, it is reflected by a direct reduction to Retained Earnings.

12-17 At year end, payroll expense for the last few days was estimated for accrual at $400; $300 would be recorded as payable to employees and the balance as taxes on both employees and employer.

	Dr	Cr
(11) _____	$ _____	$ _____
_____	$ _____	$ _____
_____	$ _____	$ _____

	Dr	Cr
Payroll Expense	$400	
Accrued Wages and Salaries		$300
Taxes Payable		100

Remember that to match expenses with revenues properly for the year, the accountant must accrue payroll due but unpaid.

12-18 Taxes due in the amount of $8,000 had been paid to governments throughout the year.

	Dr	Cr
(12) _____	$ _____	$ _____
_____	$ _____	$ _____

	Dr	Cr
Taxes Payable	$8,000	
Cash		$8,000

12-19 Depreciation of equipment amounted to $5,000; depreciation of buildings amounted to $1,000 for the year.

	Dr	Cr
(13) _____	$ _____	$ _____
Accumulated Depreciation— Equipment	$ _____	$ _____
Accumulated Depreciation— Buildings	$ _____	$ _____

	Dr	Cr
Depreciation Expense	$6,000	
Accumulated Depreciation—Equipment		$5,000
Accumulated Depreciation—Buildings		1,000

The expiration of fixed asset cost is not recorded directly but credited to the proper contra-asset account. The expiration is necessarily reflected as an expense for the period.

12-20 During 196B, one piece of equipment, which originally cost $5,000, had accumulated depreciation of $1,000. It was disposed of at a loss for $3,500 cash.

	Dr	Cr
(14) _____	$ _____	$ _____
_____	$ _____	$ _____
_____	$ _____	$ _____
_____	$ _____	$ _____

	Dr	Cr
Cash	$3,500	
Accumulated Depreciation—Equipment	1,000	
Loss on Disposal of Equipment	500	
Equipment		$5,000

The disposal of the fixed asset is recorded by a credit for its original cost to the appropriate asset account. The depreciation accumulated is also removed from the contra-asset account by a debit, and the increase in cash is recorded. The $500 net reduction in assets—book value less cash received—represents a loss ultimately reducing Retained Earnings.

12-21 Now make these necessary year-end adjustments:

(15) Prepaid insurance and insurance expense: $1,000
(16) Amortization of organization costs: $1,000 (This involves the Organization Costs account and an expense account called General Expense.)

(17) Write-off of a specific uncollectible account: $2,000

Make the debit to the Bad Debt Allowance account.

		Dr	Cr
(15)	_____	$_____	$_____
	_____	$_____	$_____
(16)	_____	$_____	$_____
	_____	$_____	$_____
(17)	_____	$_____	$_____
	_____	$_____	$_____

	Dr	Cr
Insurance Expense	$1,000	
Prepaid Insurance		$1,000
General Expense	1,000	
Organization Costs		1,000
Bad Debt Allowance	2,000	
Accounts Receivable		2,000

In the first two entries (15 and 16) the asset reduction is accompanied by a charge to the appropriate expense account for the period. The receivable asset is written off to the contra-account with the assumption that the Bad Debt Allowance account will be credited later.

12-22 Turn to Panel T, which contains the expanded
Ledger accounts for the New Company. Note that the opening balances for the year are shown and correspond to the
closing balances of the prior year on Panels R and S. Now
post to Panel T the correct entries for frames 12-8 to 12-21
After posting, the Cash balance is $_____ Dr, and
the Accounts Payable balance is $_____ Cr.

Cash: $53,500 Dr   Accounts Payable: $55,000 Cr

The Cash account balance is a net of the opening balance
of $23,000 plus debits of $270,000 (frame 12-11) plus
$3,500 (frame 12-20) less credits of $195,000 (frame
12-12), $30,000 (frame 12-13), $10,000 (frame 12-16)
and $8,000 (frame 12-18). The Accounts Payable bal-
ance is the net of an opening balance of $26,000 plus
credits of $215,000 (frame 12-8) less debits of $185,000
(frame 12-12) and $1,000 (frame 12-15).

12-23 Assume that, at the end of the year 196B, management decides that the bad debt allowance should be 1 per
cent of the outstanding receivables. Panel T shows that the
year-end Accounts Receivable balance is $_____ , and
therefore the balance in Bad Debt Allowance should be
$_____ .

Accounts Receivable: $38,000   Bad Debt Allowance: $380

The Accounts Receivable balance is the net of a $315,000
debit (frame 12-9) less credits of $270,000 (frame 12-11),
$5,000 (frame 12-14), and $2,000 (frame 12-21). The allow-
anee is 1 per cent of this balance. Therefore, the balance
in Bad Debt Allowance, to be carried to the new period, is
$380.

12-24   You will note that the Bad Debt Allowance account now has a debit balance. In recording the bad debt expense for the period, the accountant credits the Bad Debt Allowance account by an amount sufficient to make a $380 credit balance. Make the entry required to record bad debt expense for the period.

		Dr	*Cr*
(18)	_____	$ _____	$ _____
	_____	$ _____	$ _____

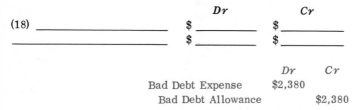

	Dr	*Cr*
Bad Debt Expense	$2,380	
Bad Debt Allowance		$2,380

Remember that Bad Debt Expense includes both actual accounts written off during the period and an adjustment to leave the residual balance reflecting anticipated future losses—in this example, $380.

12-25   Post the correct entry from frame 12-24 to Panel T. Now close Sales to Income Summary.

		Dr	*Cr*
(19)	_____	$ _____	$ _____
	_____	$ _____	$ _____

	Dr	*Cr*
Sales	$295,000	
Income Summary		$295,000

12-26 Post the correct entry from frame **12-25** to Panel T. Now prepare the compound entry closing all expense accounts, including the loss accounts, to Income Summary.

	Dr	Cr
(20) _____	$_____	$_____
_____	$_____	$_____
_____	$_____	$_____
_____	$_____	$_____
_____	$_____	$_____
_____	$_____	$_____
_____	$_____	$_____
_____	$_____	$_____

	Dr	Cr
Income Summary	$243,280	
Cost of Goods Sold		$192,000
Payroll Expense		40,400
Insurance Expense		1,000
Bad Debt Expense		2,380
Depreciation Expense		6,000
General Expense		1,000
Loss on Disposal of Equipment		500

12-27 Post the correct entry from frame **12-26** to Panel T. The earnings before taxes can now be determined as $_____ , represented by the credit balance in Income Summary. Assume now that income taxes are estimated to be $22,000. Make the entry setting up the anticipated tax liability and charging Income Summary.

	Dr	Cr
(21) _____	$_____	$_____
_____	$_____	$_____

Earnings before taxes: $51,720

	Dr	Cr
Income Summary	$22,000	
Taxes Payable		$22,000

12-28 Post the correct entry from frame 12-27 to Panel T.
Net profit after taxes can now be determined as
$_____. Make the entry closing Income Summary to
Retained Earnings and then post this entry to Panel T.

	Dr	*Cr*
(22) _____	$_____	$_____
_____	$_____	$_____

Net profit after taxes: $29,720

	Dr	*Cr*
Income Summary	$29,720	
Retained Earnings		$29,720

Turn to Panel U and complete the Income Statement and the
Balance Sheet. Then check your work by turning to Panels
V and W. Panel W shows the postings keyed to the Journal
entries by reference number. Note that, for the real accounts,
any opening balance as of January 1, 196B, and ending balances to be carried forward to 196C are marked B. All temporary holding accounts are closed. Also note the variety
of ways that accountants can use to "rule-off" accounts.

12-29 This frame introduces a sequence dealing with entries related to cost accounting. Begin only if you have completed Parts 9 and 10.

A distributor of garden equipment maintains a single Inventory account on a perpetual basis. He uses the LIFO method of inventory valuation. During the year 196A his purchases of lawnmowers were:

1. January, 100 at $90 each
2. June, 200 at $100 each
3. October, 50 at $102 each

These were all purchased on credit. Make the entry summarizing all these purchases.

	Dr	*Cr*
_____ $ _____	$ _____
_____ $ _____	$ _____

	Dr	*Cr*
Inventory	$34,100	
Accounts Payable		$34,100

In practice, the accountant would have journalized each transaction at the time of purchase. Remember that whether specific identification, average cost, FIFO, or LIFO is used, the purchase is always recorded at original cost.

12-30 This distributor had a beginning inventory balance of $5,000; the firm was out of stock before the June shipment arrived; seventy-five lawnmowers were on hand on December 31. At this date, the account balances were:

Inventory: $ _____
Cost of Goods Sold: $ _____

Inventory: $7,500   Cost of Goods Sold: $31,600

Since the distributor was on a perpetual inventory basis, he would have recorded zero inventory before the June shipment. Hence the oldest remaining costs at year end were the June costs. Deducting $7,500 from the sum of $5,000 Beginning Inventory plus $34,100 Purchases equals Cost of Goods Sold, $31,600.

12-31 The $5,000 beginning inventory was the LIFO cost
of 100 lawnmowers. Now if this distributor used a periodic
inventory instead of a perpetual inventory, the accountant
would not have recorded a zero balance before the June
receipt. The balances on December 31 would have been:

Inventory: $_____
Cost of Goods Sold: $ _____

> Inventory: $3,750   Cost of Goods Sold: $35,350
>
> In this case, the seventy-five lawnmowers on hand would
> carry the oldest remaining cost, the $50 per lawnmower
> recorded in the beginning inventory, a total for the ending
> inventory of $3,750.

12-32 A second distributor uses FIFO and periodic inventories. His purchases during the year, all on credit,
were:

> January, 100 at $90 . . . $ 9,000
> June, 200 at $100 20,000
> October, 50 at $102 . . .   5,100
> Total, 350 . . . . $34,100

This distributor does not use a separate Purchases account
but charges all purchases directly to Inventory. Make a
summary entry for the purchases.

	Dr	Cr
_____	$_____	$_____
_____	$_____	$_____

> | | Dr | Cr |
> |---|---|---|
> | Inventory | $34,100 | |
> | Accounts Payable | | $34,100 |

12-33 This distributor had a balance in the Inventory account on January 1, 196A, of $5,000. Make the entry necessary on December 31, 196A, to charge Cost of Goods Sold with the beginning Inventory balance plus the year's additions recorded by the entries in the preceding frame.

	Dr	Cr
_____	$ _____	$ _____
_____	$ _____	$ _____

	Dr	Cr
Cost of Goods Sold	$39,100	
Inventory		$39,100

12-34 The periodic inventory taken at the end of this same year, December 31, 196A, disclosed fifty lawnmowers on hand. Make the entry necessary to relieve Cost of Goods Sold of the amount of ending inventory.

	Dr	Cr
_____	$ _____	$ _____
_____	$ _____	$ _____

	Dr	Cr
Inventory	$5,100	
Cost of Goods Sold		$5,100

Note how these last two frames illustrate the formulas: Beginning Inventory plus Purchases equals goods available for sale; goods available for sale minus Ending Inventory equals Cost of Goods Sold. Instead of the last two entries, the accountant could have applied the formula separately, and then made a single entry charging Cost of Goods Sold with the resultant $34,000 figure and crediting Inventory accordingly. However, making two entries not only is simpler, but also provides a better audit trail.

12-35 Assume that this same distributor uses a Purchases account to record temporarily those costs which will be segregated into Inventory and Cost of Goods Sold at year end. Suppose that you received this data at year end, December 31, 196A.

Purchases, $34,100
Inventory, $5,000 balance on 1/1/196A
Lawnmowers on hand, 12/31/196A, 50

Make the required entries (1) to close the Purchases account, (2) to charge Cost of Goods Sold with the Beginning Inventory figure, and (3) to record the Ending Inventory by the FIFO method.

		Dr	*Cr*
(1)	_____	$_____	$_____
	_____	$_____	$_____
(2)	_____	$_____	$_____
	_____	$_____	$_____
(3)	_____	$_____	$_____
	_____	$_____	$_____

		Dr	*Cr*
(1)	Cost of Goods Sold	$34,100	
	Purchases		$34,100
(2)	Cost of Goods Sold	$ 5,000	
	Inventory		$ 5,000
(3)	Inventory	$ 5,100	
	Cost of Goods Sold		$ 5,100

Note that while the results would be the same if purchases were debited directly to Inventory, the use of a Purchases account segregates information concerning purchases.

12-36 Suppose that the hardware store selling these power mowers uses the retail method of inventory valuation. The records indicate the following:

Date	Units	Unit cost	Unit selling price
On hand, 1/1	8	$108	$180
Purchases, 5/1	24	114	190
On hand, 12/31	10	. . .	190

The ending inventory balance would be $ _____.

Ending Inventory: $1,140

This dealer maintained his gross profit ratio, or mark-up, at 40 per cent: ($180 – $108)/$180 = 40 per cent and ($190 – $114)/$190 = 40 per cent. Therefore, he would compute the cost of each lawnmower on hand on December 31 as 60 per cent of $190, or $114. Note that this is a simplified example; reductions in selling price (mark-downs) have been ignored.

12-37 What was this dealer's cost of goods sold? $ _____

$2,460

Beginning Inventory (8 × $108)	$ 864
Purchases (24 × $114)	2,736
Goods Available	3,600
Ending Inventory	1,140
Cost of Goods Sold	$2,460

You may have noticed that when a perpetual inventory is maintained, transfers from inventory are used to obtain the inventory balance. When periodic inventory is used, even with the retail method illustrated here, the cost of the transfers from inventory is obtained by valuing the ending inventory.

12-38 Suppose that a manufacturer of power lawnmowers uses an actual cost system. During a period, the production department requisitioned $5,000 of raw materials. Make the appropriate entry to the two inventory accounts involved.

	Dr	Cr
_____	$_____	$_____
_____	$_____	$_____

	Dr	Cr
Work in Process Inventory	$5,000	
Materials Inventory		$5,000

This charges production and relieves raw materials stores of the material element of product cost.

12-39 The debit balance in the Factory Payroll Expense account at this time was $14,000, of which $4,000 represented indirect labor. Make the two entries closing Factory Payroll Expense to the appropriate inventory account and to the temporary holding account for overhead, Factory Overhead.

	Dr	Cr
_____	$_____	$_____
_____	$_____	$_____
_____	$_____	$_____
_____	$_____	$_____

	Dr	Cr
Work in Process Inventory	$10,000	
Factory Payroll Expense		$10,000
Factory Overhead	$ 4,000	
Factory Payroll Expense		$ 4,000

Remember that Factory Overhead is a temporary holding account closed to Inventory at a standard rate. Variances are charged directly to Cost of Goods Sold at period end.

12-40 Let's look at another example. A lawnmower manufacturer uses an actual cost system in which materials and
direct labor are charged to Work in Process at the actual
amounts incurred, and overhead is charged at a predetermined overhead rate. Prior to the start of the year 196A,
these estimates were made for 196A:

Direct Labor, $10,000 per month
Total Overhead Cost, $240,000 per year

The overhead rate per direct labor dollar (DLD) was set at
$____.

Overhead rate: $2

Overhead rates are usually calculated on an annual basis
to avoid a changing rate due to monthly differences in
hours worked and overhead charges made. The rate here is
$240,000/(12 × $10,000) = $2 per DLD.

12-41 During the year, this firm's production department requisitioned $120,000 of materials. The total debits to the Factory Payroll Expense account were $150,000, of which $40,000 represented indirect labor. Make summary entries (1) to charge Work in Process with the materials, (2) to close the Factory Payroll Expense account to the proper accounts using a compound entry, and (3) to credit Factory Overhead at the $2 DLD rate.

		Dr	Cr
(1)	_____	$ _____	$ _____
	_____	$ _____	$ _____
(2)	_____	$ _____	$ _____
	_____	$ _____	$ _____
	_____	$ _____	$ _____
(3)	_____	$ _____	$ _____
	_____	$ _____	$ _____

		Dr	Cr
(1)	Work in Process Inventory	$120,000	
	Materials Inventory		$120,000
	(This relieves Materials Inventory and charges production for the materials requisitioned.)		
(2)	Work in Process Inventory	$110,000	
	Factory Overhead	40,000	
	Factory Payroll Expense		$150,000
	(This closes Factory Payroll Expense, charges production with the direct labor and Factory Overhead for the indirect labor.)		
(3)	Work in Process	$220,000	
	Factory Overhead		$220,000
	(This charges Work in Process for Factory Overhead at the $2 per DLD rate, $2 × 110,000 = $220,000.)		

12-42 After posting the $40,000 indirect labor to Factory
Overhead, the total debits to this account amounted to
$226,000. By entry 3 in frame 12-41, you credited
Factory Overhead with $220,000. Now close the [underab-
sorbed/overabsorbed] _____ overhead to Cost of
Goods Sold.

	Dr	Cr
_____	$ _____	$ _____
_____	$ _____	$ _____

underabsorbed

	Dr	Cr
Cost of Goods Sold	$6,000	
Factory Overhead		$6,000

On Panel X you will find T accounts, some with balances,
for the power-lawnmower division of the Smith Company.
Standard costs and perpetual inventory systems are used
in this division. From the information given, make the
required entries; post each entry to Panel X as soon as you
have checked to see if it is correct. Each entry in this sequence has a journal number. Key the postings by entry, in
the manner shown on Panel W.

12-43 The standard price for steel tubing is 10 cents per
foot. During the year, 5,000 feet were purchased on credit
at the standard price.

		Dr	Cr
(1)	_____	$ _____	$ _____
	_____	$ _____	$ _____

	Dr	Cr
Materials Inventory	$500	
Accounts Payable		$500

12-44 For the year, Stores Requisitions for steel tubing totaled 5,100 feet. However, the standard allowance for tubing for the year's production was 5,000 feet at 10 cents per foot. Make the summary entry, using a Materials Variance account to record the variance.

		Dr	Cr
(2)	_____	$ _____	$ _____
	_____	$ _____	$ _____
	_____	$ _____	$ _____

	Dr	Cr
Work in Process Inventory	$500	
Materials Variance	10	
Materials Inventory		$510

12-45 Other materials were requisitioned from raw materials stores totaling $20,400. The accountant charges these materials to Work in Process at the standard amount, which is $20,000. The compound entry to charge this figure and to record the variance is:

		Dr	Cr
(3)	_____	$ _____	$ _____
	_____	$ _____	$ _____
	_____	$ _____	$ _____

	Dr	Cr
Work in Process Inventory	$20,000	
Materials Variance	400	
Materials Inventory		$20,400

This entry illustrates the rule that "unfavorable" variances are debits.

12-46 The gross earnings of factory employees amounted to $21,000. Of this amount, $7,000 was withheld for income taxes and $1,260 for Social Security taxes. The employer was required to match the employees' Social Security taxes. Make two summary entries: the first for employees' gross earnings, the cash paid to them, and the tax liability; the second for the employer's Social Security tax liability. Remember that the Factory Payroll Expense account has a debit balance.

	Dr	Cr
(4) _____	$ _____	$ _____
_____	$ _____	$ _____
_____	$ _____	$ _____
(5) _____	$ _____	$ _____
_____	$ _____	$ _____

	Dr	Cr
Factory Payroll Expense	$21,000	
Cash		$12,740
Taxes Payable		8,260
Factory Payroll Expense	$ 1,260	
Taxes Payable		$ 1,260

12-47 During the year, productive effort was considered equivalent to 500 completed lawnmowers, each containing $30 direct labor at standard. On receipt of this information, the accountant charges Work in Process for the standard direct labor allowance. The summary entry would be:

	Dr	Cr
(6) _____	$ _____	$ _____
_____	$ _____	$ _____

	Dr	Cr
Work in Process	$15,000	
Factory Payroll Expense		$15,000

12-48   The check of Timecards indicated that $7,400 was
the actual amount of indirect labor for the year. The
Smith Company's cost accountant follows the practice of
closing the Factory Payroll Expense account when he
transfers indirect labor to the Factory Overhead account.
Before making the entry, compute the variance figure from
the balance now in the Factory Payroll Expense account so
that you can post the correct amount to the Labor Variance
account as part of this compound entry.

	Dr	Cr
(7) _____	$ _____	$ _____
_____	$ _____	$ _____
_____	$ _____	$ _____

	Dr	Cr
Factory Overhead	$7,400	
Labor Variance		$ 140
Factory Payroll Expense		7,260

This is a direct labor variance. Of the $22,260 charged to
Factory Payroll Expense, $7,400 represented indirect
labor; $22,260 − $7,400 = $14,860 represented the direct
labor cost, although $15,000 was credited to Factory Pay-
roll Expense for the direct labor. This means that actual
direct labor costs were less than standard, and as a result
there is a favorable labor variance. This variance could be
due to a more efficient use of labor, to lower wage rates, or
to some combination of these factors.

12-49 The $15,500 shown on Panel X as the balance in
Factory Overhead came from closing to Factory Overhead
various expense accounts not shown. The standard overhead rate is $1.50 per standard direct labor dollar. Make
the compound entry which will close the Factory Overhead
account to the appropriate inventory and variance accounts.

		Dr	Cr
(8)	_____	$ _____	$ _____
	_____	$ _____	$ _____
	_____	$ _____	$ _____

	Dr	Cr
Work in Process Inventory	$22,500	
Overhead Variance	400	
Factory Overhead		$22,900

$15,000 DLD times $1.50 equals $22,500, the charge to
Work in Process for overhead.

12-50 A common practice is to list standard costs for
products on a Standard Cost Card for each product. For
these lawnmowers, the card shows:

Materials	$ 41.00
Direct labor	30.00
Overhead	45.00
Total standard cost	$116.00

During the year, 450 power mowers were transferred from
production to the finished goods storeroom. Make the summary entry for the transfer:

		Dr	Cr
(9)	_____	$ _____	$ _____
	_____	$ _____	$ _____

	Dr	Cr
Finished Goods Inventory	$52,200	
Work in Process Inventory		$52,200

An almost universal characteristic of standard costing is
to charge Finished Goods with standard costs.

12-51 Since the Smith Company uses the perpetual inventory method, the accountant uses the Shipping Notices to transfer inventory to Cost of Goods Sold. During the year, he transferred 440 lawnmowers. Make and post a summary entry for these transfers:

		Dr	Cr
(10)	_____	$ _____	$ _____
	_____	$ _____	$ _____

	Dr	Cr
Cost of Goods Sold	$51,040	
Finished Goods Inventory		$51,040

Note again that, in contrast to the periodic inventory method, the inventory balances are determined from the transfers made. However, even the use of the perpetual method does not eliminate the need for a physical count for audit purposes, although these counts are not always at year end and may be made principally to check how well the firm controls its assets.

12-52 This division closes all variance accounts at year end to Cost of Goods Sold. Do this with a single compound entry:

		Dr	Cr
(11)	_____	$ _____	$ _____
	_____	$ _____	$ _____
	_____	$ _____	$ _____
	_____	$ _____	$ _____

	Dr	Cr
Cost of Goods Sold	$670	
Labor Variance	140	
Material Variance		$410
Overhead Variance		400

Inasmuch as the variances relate to the year's manufacturing and Cost of Goods Sold to the year's sales, it would be preferable to leave Cost of Goods Sold at standard in the Income Statement for management and to show the variances separately.

12-53 Note on Panel X that Cash has been debited with $32,000 and keyed (12), with the credits to other accounts not specifically shown. Now make and post summary entries reflecting:

(13) Additional credit purchases of materials totaling $18,500

	Dr	Cr
_____	$ _____	$ _____
_____	$ _____	$ _____

(14) Cash paid out: Taxes Payable, $11,400; Accounts Payable, $28,900

	Dr	Cr
_____	$ _____	$ _____
_____	$ _____	$ _____
_____	$ _____	$ _____

		Dr	Cr
(13)	Materials Inventory	$18,500	
	Accounts Payable		$18,500
(14)	Taxes Payable	$11,400	
	Accounts Payable	28,900	
	Cash		$40,300

Note that since all accounts are not given, a trial balance of those listed would not be useful.

12-54 The only open accounts, except for Cost of Goods Sold, shown on Panel X are the real accounts. Determine the balances of these open accounts and list them:

	Dr	Cr
_____	$ _____	$ _____
_____	$ _____	$ _____
_____	$ _____	$ _____
_____	$ _____	$ _____
_____	$ _____	$ _____
_____	$ _____	$ _____
_____	$ _____	$ _____

Here are a few check balances. If you are in disagreement, first check your postings for possible errors before going on to Panel Y.

Work in Process Inventory $21,800
Finished Goods Inventory 26,680
Cost of Goods Sold 51,710

12-55 Panel Y illustrates postings keyed to entries, as well as a minor point—the variety of ways accounts are "ruled off" in manually kept ledgers. Of greater importance is the implication in closing the variance accounts to Cost of Goods Sold. The variances do not become a part of inventories, and since they do become an expense item in the year of occurrence, they do affect one account on the Balance Sheet, the _____ _____ account. The reader should be aware that many more variations in practice exist than those mentioned in this illustration of standard costing; he may find examples in any standard cost text.

Retained
Earnings

answers to review quizzes

part 1

1. business decisions   2. earn [a] profit,
remain solvent   3. solvent   4. "events"
(transactions), financial position
5. (a) managers
   (b) owners
   (c) creditors
   (d) government agencies (Federal, state,
       and local)
6. inputs   7. outputs

part 2

1. D   2. F   3. B   4. A   5. I   6. E
7. C   8. J   9. H   10. G   11. units, dollars   12. customer, product, salesman,
sales territory   13. units   14. on order,
forecasted (required, demanded)   15. profit
center (responsibility center)   16. date
17. assets (properties) [and] equities
18. period [of] time

part 3

1. O   2. O   3. I   4. O   5. I   6. I   7. O
8. I   9. O   10. O   11. I   12. I   13. I
14. O   15. I   16. I   17. O   18. I   19. O
20. I   21. O   22. I   23. I   24. L   25. I
26. F   27. B   28. K   29. J   30. A
31. H   32. D   33. G   34. C   35. E
36. A, B   37. C, D, E, F   38. I, J
39. G, H   40. D, E

part 4

1. (a) processing [and] recording
   (b) financial [reporting]
   (c) control [reporting]
2. CR   3. FR   4. PR   5. PR   6. FR
7. CR   8. CR   9. PR   10. CR   11. PR
12. PR   13. CR   14. payroll, Payroll
Check   15. billing, Customer Invoice
16. payables, Checks [to] Creditors
17. cash receipt [and] reconciliation, Bank
Statements   18. financial reporting, Balance
Sheet   19. Budget Information   20. planned,
actual

part 5

1. C   2. L   3. H   4. D   5. J   6. I
7. E   8. F   9. M   10. K   11. B   12. G
13. A   14. G, H, I, J   15. D, E, F   16. A,
B, C   17. L, M   18. K   19. G, H, I, J, K,
L, M   20. E   21. B   22. C   23. A
24. D   25. dollars   26. assets, assets,
equities   27. liabilities
28. (a) Assets = Equities
    (b) Assets = Liabilities + Net Worth
            (Owners' Equity)
    (c) Assets = Current Liabilities + Long-
            term Debt + Net Worth
            (Owners' Equity)
    (d) Net Worth = Assets − Liabilities
    (e) Net Assets = Assets − Liabilities
29. Owners' Equity   30. do *not*   31. Ledger
32. Journal   33. entry   34. journalizing
35. posting   36. balance   37. increase
38. Equipment, reduction   39. increase,
Inventory, Cash   40. increase, increase,
Accounts Payable   41. reduce, reduce

part 6

1. left, right   2. debit balance, credit balance   3. debit, credit   4. credit, debit
5. debits, credits   6. credit, (a) equity, (b) revenue, (c) asset   7. net, profit   8. revenues   9. expenses
10. Income Statement   11. Retained Earnings   12. temporary holding, permanent
13. Income Summary   14. Retained Earnings

15.

	Dr	Cr
Cash	$1,000	
Capital Stock and Paid-in Surplus		$1,000

16.

	Dr	Cr
Equipment	$500	
Cash		$500

17.

	Dr	Cr
Inventory	$400	
Accounts Payable		$400

18.

	Dr	Cr
Telephone Expense	$50	
Accounts Payable		$50

19.

	Dr	Cr
Accounts Payable	$50	
Cash		$50

20.

	Dr	Cr
Accounts Receivable	$200	
Sales		$200
Cost of Goods Sold	$120	
Inventory		$120

21.

	Dr	Cr
Sales	$9,000	
Income Summary		$9,000

22.

	Dr	Cr
Income Summary	$8,000	
Cost of Goods Sold		$5,400
Other Expenses		1,600
Taxes		1,000

23. $1,000

24.

	Dr	Cr
Income Summary	$1,000	
Retained Earnings		$1,000

25. $400

part 7

1. Timecard, Salary List, Payroll   2. rate [of] pay, dependents, deductions   3. gross earnings   4. take-home pay

5.

Straight time		$80.00
Overtime		15.00
Gross earnings		$95.00
Income tax	$19.00	
Social Security	4.75	
Union dues	2.00	25.75
Take-home pay		$69.25

6. (a) Payroll Expense
   (b) Cash
   (c) Taxes Payable (including Social Security)
   (d) Union Dues Payable

7.

	Dr	Cr
Payroll Expense	$99.75	
Cash		$69.25
Taxes Payable		28.50
Union Dues Payable		2.00

8. employer's (firm's)   9. Purchase Order [Copy], Receiving Record   10. payables
11. (a) Shipping Notice
    (b) Parts
    (c) Customer
12. part [number], list [price]
13. (a) [Customer name]
    (b) Shipping [address]
    (c) Billing [address]
    (d) [Trade] discounts
    (e) Payment terms
    (f) [Applicable] taxes
    (g) [Customer number]
14. $87.36
15. (a) Accounts Receivable
    (b) Sales
    (c) [Taxes Payable]
    (d) Cost [of] Goods Sold
    (e) Inventory

16.

	Dr	Cr
Accounts Receivable	$87.36	
Sales		$84.00
Taxes Payable		3.36
Cost of Goods Sold	$60.00	
Inventory		$60.00

17. $24   18. cash receipt [and] reconciliation

19.

	Dr	Cr
Cash	$392	
Discounts and Allowances	8	
Accounts Receivable		$400

part 8

1. trial balance   2. would *not*   3. 11
4. 110
5. On order: X
   On hand: X
6. A   7. B   8. C   9. A   10. A   11. B
12. variance (difference)   13. percentage
14. balance   15. audit   16. reversing, correct

17.

	Dr	Cr
Accounts Payable	$70	
Supplies Expense		$70
Supplies Expense	$700	
Cash		$70

part 9

1. does not   2. may   3. freight-in, installation   4. freight-in
5. (a) average cost
   (b) specific identification
   (c) FIFO
   (d) LIFO
6. FIFO   7. is   8. LIFO   9. FIFO
10. (a) material
    (b) direct labor
    (c) overhead
11. (a) Materials
    (b) Work in Process
    (c) Finished Goods
12. direct, indirect   13. period   14. sold, are not   15. are not   16. P   17. P   18. O
19. P   20. L   21. O   22. O   23. P
24. P   25. overhead   26. absorbed   27. direct labor dollars   28. underabsorbed
29. overabsorbed
30. Step 1: debit Materials Inventory, credit Accounts Payable

Step 2: credit Materials Inventory, debit Work in Process Inventory
Step 3: debit Finished Goods Inventory, credit Work in Process Inventory
Step 4: credit Finished Goods Inventory, debit Cost of Goods Sold

part 10

1. standard, actual   2. Cost of Goods Sold
3. variance   4. periodic, low
5. Beginning [Inventory plus] Cost [of Goods] Manufactured [less] Ending [Inventory equals] Cost of Goods Sold
6. Beginning [Inventory plus] Cost [of Goods] Purchased [less] Ending [Inventory equals] Cost of Goods Sold
7. retail method   8. income (profit), Income Statement   9. overstated, income, Retained Earnings   10. two   11. materiality   12. does not, Shipping Notice
13. consistent   14. fixed   15. variable
16. break-even   17. contribution   18. 10,000 [units], $50,000   19. profit, loss   20. expense, income (profit, loss), volume

part 11

1. transactions   2. adjusting
3. (a) error correction
   (b) depreciation
   (c) bad debts
   (d) accruals
   (e) prepaids
4. (a) depreciation
   (b) bad debts
   (c) prepaid
   (d) accrued
   (e) accrued
5. does not   6. usefulness, fixed asset
7. straight-line   8. $4,000, $5,000 debit balance, $1,000 credit balance
9.

	Dr	Cr
Depreciation Expense	$500	
Accumulated Depreciation		$500

10.

	Dr	Cr
Cash	$1,000	
Accumulated Depreciation	3,500	
Loss on Sale of Equipment	500	
Equipment		$5,000

11. zero, zero, $5,000, $5,000

12.

	Dr	Cr
Accumulated Depreci- ation	$5,000	
Equipment		$5,000

13. Land

14.

	Dr	Cr
Bad Debt Expense	$1,300	
Allowance for Bad Debts		$1,300

15.

	Dr	Cr
Bad Debt Allowance	$100	
Accounts Receivable		$100

16. accrual

	Cr	Dr
Telephone Expense	$200	
Accounts Payable		$200

17.

	Dr	Cr
Prepaid Insurance	$400	
Insurance Expense		$400

18. reverse, reverse, depreciation [and] bad debts

19. (a) volume
    (b) standardized
    (c) master (reference)
    (d) updating
    (e) multiple

20. man-[language], machine-[language]

21. (a) low-cost
    (b) timely
    (c) cost

22. classifications (sorts)

23. aged   24. trends

glossary

This glossary provides a brief definition of the terms used in the program, together with related terms and common synonyms. The abbreviations *n*. and *v*. stand for noun and verb, respectively. Note that following many definitions is a number signifying the part and frame in which treatment of the term begins. For instance, the number 4-57 refers you to frame 4-57 in Part 4. Use these references for a selective review if you are uncertain of the concepts related to particular terms.

absorbed cost   In cost accounting, the costs and expenses included in the product costs. *See* Product Cost; Cost Elements; Cost Absorption. [9-90; 10-18]

absorption costing   In cost accounting, a system whereby variable and all fixed costs related to production are absorbed or assigned so as to arrive at a "full" product cost. *See* Direct Cost; Cost Absorption. [9-90; 10-18]

abstract (often called Summary)   *n*. A condensed version of all or part of a record or report. *v*. To take data required for a particular use from a record or report.

account   *n*. 1. The formal record of the results of financial transactions in terms of money; kept in a Ledger. 2. In the plural, the "books of account," or accounting records. *v*. Generally, to provide a reckoning. [5-4; 6-4]

accounting   1. A report by one responsible for assets or the results of transactions. 2. The recording and reporting of transactions according to certain rules or principles, including devising, maintaining, and testing a system for recording transac-

tions and interpreting their results.

accounting cycle   The accounting steps taken during the accounting period: journalizing, posting, adjusting, and closing the accounts to obtain the financial statements.

accounting period   The period of time adopted by a firm for reporting purposes; the time between closings or Balance Sheet dates. *See* Accounting Cycle.

accounting system   Generally, the plan for the flow and control of financial data from origination, through processing, to the final output; includes the manual, mechanical, or electronic devices used and the methods of use. In this text, the term has been enlarged to include the individuals responsible for, or engaged in, the accounting function and also the purpose of accounting. [2-1]

accounts payable (also called Trade Payables)   1. The money obligations a firm has to its suppliers in return for goods and services purchased on short-term credit (i.e., payment usually to be made within ninety days). 2. The current liability account recording such obligations; sometimes this term refers only to the control account. [5-76]

accounts receivable (often called Receivables)   1. The money claims a firm has against its customers which are expected to be settled within a year of a given date and which are on "open account" (i.e., are not evidenced by a promissory note). 2. The current asset account recording such claims. *See also* Notes Receivable; Bad Debt Allowance. [3-69; 5-46]

accrual   A revenue earned or expense incurred not contractually due at statement date but recognized in order to match revenues and expenses more properly. Accruals generally are recorded by means of an adjusting entry. *See* Deferral; Prepaid. [11-56]

accrue 1. To make an accrual. 2. To accumulate (e.g., interest not payable until a future date is accruing daily).

accrued depreciation *See* Accumulated Depreciation.

accrued expenses *See* Accrual.

accrued revenues *See* Accrual.

accrued taxes 1. The amount of the tax liabilities, frequently estimated, to various governments at the date of the financial statement. 2. The current liability account in which these amounts are recorded. Other terms used for this account are Accrued Taxes Payable, Estimated Tax Liability, and Provision for Taxes. [5-81]

accrued wages and salaries 1. The amount of wages and salaries earned by employees but not due to be paid until after the statement date. 2. The current liability account to which these accruals are posted. [5-60; 5-78; 11-61]

accumulated depreciation (also called Accrued Depreciation; Allowance or Provision for Depreciation; Reserve for Depreciation; Depreciation) 1. The amount of depreciation recorded against fixed assets held by the firm at the date of the Balance Sheet. 2. The contra-asset account in which depreciation accrues or is accumulated. See Depreciation; Book Value. [11-21]

actual cost In cost accounting, the use (to determine a product cost) of actual rather than predetermined material and direct labor cost elements together with overhead, either at actual or assigned by a rate. *See* Costing; Stanford Cost. [10-15]

adjusting entry An entry, which is not the result of a specific input, designed to reflect properly all transactions that have occurred. Examples are error-correction entries, accruals, deferrals, and entries to reflect depreciation, amortization and adjustments to Bad Debt Allowance. [8-7; 11-5; 11-41; 11-56; 11-68]

ageing, aging Analysis of one or more accounts by dates of entries; most often applied to individual Accounts Receivable to determine amounts past due which might require special action to ensure prompt collection.

allowance for bad debts *See* Bad Debt Allowance.

allowance for depreciation *See* Accumulated Depreciation.

allowance for income taxes *See* Provision for Income Taxes.

amortization The reduction of the carrying value of an asset by a systematic write-off, either directly to the asset account or by means of a contra-asset account. Generally, the term is restricted to include only the write-off of intangible assets such as Leasehold Improvements, Organization Cost, Patents, and Goodwill. *See* Depletion; Depreciation. [12-5]

applied overhead The overhead cost absorbed by means of an overhead rate. *See* Overhead Rate; Cost Absorption.

asset Tangible or intangible property in the firm's legal possession which has a present or future money value. [2-59; 5-35; 6-9; 9-102]

asset account Any of several accounts in which a given kind of asset or group of similar assets and the changes affecting these assets are recorded. Normally, asset accounts have debit balances. [5-35]

audit *n.* An examination to test the effectiveness of an accounting system and to appraise the reasonableness of the results, or statements, produced. *v.* To conduct such an examination.

audit trail The cross references between Ledgers, Journals, and input documents, together with records of changes in accounts since a prior inspection; generally, any device incorporated into the accounting system to facilitate audits. *See* Audit. [8-75]

auditing *n.* The practice of making audits. *v.* To make an audit. *See* Audit.

average, or weighted average, cost A method of inventory valuation or pricing. The cost of beginning inventory and subsequent inventory acquisitions are averaged, and this average is used to value both withdrawals and ending inventory. A simple average may be used if no serious distortions would arise from price and quantity fluctuations. Otherwise, a *weighted average* is to be preferred. For example; 10 units at 50 cents plus 20 units at $2 would give either: 30 units at $1.25 each (simple average) or 30 units at $45 or $1.50 each (weighted average). *See* Inventory Valuation. [9-16]

bad debt allowance (Allowance, Provision, or Reserve for Bad Debts)   1. The estimated amount of Accounts Receivable that will not be collected. 2. The contra-asset account carrying such amounts. *See* Bad Debt Expense. [11-46]

bad debt expense   1. The amount of credit sales or accounts receivable that have proved uncollectible during the accounting period, together with any necessary adjustments to Bad Debt Allowance in anticipation of future inability to collect on certain receivables. 2. The expense account recording such amounts. *See also* Bad Debt Allowance. [11-41]

balance   *n.* The amount in any account at a particular moment (the difference between debits and credits in that account). *v.* To check all General Ledger accounts to see if total debits equal total credits. *See* Trial Balance. [5-6]

balance sheet   An output prepared as part of the financial reporting responsibility; a report of the firm's financial position at the date of the Balance Sheet. Conventionally, asset and equity accounts are listed in parallel columns with, in the United States, the assets in the left column and equities in the right. *See* Statement of Financial Position; Income Statement. [2-58; 5-3; 5-31; 8-3; Panel P]

bank statement   An input; a list of a firm's checks paid, bank deposits made, and the opening and closing bank balances, prepared at least monthly by the bank; used in the cash receipt and reconciliation activity. [3-100]

basic inventory equation (also called Inventory Equation)   The equation used to determine cost of goods sold under the periodic inventory method. Its simplest form is: Goods Available for Sale less Ending Inventory equals Cost of Goods Sold. For a wholesaler or merchandising firm having no direct labor or production overhead costs, Goods Available for Sale is merely the sum of Beginning Inventory and Purchases. For a manufacturer, the equations are: Beginning Materials Inventory plus Purchases less Ending Materials Inventory equals Cost of Materials Used; Beginning Work in Process Inventory plus Manufacturing Costs (materials used plus direct labor plus overhead costs) less Ending Work in Process Inventory equals Cost of Good Manufactured; finally, Beginning Finished Goods Inventory plus Cost of Goods Manufactured less Ending Finished Goods Inventory equals Cost of Goods Sold. *See* Periodic Inventory Method. [10-54; 10-73; Panel M]

batching   Accumulating similar data for periodic processing; contrasted to continuous, or real-time, data processing. [2-11; 7-43]

beginning inventory   The dollar cost amount of inventory owned by the firm at the start of an accounting period. The opening debit balance in the Inventory account. *See* Basic Inventory Equation; Inventory.

bill (also called Invoice)   A statement covering goods received or services rendered sent to a customer by the firm supplying the goods or services. *See* Customer Invoice; Incoming Invoice.

billing activity   1. That function of the accounting system primarily concerned with the preparation of Customer Invoices; part of the processing and recording responsibility. 2. The processing of incoming Shipping Orders in conjunction with Parts Master Files and Customer Master Files in the preparation of Customer Invoices. [4-26; 7-51; Panel B]

billing address   The address to which all invoices for a particular customer are sent, regardless of the destination of any particular shipment made. *See* Shipping Address. [7-59]

bonds Certificates of indebtedness issued for long-term debt whenever it is presumed that the original creditors may wish to transfer all or part of their claims to others. Bonds have differing kinds of security or collateral behind them for the protection of the creditor. *See* Debenture; Note; Notes Payable.

book value The net amount of an asset or equity account. Whenever a contra-account or valuation account is used, the net amount is found by subtracting from the balance of the asset or equity account the balance of the contra-account. For example, the book value of a fixed asset, such as a building, is the original cost less the accumulated depreciation. [11-38]

bookkeeping activity The processing and recording of the results of transactions that affect the firm's financial position according to the relevant accounting rules applied. [4-39; 7-78; Panel B]

books The various journals and ledgers maintained as part of the accounting system. In mechanized systems, these are in the form of tapes or punched cards.

break-even analysis An analysis of the volume required to cover fixed costs and to make a profit. Total fixed costs for the period divided by the contribution margin equals the break-even volume. The analysis is often presented as a chart or graph. [10-112; 10-121]

break-even chart or graph Graphical presentation of the cost-volume-profit relationship. A common form has two intersecting straight lines, one for total revenues and one for total costs, plotted against a dollar scale on the vertical axis and a volume scale, in units or dollars, on the horizontal axis. The point of intersection is the break-even point at which revenues equal costs. Volume in excess of break-even is the "safety margin." [10-114; Panel 0]

budget *n.* A plan for operations during a specific period, generally expressed in financial terms. Budgets are part of the control reporting responsibility and may be prepared for subdivisions of the firm—re-

sponsibility or profit centers—as well as for the firm as a whole. *v.* To make such a plan from Budget Information. [2-45; 8-57]

budget information An input; the raw input data or planning information from which Budgets are prepared. *See also* Budget. [3-104]

budget performance analysis An output or report prepared as part of the control reporting responsibility, providing a comparison of the planned or budgeted operations with actual operations for a specific period. Differences, or variances, are often shown both for the current period and on a cumulative year-to-date basis. Such figures may be expressed in dollars, percentages, or both. [2-53; 8-59]

budget period A period or specific segment of time over which a plan or Budget applies; the time covered by a given Budget. *See* Budget; Budget Performance Analysis.

buildings The fixed asset account in which structures owned by the firm are recorded, usually at the original cost to the firm. *See* Depreciation. [5-54; 11-21]

burden *See* Overhead Cost.

canceled check An input; a Check to Creditor or Payroll Check which has been paid by the bank and returned to the firm as a record of the payment. Used in the cash receipt and reconcilation activity. [3-100]

capital 1. That portion of a firm's resources attributed to owners and long-term creditors (invested capital). 2. That portion attributed to owners (Owners' Equity). 3. The amount carried in the capital stock accounts (legal or stated capital). *See* Capital Stock.

capital stock 1. Shares of corporate ownership authorized for issue to stockholders. 2. Certificates for such shares, describing the type of stock and the par or stated value, if any. 3. The equity account (one for each class of stock issued) in which the total amounts received by a firm for its no-par or no-stated-value shares is recorded. If the shares have a par or stated value, then (in most states) the amount recorded in this account is determined by multiplying the number of shares issued by the par or stated value; any amounts received by the firm in excess of this amount are carried in Paid-in Surplus. In the event the firm distributes to its stockholders additional shares as a stock dividend, Retained Earnings is reduced by an amount at least equal to the total par or stated value of the shares distributed, and this amount is added to the appropriate capital stock account. *See* Capital Stock and Paid-in Surplus; Common Stock; Paid-in Surplus; Preferred Stock. [5-95]

capital stock and paid-in surplus The term used in this text to represent all equity accounts in which the amounts received by a corporation for shares issued are recorded. *See* Capital Stock; Paid-in Surplus; Common Stock; Preferred Stock. [5-95]

capital surplus *See* Paid-in Surplus; Capital Stock and Paid-in Surplus.

cash The current asset account reflecting the balance of cash in the possession of the firm—checks and currency on hand and enroute to, or on deposit in, banks—as of a specific date. [5-45]

cash discount Amount a customer may deduct from the net invoice price if he pays on or before a specified date. [7-109]

cash dividend A cash distribution of profits of the current year or prior years to stockholders, reducing the Cash and the Retained Earnings accounts. Any distribution in excess of the amount of retained earnings is, properly, a return of capital. *See* Stock Dividend. [12-16]

cash receipt and reconciliation activity The processing and recording of Checks from Customers and the reconciliation of the Cash account. *See* Cash Reconciliation. [4-36; 7-73; Panel B]

cash reconciliation Verifying the accuracy of the balance shown in the Cash account, using Bank Statements, Canceled Checks, and duplicate Deposit Slips, and fully explaining or reconciling any differences between bank and company records. [3-95]

cash statement *See* Funds Statement.

charge *See* Debit.

check *n.* A written order to a bank authorizing payment of a specific amount of money. *v.* To compare for accuracy. *See also* Check to Creditor; Payroll Check; Check from Customer.

check from customer (also called Check in Settlement) An input; a check received from a customer in settlement of all or part of his account. Processed as part of the cash receipt and reconciliation activity. [3-95]

check in settlement *See* Check from Customer.

check to creditor An output prepared as part of the payables activity; a check issued in full or partial payment of one of the firm's liabilities. *See* Creditor. [2-7]

close *See* Closing.

closing The procedure followed at the end of the accounting period: (*a*) subsidiary accounts are reconciled with their control accounts; (*b*) the necessary adjusting entries are made; (*c*) nominal accounts are closed to the Income Summary account, which in turn is closed to Retained Earnings; and (*d*) any necessary trial balances are taken. *See* Work Sheet. [6-93; 8-7; Panel W]

closing entry *See* Closing.

common stock 1. The type of stock representing true corporate ownership. Common stockholders ordinarily have the right to vote and to share in any profit distribution in proportion to the number of shares held; in case of liquidation, common stockholders receive proportionate shares of any assets remaining after all other claims are settled; hence they have only a residual claim against assets. 2. The equity account established for common stock in which are recorded the amounts received by the corporation for shares issued; if the shares have a par or stated value at which they must legally be recorded, any excess received is recorded in Paid-in Surplus. *See* Capital Stock; Preferred Stock; Capital Stock and Paid-in Surplus; Paid-in Surplus. [5-95]

compound entry An entry arising from a single transaction which, although balanced, affects more than two accounts. [7-105] For example:

	Dr	Cr
Payroll Expense	$1,000	
Cash		$750
Taxes Payable		$250

consistency The accounting principle that restricts changes in accounting methods to those necessary for a more accurate financial reporting, thereby minimizing distortions of reported income due to change of method. The principle further requires that any changes made be specifically identified and their effects separately noted on the financial statements for the period in which the change occurred. [10-89]

contra-account An account related to, and partially or wholly offsetting, another account. A contra-asset account relates to an asset account and acts to reduce that account when the two are combined. An example is Accumulated Depreciation, which is related to the fixed asset being depreciated. The use of the contra-account permits the original cost of the fixed asset to be carried forward, a significant figure which otherwise would not appear if any depreciation taken was recorded as a reduction of the fixed asset instead of being accumulated in the contra-asset account. An example of a contra-equity account is Bond Discount, an account not illustrated in this text. An example of a contra-revenue account is Sales Returns and Allowances. [11-24; 11-46]

contribution (also called Contribution Margin) The difference between the selling price and the variable costs and expenses required to buy or produce and sell products. See Break-even Analysis. [10-110]

control The direction of an enterprise to conform with a plan of action or, if a plan is lacking, with the most desirable course of action under a given set of circumstances. Control is facilitated by various reporting devices but must always be effected by and through people. See Control Reporting.

control account Firms often maintain many accounts of the same kind, such as individual Accounts Receivable for each customer. A control account is maintained to show the total of the individual, or subsidiary, accounts. Control accounts are kept in the General Ledger, subsidiary accounts in Subsidiary Ledgers. See Ledger.

control area A specific area, often physically delineated, set aside as distinct for management control purposes. For example, raw material stores represents a segregation of purchased raw materials received but not yet started into production. [3-76]

control reporting (also called Management Reporting) One of the three major responsibilities of the accounting system, involving the preparation of reports which aid management in making decisions. Among these are Inventory Control Records, Sales Performance Analyses, Budgets, Budget Performance Analyses, Cost Analysis Reports, and various other financial reports, such as those dealing with cost variances. [4-4; 4-15; 4-52; 8-19; Panel B

control total(s) A checking device whereby the totals of related accounts are compared for balance. [11-86]

copyright See Intangible Assets.

cost n. 1. Commonly, any expenditure or outlay except one made to settle a liability, pay a dividend, or return capital. 2. More properly, any portion of an expenditure which, after adjustment for accruals and deferrals, has a future value at Balance Sheet date. 3. The accepted basis for accounting, as defined in definition 2. v. To assign a monetary value to an asset acquired, goods or services sold, or to any activity or function of the firm. See Expense; Costing. [9-1]

cost absorption In cost accounting, the process or rate at which cost elements are assigned as product costs. If the rate assigns more than the actual cost incurred, the difference is "overabsorbed," a favorable variance if the rate is accurate. If the reverse is true, the difference is "underabsorbed," an unfavorable variance. *See* Variance. [9-89; 9-97]

cost accounting Originally, the portion of the overall accounting activity concerned with manufacturing costs; now extended to other functions (sales, credit collections, etc.) and to the analysis of present and future costs for management. *See* Costing. [Parts 9 and 10]

cost accounting system *See* Costing.

cost accounts Generally, accounts in which production costs are recorded, such as Factory Payroll Expense, Factory Overhead Cost, Work in Process, and Finished Goods. More recently, accounts for distribution costs. Cost of Goods Sold is ordinarily not considered a cost account. [10-50]

cost analysis report Any of several outputs produced as part of the control reporting activity; such reports indicate the cost of purchasing, producing, storing, selling, and shipping a firm's products. They are prepared periodically to facilitate management's control of operating costs. [2-40; 8-50]

cost basis *See* Cost.

cost elements In cost accounting, the several components of total product cost. Included are raw materials or materials cost, direct labor cost, and overhead cost. Direct labor and materials cost are often referred to as "prime costs," and also, separately, direct labor and overhead cost may be referred to as "conversion costs." *See* Materials Cost; Direct Labor Cost; Overhead Cost. [9-38]

cost of goods manufactured *See* Basic Inventory Equation.

cost of goods sold 1. In a merchandising firm, the acquisition cost of goods sold, which includes the price paid and related costs, such as freight-in. 2. In a manufacturing firm, the cost of manufacturing the products sold. 3. The account in which these costs are recorded. Since these costs have expired, i.e., have been ex-

changed for revenues, this account is, properly, an expense account. *See* Inventory Valuation. [6-77; 10-13]

cost of sales *See* Cost of Goods Sold.

cost or market *See* Inventory Valuation.

cost-volume-profit relationship *See* Break-even Analysis; Break-even Chart or Graph.

costing 1. Determination of cost by any method. 2. The cost reported by a cost accounting system of either of two basic types: (*a*) job order systems, in which costs are assigned directly to products, used where production of a particular product is intermittent and (*b*) process cost systems, in which all costs are first assigned to a process and the resulting total divided by units produced to arrive at a product cost, used where production of like items is continuous. Either type of system may incorporate actual or standard costs, and a particular firm may use both systems. *See* Actual Cost; Standard Cost.

coverage A term often used with respect to Inventory Control Records denoting the amount of supply (on hand plus on order) in excess of requirements. Coverage would be negative for any item where requirements exceeded supply. *See* Inventory Control Record. [8-30]

credit *n.* 1. An entry or posting on the right side of an account, or the amount entered or posted. A credit reduces asset and expense account balances, increases equity and revenue account balances. 2. Trust that an individual will repay, e.g., sale on credit. *v.* To make a credit entry or posting. *See* Debit. [6-4]

credit balance The balance in an account in which total credits exceed total debits. [6-7]

creditor One to whom a debt is owed; one who has a legal claim against a firm's assets which takes precedence over the residual claims of owners or stockholders.

current assets Properties which, in the normal course of business, will be converted to cash within a year of the Balance Sheet date. These usually include cash, accounts receivable, inventories, and various prepaid expenses. *See* Asset. [5-38]

current liabilities Claims by creditors which the firm must settle within a year of the date of the Balance Sheet. Included are accounts payable, notes payable, accrued taxes, accrued wages and salaries, any dividends declared but unpaid, and any portion of long-term debt due within a year. [5-67]

customer invoice An output prepared as part of the billing activity; a notice, or bill, sent to a customer advising him of the amount owed for goods or services rendered, the date of shipment or performance, a description of the goods or services, and the due date and payment terms. *See* Discount. [2-13]

customer master file A file or record of up-to-date reference information maintained for use in the billing activity. This usually contains data for each customer: shipping address, billing address, trade discount category, tax category, payment terms, and possible credit limit. [7-57; 8-69]

customer order An input; a written request from a customer for goods or services. [3-55]

debenture A bond secured only by the earning power of the issuing corporation.

debit *n.* An entry or posting on the left side of an account; the amount entered or posted. Increasingly, the term "charge" is substituted. A debit increases asset and expense accounts, reduces equity and revenue accounts. *v.* To make such entry or posting. [6-4]

debit balance The balance in an account in which total debits exceed total credits. [6-7]

debtor One who owes money to the firm.

deductions Amounts subtracted from an employee's gross earnings for withholding taxes, Social Security, union dues, and the like. *See also* Take-home Pay. [7-5]

defer To postpone. *See* Deferral.

deferral Postponement of the inclusion in the Income Statement to some future accounting period of revenues received but not earned or expenses prepaid at the Balance Sheet date. Unearned revenues are recorded in the Deferred Income account, included in the Current Liabilities section of the Balance Sheet; prepaid expenses are recorded either in an asset account by that name or in Deferred Charges another asset account. Both are asset accounts. *See* Accrual.

deferred charges Asset accounts carrying expense deferrals which will not be charged as current expenses in the entire amount of the deferral within a year of the Balance Sheet date. These accounts are included under the Balance Sheet captions Other Assets or Deferred Charges. *See* Deferral; Prepaid. [11-68]

deferred income 1. Revenue received but which, at the Balance Sheet date, has not been earned by the delivery of goods or the rendering of services. 2. The account in which deferred income is recorded, generally included in the Current Liabilities section of the equities on the Balance Sheet. *See* Deferral.

deferred revenue *See* Deferred Income; Deferral.

depletion As distinguished from depreciation, depletion refers to the reduction of such natural-resource assets as mineral deposits and oil reserves.

deposit slip A record of cash and Checks in Settlement turned over to a bank for addition to the firm's bank account.

depreciation 1. The gradual expiration of the future usefulness of a fixed asset by operation of natural causes such as wear, tear, and obsolescence. 2. The systematic reduction of the original cost of a fixed asset by debits to the Depreciation Expense account and credits to the Accumulated Depreciation account. *See* Amortization; Contra-account; Depletion; Depreciation Methods. [11-13]

depreciation expense The expense account in which amounts of depreciation taken during the accounting period are recorded. *See* Depreciation. [11-19]

depreciation methods Systematic allocations of the cost of a fixed asset by periodic charges to Depreciation Expense and credits to Accumulated Depreciation, not to exceed the original cost of the fixed asset. In the descriptions of three of the methods used which follow, a fixed asset costing $10,000 is to be depreciated over four years, at which time it will have no salvage value. (a) Straight-line depreciation: The yearly rate is a constant, one-fourth or 25 per cent. The rate times the cost equals $2,500, the yearly depreciation expense. This method is the one illustrated in the text. (b) Double-declining balance depreciation: The yearly rate is a constant, twice the straight-line rate and hence, in this example, 50 per cent. It is applied to the remaining book value to determine the yearly charge. The first year depreciation expense would be $10,000 times 50 per cent, or $5,000; the second year it would be ($10,000 minus $5,000) times 50 per cent, or $2,500; and so on. To reduce the book value to zero requires a conversion from this method to straight-line. (c) Years digits, or sum of the years digits, depreciation. The yearly rate is a declining fraction whose denominator is the total of the digits of life and whose numerator is the years of life remaining. The yearly rates in this example would be $\frac{4}{10}$, $\frac{3}{10}$, $\frac{2}{10}$, and $\frac{1}{10}$, which are applied to the original cost to determine the yearly charge. This is similar to double-declining balance in that both methods yield higher initial and lower final yearly depreciation charges than does the straight-line method. [11-15]

direct cost 1. Any cost directly related to a function or activity. 2. In cost accounting, the inclusion in product costs of only those costs that vary directly with production volume, fixed costs being considered wholly period costs. Hence a direct product cost will normally be lower than a full product cost. See Absorption Costing.

direct costing 1. A cost system incorporating direct costs. Growing in relative importance owing to advantages for control reporting. See Direct Cost; Absorption Costing. [7-52; 7-60; 7-109]

direct labor As distinguished from indirect labor, direct labor represents that portion of factory labor costs readily identifiable and assignable as involved in the manufacture of a product. See Cost Elements; Direct Labor Cost; Indirect Labor. [9-55; 10-4]

direct labor cost (often simply Labor Cost) The element of total product cost attributable to direct labor. May be at actual cost or standard cost. See Actual Cost; Cost Elements; Direct Labor; Standard Cost. [9-39]

discount A deduction from a given price granted to a customer for a specific reason or purpose. See Cash Discount; Trade Discount.

discounts and allowances See Sales Returns and Allowances; Purchase Returns and Allowances.

dividend See Cash Dividend; Stock Dividend; Dividends Payable. [6-58; 12-16]

dividends payable The current liability account in which is recorded the amount of any dividends declared but unpaid at the Balance Sheet date.

double-declining balance depreciation See Depreciation Methods.

double-entry bookkeeping A self-balancing system for keeping financial records which facilitates accuracy and analysis. Each entry in this system is composed of equal debits and credits, posted to at least two accounts. [5-129; 6-27]

earned surplus See Retained Earnings.

earnings See Profit.

earnings statement See Income Statement; Statement of Retained Earnings.

ending inventory The dollar cost amount of inventory owned by the firm at the close of an accounting period. Often verified by an actual physical count. See Basic Inventory Equation; Periodic Inventory Method; Physical Inventory.

entry The instructions listing the accounts affected and the amounts to be posted to these accounts; the result of analyzing a transaction. In double-entry bookkeeping, the debits must exactly equal the credits of each entry. *See* Compound Entry. [5-15; 11-4]

equipment 1. Machinery, tools, dies, fixtures, and the like. 2. The fixed asset account in which such items are recorded at original cost. Note that equipment is always depreciated. *See* Depreciation. [5-54; 11-21]

equities The sources of a firm's assets: the current and long-term credit received and the stockholders' contribution. Conversely, these sources have claims against the total assets, although in the event of liquidation the stockholders have only a residual claim. Frequently, the term ''equity'' is restricted to mean the stockholders' or owners' equity only. *See* Asset; Balance Sheet. [2-59; 5-59; 6-9]

equity account Any account recording equities, normally having a credit balance. On the Balance Sheet, the current creditors' equity accounts are listed under Current Liabilities, the long-term creditors' accounts under Long-term Debt, and the ownership accounts in the Owners' Equity or Net Worth grouping. *See* Asset; Balance Sheet. [5-58]

estimated cost 1. A cost determined before the fact or a cost figure used when facts are unknown. 2. A product cost determined by an estimated cost system, which incorporates estimated product costs that are ultimately converted to actual costs in Inventory and Cost of Goods Sold. *See* Costing; Standard Cost.

estimated tax liability *See* Accrued Taxes.

estimated taxes payable *See* Accrued Taxes.

expenditure An outflow of assets or the incurrence of a liability during an accounting period (although not necessarily related to that period) in exchange for services or other assets. *See* Cost; Expense; Accrual; Deferral.

expense 1. An asset outflow occurring in, accrued in, or deferred to the current

period to properly match expenses with revenues realized. Fixed asset costs are deferrals, becoming expenses through depreciation, depletion, or amortization charges. 2. A loss; an asset outflow which presumably will benefit no accounting period in the form of securing revenues; may be classified as an expense. Unusual losses, particularly if material in amount, are generally recorded as such and separately listed on the Income Statement. *See* Cost. [6-68; 9-102]

expense account 1. Any account used to record a specific type of the firm's expenses. Expense accounts have debit balances, are shown on the Income Statement, and are closed ultimately to Retained Earnings. 2. Often refers to the single account used to record travel and entertainment expense. *See* Expense. [6-75]

extension The result obtained by multiplying price times quantity. An example is seen on invoices, on which each product shipped is listed as a line item, showing the quantity shipped, the price, and the extension. Another example is the determination of an employee's gross earnings by multiplying rate of pay by hours worked. [6-65]

factory overhead *See* Overhead Cost.

financial position The status of a firm in terms of its assets and equities, as reported on the Balance Sheet or Statement of Financial Position. [1-9; 2-61]

financial reporting One of the major responsibilities of the accounting system; it involves the preparation of outputs such as the Balance Sheet and Income Statement, both of which are illustrated in this text, and other statements of a financial nature. Financial reporting also involves the interpretation of these reports for the benefit of management. [4-4; 4-11; 4-45; 8-1; Panel B]

financial statement 1. Individual financial reports such as Income Statements and Balance Sheets. 2. Collectively, a presentation including an Income Statement, a Balance Sheet, and frequently other financial reports, such as that made in corporate annual reports to stockholders. *See* Financial Reporting.

finished goods   1. Completed goods. 2. The inventory account in which completed goods on hand are recorded at cost. *See* Cost of Goods Sold. [9-41]

first-in, first-out (FIFO)   Under this method of inventory valuation or pricing, costs are debited and credited to the inventory accounts in the order of their occurrence. Consequently, the amount of Cost of Goods Sold shown on the Income Statement reflects the older costs of acquiring or manufacturing inventoried items. The amount of Inventory on the Balance Sheet would then reflect the most recent costs. *See* Inventory Valuation; Last-In, First-Out. [9-20]

fiscal year   1. An accounting period of any twelve consecutive months. 2. Commonly an accounting year that does not coincide with the calendar year; generally selected to end at a time of low inventories.

fixed and other assets   1. As used in this text, a Balance Sheet heading under which are listed all assets other than current assets. "Other Assets" may then include intangible assets and deferred charges. *See* Fixed Assets. [5-40]

fixed assets   1. Properties which, in the normal course of business, are not expected to be converted to cash within a year of acquisition. 2. The grouping of accounts for fixed assets on the Balance Sheet, sometimes limited to tangible fixed assets such as land, buildings, and equipment. *See* Fixed and Other Assets; Intangible Assets; Deferred Charges. [5-40; 11-21]

fixed cost or expense   Any cost or expense whose total over a given range of activity does not change as the rate of activity changes. *See* Variable Cost or Expense. [10-103]

flag   n. A device used to single out an item or record for special attention. v. To make or note a record for special attention.

flow chart   A chart that shows schematically a system for handling data. [11-121; Panel Q]

freight-in   1. Freight charges on incoming items paid by the firm. 2. An account for such freight charges, if not assigned directly to an inventory account. *See* Inventory. [9-4]

freight-out   1. Freight charges on goods shipped by the firm. 2. An account recording such charges, sometimes limited to charges which will not be paid by the customer. In this event, those charges may be included in the Sales Returns and Allowances account. *See* Sales Returns and Allowances.

full cost   *See* Absorption Costing.

fully depreciated   A term applied to a fixed asset when the total of the accumulated depreciation equals the original or recorded cost, thus making the book value of the asset equal zero. [11-33]

fundamental accounting equation   In its simplest form, this equation is that shown on a conventional Balance Sheet: Assets = Equities. Without impairment of the equality it may also be expressed in "report" or Statement of Financial Position form, in a vertical arrangement: Current Assets − Current Liabilities + Fixed and Other Assets − Long-term Debt = Owners' Equity or Net Worth. [5-103; 6-24]

funds statement   (also called Working Capital Statement)   1. A statement showing the causes of changes in working capital during a period. 2. Sometimes refers to a statement giving the causes for changes in cash, or cash and marketable securities, during a period. *See* Working Capital.

general ledger   *See* Ledger.

general, selling, and administrative expense   *See* Operating Expense.

goods available for sale   *See* Basic Inventory Equation.

goodwill   1. Any portion of a firm's earning power in excess of that attributable to the assets owned. 2. An asset, recognized only when the purchase price of other assets exceeds the total amount at which they can justifiably be recorded on the acquirer's books, as when an entire firm is acquired at a price in excess of its asset values even after their adjustment to a fair market figure. 3. The asset account for goodwill, included on the Balance Sheet under Other Assets, Intangible Assets, or Deferred Charges; generally amortized.

gross earnings The total amount due to an employee for work performed. An hourly paid employee's gross earnings is the rate of pay times the hours worked during the pay period; a salaried employee's gross pay is the total salary for the pay period. See also Deductions; Take-home Pay. [7-4]

gross profit The figure obtained by subtracting Cost of Goods Sold from Net Sales; profit before the deduction of operating expenses and income taxes. See Gross Profit Ratio; Net Sales. [6-78]

gross profit ratio The amount of Gross Profit divided by the amount of Net Sales and usually expressed as a percentage of Net Sales. See Gross Profit; Retail Inventory Method. [10-74]

gross sales Total sales before any deductions made for returns, cash discounts, or allowances. See Net Sales; Sales Returns and Allowances.

income Variously equivalent to revenues, net income, or profit; hence an imprecise term.

income statement (also called Operating Statement; Profit and Loss Statement; Earnings Statement) An output prepared as part of the financial reporting responsibility; a report which lists or matches the revenues and expenses (the profit or loss or net income for the period) is added alge- revenues and expenses, the profit or loss or net income for the period is added algebraically to the Retained Earnings account. [2-64; 5-3; 6-59; 6-109; 8-14; Panel L)

income summary account (also called Profit and Loss; Profit and Loss Summary; Income Summary) A nominal or temporary holding account to which revenue and expense accounts are closed and which in turn is closed to Retained Earnings. [6-93]

income tax The tax levied on earnings or profits as adjusted to accord with the applicable tax regulations. See Accrued Taxes; Provision for Income Taxes.

income taxes due See Provision for Income Taxes.

incoming invoice An input; a notice, or "bill," which the firm receives for goods or services provided by a supplier. The two kinds of Incoming Invoices are the Materials Invoice, covering goods purchased for inventory, and the Other Incoming Invoice, covering noninventoried goods or services. [3-23; 3-24]

indirect cost See Overhead Cost.

indirect labor The portion of factory labor costs not readily identifiable and assignable to products as direct labor. Included in product cost as part of overhead. See Cost Elements; Overhead Cost; Direct Labor. [9-55; 10-5]

input Any of several documents that provide the accounting system with data from which it prepares outputs. [1-19; Part 3; Panel A]

intangible assets 1. Assets which may or may not have a physical existence and whose value depends upon the "right of use." Intangibles without physical existence include patents, copyrights, goodwill, trademarks, etc. However, securities are not, in accounting, considered to be intangible assets. An example of an intangible having a physical existence is an improvement to a leasehold. 2. The account in which intangible assets are recorded or the Balance Sheet caption under which the balances of several such accounts may be summarized if not listed separately. See Marketable Securities; Investments; Leasehold Improvements.

interest 1. The rent paid for the use of money. 2. The expense account for interest. See Operating Expense; Prepaid.

inventory n. 1. Any stock or supply. 2. Items held for sale; in manufacturing, materials to be incorporated in products, as well as partially and wholly completed products to be sold. 3. The current asset account which records these properties at cost (including freight-in), or cost or market, whichever is lower. Normally, supplies are excluded from this account, any on hand being included in a Supplies account. *v.* To take a physical count of items on hand. *See* Inventory Valuation. [5-48; 10-52]

inventory control record (also called Stock Control Record; Inventory Control Report; Unit Inventory Control Record) An output maintained as part of the control reporting responsibility; a perpetual record carrying the current balance in units of items on hand, and frequently also both required and on order, which is used for management control purposes. Distinct from the Inventory Account which carries dollar totals only. [2-32; 3-32; 3-66; 4-54; 8-20]

inventory equation *See* Basic Inventory Equation.

inventory transfer information Data provided by a category of inputs reporting on the internal movement of inventory from one control area within the firm to another or out of inventory altogether. *See also* Stores Requisition; Scrap Notice. [3-76; 8-39]

inventory valuation The determination of the cost to be assigned at the end of the accounting period to any inventory items on hand, or in transit if title is held by the firm. Several methods are described in this text: specific identification; average cost; first-in, first-out (FIFO); last-in, first-out (LIFO); and retail. Not described is "cost or market," under which cost is determined by any of the foregoing methods and then compared with the current or market cost of acquiring similar items. The lower of these two valuations is accepted as the inventory value; hence the method is frequently called "lower of cost or market." [9-13]

investments An asset account in which the cost of securities held by the firm are recorded, except for notes received in exchange for goods or services. If the investments are of a temporary nature and marketable, the account may be included with Current Assets, generally under the title Marketable Securities. If the invest-

ments are considered to be more or less permanent, the account may be included in the fixed or other asset section of the Balance Sheet as Investments, Marketable Securities, or Other Assets.

invoice (often called Bill) A bill for goods shipped or services rendered. When received from a supplier, it is called an Incoming Invoice; when sent to a customer, it is called a Customer Invoice.

journal A continuous record of individual transactions in the order in which inputs advising of the transactions are received. Since entries are first journalized and then posted to the Ledgers at a later date, Journals are known as "books of original entry." *See* Journalize. [5-24]

journalize To analyze a transaction to determine the proper accounts affected and the appropriate debits and credits and to record the entry in the Journal. *See* Journal. [5-25]

labor cost *See* Direct Labor Cost.

land The fixed asset account in which land owned is recorded, normally at original cost. Since land is considered permanent, it is not a depreciable asset. If land is held under a leasehold, however, that account may be amortized over the life of the lease. *See* Leasehold. [5-57; 11-40]

last-in, first-out (LIFO) Under this method of inventory valuation or pricing, costs are debited to inventory accounts in the order of their occurrence but are credited in the reverse order. Consequently the amount carried as Inventory on the Balance Sheet reflects the older costs of acquiring or manufacturing inventoried items. The amount shown as Cost of Goods Sold on the Income Statement would then reflect the most recent costs. *See* First-In, First-Out; Inventory Valuation. [9-23]

leasehold The right to use unowned property, acquired under the terms of a lease. *See* Intangible Assets.

leasehold improvements   Improvements made to leased property which will go with the property when it reverts to the owner at the expiration of the lease. *See* Leasehold; Intangible Assets.

ledger   A collection or group of accounts in book form, on punched cards or magnetic tape, or in some other storage device. In small firms, all accounts may be contained in a single General Ledger. Larger firms may have detailed subsidiary accounts in Subsidiary Ledgers and only the related summary or control account in its General Ledger. [4-48; 5-11; 5-29]

liabilities   Creditors' claims against, or equity in, a firm's assets; the firm's legal obligations to its creditors for cash, goods, or services received. *See* Current Liabilities; Long-term Debt. [2-60; 5-67]

line item   The separate listing of each product and quantity as it appears on a Shipping Notice or Invoice.

liquidation   1. The process of terminating the existence of a company; involves payment of all liabilities to creditors and distribution of any remaining assets to stockholders. 2. In a restricted sense this term may refer to conversion of excessive assets into cash in a going concern, such as the liquidation of excess inventory.

list price   The price of a firm's product before the deduction of any applicable trade discount. *See* Trade Discount. [7-52]

long-term debt   Any liability that does not have to be settled within a year. Any portion of Long-term Debt due within a year of the Balance Sheet date such portion is classified as a current liability. [5-73]

loss   1. Any excess of expenses over related revenues. 2. An asset outflow which is not productive, such as that from fire, flood, embezzlement, etc. *See* Expense. [6-58]

lower of cost or market   *See* Inventory Valuation.

machine-language   A term used in conjunction with data-processing equipment and referring to data in a form intelligible to a machine (holes in punched cards, bits on magnetic tape, etc.) and usually not readily readable by humans. *See* Man-language. [11-99]

man-language   A term used in conjunction with, and in contrast to, "machine-language"; refers to data in a form readily readable by humans. *See* Machine-language. [11-99]

manufacturing expense   *See* Overhead Cost.

margin   *See* Contribution; Profitability.

marketable securities   1. Securities for which there is a ready market. 2. The current or fixed asset account in which the amounts of such securities held by the firm are recorded. *See also* Investments.

master file   (also called Reference File) Any file of reference information maintained in a current status and used in the accounting process. *See* Customer Master File; Parts Master File; Payroll Master File.

matching   1. A process which is part of the payables activity; Purchase Order Copies and Receiving Records are compared or matched with Materials Invoices to verify the accuracy of amounts and legitimacy for payment. [7-32] 2. The overriding concept in the determination of net income, requiring the accountant to make accruals and deferrals in order to match the revenues earned with the related expenses during the accounting period. [9-83] *See* Income Statement.

materiality   An accounting principle which acts to concentrate effort to achieve greatest reasonable accuracy upon those accounts or items having a significant effect upon reported earnings. The use of this principle permits departures from other accepted accounting principles whenever the effect is considered insignificant. [10-93]

materials   (also called Raw Materials) 1. Items acquired or produced which at the conclusion of the manufacturing process will become part of the completed product. 2. Sometimes used as the name of the inventory account for such items. *See* Supplies; Inventory; Incoming Invoice. [9-10]

materials cost (often called Raw Materials) The element of total product cost attributable to raw materials and other parts included therein. May be at actual cost or standard cost. *See* Actual Cost; Cost Elements; Standard Cost. [9-38]

materials invoice An Incoming Invoice from a supplier for materials purchased for inventory. *See* Incoming Invoice. [3-24]

merchandise *n.* 1. Goods acquired for resale. 2. A nominal account, synonymous with a Purchases account, in which goods for resale are recorded at acquisition costs. 3. A real account, sometimes called Merchandise Inventory. *v.* To sell.

mortgage payable The long-term debt account in which the firm's mortgage obligations are recorded. [5-74]

net amount 1. The amount remaining after deductions from an original amount. 2. Book value; the balance after amortization, depletion, or depreciation has been credited directly to an asset account, or the difference after deducting from any account balance the balance of the related contra-account.

net assets The amount of total assets remaining after subtracting total liabilities. Identical in quantity to Owners' Equity or Net Worth. [5-108]

net current assets *See* Working Capital.

net income (also called Earnings; Profit; Profit or Loss) The amount remaining after the deduction from revenues of all expenses including income taxes; the final figure on the Income Statement, which can be negative; sometimes called "Net Income after Income Taxes."

net invoice price The selling price after deducting any applicable trade discount from the list price and adding any sales taxes which the seller is obligated to collect. Cash discounts, if any, are ordinarily not used in the calculation of the net invoice price. [7-55]

net sales (often called simply Sales) The revenue amount first listed on published Income Statements. The amount is determined by subtracting from the total sales recorded in the Gross Sales account the balance in the contra-revenue account Sales Returns and Allowances. In expressing Income Statement relationships, the net sales figure is the base, or 100 per cent. [6-76]

net working capital *See* Working Capital.

net worth *See* Owners' Equity.

nominal account (also called Temporary Holding Account) Any revenue or expense account, including the Income Summary account. All are closed to Income Summary, which in turn is closed to Retained Earnings. Nominal accounts, in contrast to real accounts, never contain balances to be carried forward to the next accounting period; instead, their balances are listed on the Income Statement. *See* Real Account. [6-72; 6-86; 6-93]

note The usual term for a promissory note issued as a written promise to pay a fixed sum on a certain date or on the demand of the lender in return for assets or services received. If issued as evidence of long-term debt, the implication is that the note will not be transferred to another creditor or, if it is, that it will not be subdivided into fractions of the original amount. *See also* Bonds; Notes Payable; Notes Receivable.

notes payable The account representing the total of the firm's notes held by creditors. If the notes are due within a year of the date of the Balance Sheet, the account is listed as a current liability. Notes issued by a firm which are not due within a year of the date of the Balance Sheet are a part of its long-term debt. [5-80]

notes receivable The account in which the firm records the amount of the notes held by it and not issued by the firm itself. If the note was given to the firm by a customer in the ordinary course of business and is due within a year of the statement

date, it is a part of the current assets. If
the note does not satisfy either of these
requirements, it is classified under the
heading Other Assets, Investments, or
Marketable Securities.

oncost *See* Overhead Cost.

operating cost *See* Operating Expense.

operating expense (also called General,
Selling, and Administrative Expense; or
simply Other Expense) Any expense not
directly related to the production or acquisition of goods for sale or cost of goods
sold. Includes general overhead, selling,
and administrative expense. Interest paid
is sometimes excluded from this category
and separately identified as financial expense. *See* Overhead. [6-79; 7-92; 9-78;
10-13]

operating statement *See* Income Statement.

organization cost (also called Organization Expense) An intangible asset account
listed under Other Assets or Deferred
Charges on the Balance Sheet; the account
in which any costs incurred in setting up or
starting a company are recorded. This cost
may or may not be amortized; if it is, the
credit is made directly to the account
rather than to a contra-account.

organization expense *See* Organization
Cost.

other assets An account grouping on
the Balance Sheet for assets other than
current or fixed; under this caption on a
Balance Sheet the balances of Investments,
Intangible Assets, and Deferred Charges
accounts may be listed separately or summarized. *See* Fixed and Other Assets. [5-
40]

other expense *See* Operating Expense.

other incoming invoice *See* Incoming
Invoice.

output Any report, record, or check
prepared by the accounting system. [1-18;
Part 2; Panel A]

overabsorbed *See* Cost Absorption;
Overhead Rate.

overhead 1. Often this term is used
loosely to include costs or expenses not
obviously varying directly with the volume
of production or sales. 2. Any cost applicable to a particular period other than for
materials, merchandise, direct labor, or
an operating expense which has been separately identified and deliberately excluded
from general overhead. Overhead may include such fixed costs as depreciation,
rent, insurance, and taxes, as well as other
costs, such as indirect labor; supplies; re-
pairs; maintenance, supervisory, and executive salaries; and office payroll. In manufacturing, factory overhead is normally
treated as an element of product cost.
Other overhead, known as general overhead,
may be treated as a period cost. *See* Overhead Cost; Operating Expense. [9-59; 9-88]

overhead cost (also called Burden; Indirect Cost; Factory Overhead; Manufacturing Expense; Oncost) 1. That portion of
overhead related to factory operation which,
although not readily identifiable with a
product, is nevertheless related to its
production. Overhead cost includes such
items as indirect labor, factory supplies,
depreciation on factory buildings and equipment, and factory supervision; it is frequently incorporated as an element of
product cost by means of a rate. 2. A
factory cost account in which such amounts
are accumulated. *See* Cost Elements;
Overhead; Overhead Rate. [9-59; 9-88;
10-6]

overhead rate A rate determined prior
to the start of an accounting period by estimating the total overhead costs to be incurred and the total activity, as measured
by direct labor dollars or hours or by
machine hours, and then dividing the first
by the second. During the period the Overhead Cost account is debited for actual
costs and credited by means of the rate.
Any balance at the end of the period is a
variance—over- or underabsorbed overhead. *See* Variance; Cost Absorption;
Overhead. [9-91]

owners' equity (also called Net Worth;
Stockholders' Equity; Ownership) 1. The
amount of a firm's total resources attributed to its owners; equivalent to total as-

sets minus total liabilities, or net assets.
2. Collectively, the several equity accounts
in which the amounts are recorded, including Capital Stock and Paid-in Surplus and
Retained Earnings. 3. The owners' claims
in case of liquidation; equivalent to the residual assets after all creditors' claims
have been settled. [5-92]

paid-in surplus (also called Capital
Surplus) 1. Any amount received by the
firm in excess of the legal or stated value
of the capital stock issued. 2. The equity
account in which such amounts are recorded. *See* Capital Stock and Paid-in
Surplus; Common Stock; Preferred Stock.

parts master file A listing of part
numbers, descriptions, list prices and applicable taxes for all standard items sold
by a firm. Used in the billing activity.
[7-57; 8-69]

patents An intangible asset recorded
in an account by this name and included
under the Balance Sheet caption Other Assets or Intangible Assets. Since patents
have a limited life, they are amortized, and
the credit is usually made directly to the
account rather than to a contra-account.

payables Another term for liabilities.

payables activity The processing and
recording of Incoming Invoices, Purchase
Order Copies, and Receiving Records leading ultimately to the issuance of Checks to
Creditors in payment of the firm's accounts payable. See Matching; Check to
Creditor. [4-31; 7-29; Panel B]

payment terms Information usually
found on an invoice advising the recipient
of payment due date and cash discount
availability for prompt payment. For example, "2/10 net 30" indicates that a 2
per cent discount may be taken for payment
within ten days and that otherwise the net
invoice is due and payable within thirty
days from the invoice or shipping date.
[7-60]

payroll activity The calculation of employees' gross earnings, deductions, and
take-home pay and the preparation of Payroll Checks on the basis of Timecard and

Salary List inputs received. Part of the
processing and recording responsibility.
[4-22; 7-3; Panel B]

payroll check An output prepared as
part of the payroll activity; a check issued
to an employee for work performed in the
amount of his take-home pay. *See also*
Gross Earnings; Deductions. [2-2]

payroll expense 1. The direct cost to
the firm of employees' services including
gross earnings and additional expenditures
directly related to employment, such as
employer's Social Security contributions,
vacation pay, and accident insurance. 2. The
expense account in which such items are
recorded. [7-9; 10-3]

payroll information Input data for the
payroll activity provided by Timecards and
the Salary List. *See* Payroll Timecard;
Salary List. [3-5]

payroll master file A list of a firm's
employees, including such information as
the employee's rate of pay, number of dependents, and authorized deductions; used
in the payroll activity. [7-10; 8-69]

payroll timecard (or simply Timecard)
An input providing payroll information; a
document covering the hours worked by an
hourly paid employee. [3-6]

period cost or expense A cost or expense considered to be a function of time.
Being unrelated to productive effort, it is
not inventoried as a portion of product
cost. *See* Product Cost; Direct Cost; Expense. [9-66]

periodic inventory method Determination of the ending inventory by pricing or
valuing a physical count of the inventory.
See Perpetual Inventory Method; Retail Inventory Method. [10-49; Panel N]

permanent account *See* Real Account.

perpetual inventory control record An
Inventory Control Record maintained under
the perpetual inventory method.

perpetual inventory method A method
which maintains a current or running inventory balance in dollars, units, or both
by recording additions and withdrawals to
inventory as they occur. *See also* Periodic
Inventory Method. [10-48]

physical inventory An actual physical count of inventory owned by the firm at a particular date. Taken usually at the close of an accounting period to reconcile inventory records. *See* Ending Inventory; Periodic Inventory Method. [10-52]

post To transfer an entry amount from a Journal to a Ledger account. *See* Posting. [5-16]

posting *n*. The amount transferred or posted to an account. *v*. To post. *See* Post.

preferred stock 1. Stock taking precedence over common stock to a fixed upper limit in the distribution of profits and, in liquidation, of assets after creditors' claims have been settled. Oridinarily, voting rights are restricted. 2. The equity account in which the par or stated values of preferred shares issued is recorded, the balance received being recorded in Paid-in Surplus. *See* Capital Stock; Common Stock; Paid-in Surplus.

prepaid 1. Anything paid for but not yet received. 2. An expense which, in order to match more properly expenses and revenues, is carried forward to the accounting period the expense will benefit. 3. The account, such as Prepaid Insurance, in which prepaid expenses are recorded. If the prepayment extends beyond a year from the Balance Sheet date, it is shown as a Prepaid Charge. Otherwise, it is usually included with the current assets. [11-68]

prepaid expense *See* Prepaid.

processing and recording One of the three major responsibilities of the accounting system. Includes the payroll, billing, payables, cash receipt and reconciliation, and bookkeeping activities. *See also* Financial Reporting; Control Reporting. [4-4; 4-22; Panel B]

product cost The cost involved in the manufacture of a product; becomes an expense only when the product is sold. *See* Period Cost or Expense; Absorption Costing; Direct Costing; Cost Elements. [9-66]

profit (also called Earnings; Income; Net Income) Any excess of revenue over related expenses. *See* Gross Profit; Loss;

Income Statement; Net Income. [6-38; 6-56]

profit and loss account *See* Income Summary Account.

profit and loss statement *See* Income Statement.

profit and loss summary account *See* Income Summary Account.

profit center A center of responsibility within a firm with both expenses and revenues; the latter may arise from internal transfer pricing within the company. *See* Responsibility Center.

profit margin *See* Profitability.

profitability (also called Margin; Profit Margin) A relative term referring to the amount of profit realizable from a particular product, service, or group of products or services. *See* Contribution; Gross Profit.

promissory note *See* Note.

provision for bad debts *See* Bad Debt Allowance.

provision for depreciation *See* Accumulated Depreciation.

provision for income taxes (also called Allowance for Income Taxes; Allowance for Taxes; Income Taxes Due; or simply Income Taxes) 1. The amount of income tax expense, frequently estimated, applicable to the current period. 2. The expense account in which such amounts are recorded. 3. A term sometimes applied to the liability account for income taxes payable. *See* Accrued Taxes; Income Tax. [6-84]

provision for taxes *See* Accrued Taxes.

purchase information Input data relative to purchases; provided by the Purchase Order Copy, the Receiving Record, and the Incoming Invoice. [3-18]

purchase order copy An input; the copy of an issued Purchase Order providing purchase information to the accounting system and used in the matching operation to verify the legitimacy of incoming Materials Invoices. *See* Matching. [3-20]

purchase returns and allowances A contra-account to the Purchases account in which are recorded the amounts of any purchases returned or allowances made, generally excluding cash discounts taken.

purchases   1. Goods bought for resale.
2. Especially under the periodic inventory
method, the cost account in which such incoming inventory is accumulated for later
calculation of cost of goods sold instead of
being entered directly to the Inventory account. See Basic Inventory Equation; Purchase Information; Purchase Order Copy.
[12-35]

raw materials See Materials.

real account (sometimes called Permanent Account) An asset or equity account
listed on the Balance Sheet. A real account
is not closed as part of the closing process;
any balance contained is carried forward to
the next accounting period. See Nominal
Account. [6-73]

real-time Refers to processing data as
it is received. See Batching.

receipt (also called Voucher) A document certifying that goods, services, or
money has been received.

receivables See Accounts Receivable.

receiving record An input providing in
part data called purchase information; a
document which records the receipt of
materials from suppliers. See Matching.
[3-22]

reference file See Master File.

requisition A document requesting
delivery of inventory items. See Stores
Requisition.

reserve for bad debts See Bad Debt
Allowance.

reserve for depreciation See Accumulated Depreciation.

responsibility center (also called Center
of Responsibility) An organizational entity
within a firm (division, department, section, etc.) with separable expenses and
possibly revenues for budgetary control
purposes. See Profit Center. [2-46]

retail inventory method A variation of
the periodic inventory method wherein the
costing of ending physical inventory is ac-
complished by first valuing or pricing at
selling price and then adjusting the total to
cost by applying a ratio. The ratio used is

that of total cost to total selling price (adjusted for special markups and markdowns)
of goods available for sale; it can be thought
of as similar to the difference between the
gross profit ratio and 100 per cent. See
Gross Profit Ratio; Periodic Inventory
Method; Physical Inventory. [10-74]

retained earnings (also called Earned
Surplus; Undistributed Profits; Earnings or
Profits Retained in the Business) 1. The
reflection of net assets not accounted for by
Capital Stock and Paid-in Surplus; that
portion of net assets resulting from profits
which have not been distributed in dividends
to stockholders but have been retained in
the business. 2. The equity account in
which such amounts are recorded. [5-97;
6-45]

retained earnings statement See Statement of Retained Earnings.

returns and allowances See Sales Returns and Allowances.

revenue The inflow of assets, usually
cash or accounts receivable, from the sale
of products and services to customers and
from such other sources as interest, dividends, and rent. [6-66]

revenue account Any account recording
revenues. Revenue accounts are nominal
accounts with credit balances which appear
on the Income Statement. The most common revenue account is Sales. See Revenue.
[6-75]

reversing entry An entry which is the
exact opposite of a previous entry; that is,
the debits and the credits to the same accounts are reversed. Such an entry eliminates the effects of the previous entry and
is used as the first step in the procedure
of correcting a prior incorrect entry. Also
used at the beginning of an accounting
period to clear accounts of amounts of accruals and deferrals established by adjusting entries at the end of the prior period.
[8-85; 11-66; 11-71]

salary list An input providing payroll
information for the payroll activity; a list
of salaried personnel with their rates of
pay. [3-8; 7-28]

sales   *See* Net Sales.

sales information   A category of input data that includes the Customer Order and the Shipping Notice. *See* Customer Order; Shipping Notice. [3-55]

sales performance analysis   An output prepared as part of the control reporting responsibility; any report providing management with specific information on a firm's sales and based on orders received or shipments made. Sales may be classified and summarized in dollars, units, or both, according to product, territory, customer, period, or any other meaningful way. This output may also provide cumulative figures from prior periods for comparison. [2-19; 8-41]

sales returns and allowances (often called Discounts and Allowances)   A contra-revenue account to the Gross Sales account in which is recorded cash discounts, sales returns, and any special adjustments or allowances. *See* Net Sales. [7-112; 11-75; 12-14]

scrap notice   An input which in part provides inventory transfer information; a record of materials, parts, or products scrapped or discarded as unusable. [3-84]

shareholder   *See* Stockholder.

shipping address   The address to which a shipment for a customer is forwarded; may be different than the address to which the customer wishes his invoice sent. *See* Billing Address. [7-59]

shipping notice   An input providing sales information; a document reporting items and quantities shipped to a particular customer. [3-55]

solvent   The ability to meet financial obligations as they become due. [1-4]

specific identification (sometimes called Actual)   A method of inventory valuation or pricing by which actual acquisition or manufacturing costs are related to each specific item; the specific item's cost is used both in the inventory accounts and in Cost of Goods Sold. This method, generally, is used only for items which are readily identifiable and are of relatively high value—

fine jewelry, automobiles, etc. *See* Inventory Valuation. [9-14]

standard cost   1. Any predetermined cost. 2. In a standard cost system, when it is judged that the standard cost can be predetermined with reasonable accuracy, the differences between actual and standard manufacturing costs (or the variances) become measures of efficiency and can be used for control. Since standard costs are then considered the proper costs, only standard costs are used for inventory valuation; the variances represent manufacturing losses or gains and are related to the period of occurrence by closing them to Cost of Goods Sold or to some other expense account. *See* Standard Cost Variance. [10-17]

standard cost system   A cost accounting system incorporating standard costs. *See* Standard Cost; Standard Cost Variance. [10-17]

standard cost variance   Any difference between the actual and the standard manufacturing cost. The total variance for each cost element is the accounting variance. The accounting variance is usually further broken down into more meaningful components for management. As variances are exceptions to the planned or expected costs, management will concentrate on them as having more significance for control than the total manufacturing costs. *See* Standard Cost. [10-20; 10-38]

standard costing   Procedures used in, or the results obtained by, a standard cost system. [10-17]

statement of financial position   Sometimes referring to the conventional Balance Sheet, more often to the "report form" of presenting a firm's financial position, in that it is a succession of additions and subtractions similar to those made on the Income Statement. One formula in common useage is Current Assets minus Current Liabilities equals Working Capital; Working Capital plus Fixed and Other Assets minus Long-term Debt equals Owners' Equity. *See* Balance Sheet. [2-58; 5-3; 5-31; 8-3]

statement of retained earnings (also called Retained Earnings Statement; Statement of Earned Surplus) A report showing the cause of changes in the Retained Earnings account between successive Balance Sheets. Profit or loss for the period covered is added to the beginning Retained Earnings balance, and dividends declared are subtracted, to arrive at ending Retained Earnings. Other items which may appear in this statement are any extraordinary gains or losses which do not appear on the Income Statement and any portion of Retained Earnings which has been reclassified into other accounts, such as Capital Stock and Paid-in Surplus. This statement is sometimes incorporated in the Income Statement.

statement of working capital *See* Funds Statement.

stock control record *See* Inventory Control Record.

stock dividend A distribution of additional shares of a firm's capital stock, made to stockholders in the proportion their holdings bear to the total stock before the dividend. If a stockholder sells the shares received from a stock dividend, he reduces his proportionate holding of the new total of shares outstanding. See Dividends Payable; Cash Dividend; Capital Stock; Statement of Retained Earnings.

stockholder A shareholder; one who owns shares of the capital stock of a firm. *See* Owners' Equity; Capital Stock.

stockholders' equity *See* Owners' Equity.

stores receipt *See* Stores Requisition.

stores requisition (Stores Requisition and Receipt) An input providing inventory transfer information; a document originating with the requisitioning control area is a Stores Requisition, while a document recording receipt of inventory items not requisitioned is a Stores Receipt. Generally, a single multicopy form serves as either a receipt or a requisition, depending on the direction of the movement of the items. [3-78; 3-79]

straight-line depreciation *See* Depreciation Methods.

subsidiary accounts Accounts of like kind whose total balances equal the balance of the master or control account maintained in the General Ledger; subsidiary accounts are maintained in Subsidiary Ledgers. *See* Control Account; Ledger.

subsidiary ledger *See* Ledger.

sum of the years digits (or Years Digits Depreciation) *See* Depreciation Methods.

summarize 1. To select and regroup significant data from a record or report for a more concise version. 2. To total to a net figure any data or group of data. *See* Abstract.

supplier Any person or company selling goods or supplies to the firm. The liability from such sales is recorded in the Accounts Payable account.

supplies 1. Items acquired not for incorporation in a finished product or for resale: stationery, maintenance supplies, and the like. 2. The accounts for such items: Supplies Expense for the supplies used during the accounting period; Supplies Inventory or simply Supplies for items on hand at the date of the Balance Sheet. Usually, supplies on hand are not included under the Balance Sheet caption Inventories, but are listed separately. *See* Inventory.

surplus *See* Paid-in Surplus; Retained Earnings.

take-home pay The net pay or net amount actually paid to an employee after all deductions have been subtracted from gross earnings. *See* Deductions; Gross Earnings. [7-5]

taxes payable *See* Accrued Taxes.

temporary holding account or temporary account *See* Nominal Account.

timecard *See* Payroll Timecard.

trade discount A reduction from list price. Different trade discounts are granted to different classifications of customers (wholesalers, manufacturers' representatives, retailers, etc.). [7-52; 7-60]

trade payables *See* Accounts Payable.

transaction An event recognized as affecting the financial position of the firm; this recognition is the basis for an entry.

Transactions are of two kinds: One is between the firm and outsiders (purchases, sales, etc.); the other is internal (depreciation, accruals, deferrals, etc.). [4-6]

transportation-in *See* Freight-in.

transportation-out *See* Freight-out.

trial balance A method for checking the accuracy of accounting records involving the listing of all account balances to determine if total debits equal total credits. Trial balances are often taken before books are closed (pre-closing) and afterwards (post-closing). [8-4]

undistributed profits *See* Retained Earnings.

unearned income *See* Deferred Income.

underabsorbed *See* Cost Absorption; Overhead Rate.

unit inventory control record *See* Inventory Control Record.

valuation The assignment of a cost, frequently on a judgment basis. *See* Depreciation Methods; Inventory Valuation.

valuation account *See* Contra-account.

variable cost or expense 1. Any cost or expense which varies in total amount as the activity varies. 2. Sometimes refers direct cost. See Direct Cost; Fixed Cost or Expense. [10-107]

variance Any difference between budgeted amounts and actual amounts; in a standard cost system, the difference between standard and actual costs. Variances are reported on the Budget Performance Analysis and may be analyzed in detail on the Cost Analysis Report. *See* Standard Cost Variance. [8-66; 9-100; 10-20]

variance analysis The study of the causes of variances in order to determine what corrective action, if any, is indicated.

vendor *See* Supplier.

voucher A receipt.

wages and salaries payable *See* Accrued Wages and Salaries.

withholding tax The personal income tax the employer is required to deduct from the employee's gross earnings and to remit to the government levying the tax.

See Deductions. [7-5]

work in process (also called Work in Progress; Goods in Process) 1. Work started out but not yet completed. 2. The inventory account recording product costs as incurred; manufacturing account. [9-40]

work sheet A form with several money columns. One such form has eight columns: The first two columns are for the balances of the Ledger accounts before closing; the next two are used for any required adjustments; extensions after are made to the third pair of columns for the accounts that will be on the Income Statement or to the last pair for the accounts to appear on the Balance Sheet. This device facilitates the preparation of adjusting and closing entries; it also permits a "constructive" closing since monthly Income Statements and Balance Sheets can be made from the work sheet without the necessity of going through the formal closing procedures.

working capital (also called Net Working Capital; Net Current Assets) The difference between total current assets and total current liabilities. In Statements of Financial Position, this figure is highlighted by a caption. *See* Statement of Financial Position.

working capital statement *See* Funds Statement.

write-off 1. Any entry recording the expiration of usefulness of an asset by a debit to the appropriate expense account and a credit to the asset account or to a corresponding contra-asset account, e.g., recording bad debt expense, reduction of prepaids, depreciation of fixed assets, or amortization of other assets. 2. An entry recording the disposition or loss of an asset by a credit to the appropriate asset account and a corresponding debit to an expense or loss account. When a contra-asset account has been previously established and carries accumulated credits in anticipation of the eventual disposition or loss, the debit may be made to this account, e.g., when a fully depreciated asset is discarded, the credit is to Accumulated Depreciation and the debit to the asset account.

Simplified input-ouput connections

Inputs	Outputs				
	Balance Sheet	Income Statement	Inventory Control Records	Cost Analysis Report	Other
Payroll Information:					
Payroll Timecard ...	X	X		X	Payroll Check
Salary List	X	X		X	Payroll Check
Purchase Information:					
Purchase Order Copy .			X		
Receiving Record....			X		
Material Invoice.....	X			X	Check to Creditor
Other Incoming					
Invoice	X	X		X	Check to Creditor
Sales Information:					
Customer Order.....					Sales Perform-ance Analysis
Shipping Notice	X	X	X		Sales Perform-ance Analysis; Customer Invoice
Inventory Transfer Information:					
Stores Requisition ...	X		X		
Scrap Notice	X	X	X	X	
Cash and cash recon-ciliation inputs:					
Check from Customer.	X	X			
Canceled Checks					No specific output
Bank Statements					No specific output
Budget Information					Budget; Budget Performance Analysis

Outline of accounting responsibilities

Major responsibilities	Activities	Outputs
Processing and recording ...	(a) Payroll	Payroll Check
	(b) Billing	Customer Invoice
	(c) Payables	Check to Creditor
	(d) Cash receipt and reconciliation	
	(e) Bookkeeping	Journals, Ledgers
Financial reporting	Adjusting, closing	Balance Sheet, Income Statement
Control reporting	(a) Inventory control	Inventory Control Record
	(b) Sales analysis	Sales Performance Analysis
	(c) Cost analysis	Cost Analysis Report
	(d) Budgeting	Budget
	(e) Budget analysis	Budget Performance Analysis

panel C balance sheet

Example of Balance Sheet (greatly simplified)
Jones Company, Statement of Financial Position, 12/31/6B

Assets				Equities		
Cash.	$12,000			Accounts Payable.	$15,000	
Accounts Receivable	18,000			Wages and Salaries Payable.	5,000	
Inventory.	40,000	$ 70,000		Notes Payable.	9,000	
Total Current Assets				Taxes Payable.	15,000	
Land.	$ 9,000			Total Current Liabilities		$ 44,000
Buildings.	15,000			Mortgage Payable.	$20,000	
Equipment.	6,000			Long-term Debt		20,000
				Total Liabilities		$ 64,000
Total Fixed Assets.		30,000		Capital Stock and Paid-in Surplus	$15,000	
				Retained Earnings	21,000	
				Total Net Worth.		$ 36,000
Total Assets		$100,000		Total Equities		$100,000

panel D

Partial Balance Sheet

Cash	$15,000			
		Capital Stock and Paid-in Surplus	$15,000
Total Assets . .	$15,000	Total Equities.	$15,000

panel E

Partial Balance Sheet

Cash	$ 9,000		
Equipment · · ·	6,000	Capital Stock and Paid-in Surplus	$15,000
Total Assets . .	$15,000	Total Equities.	$15,000

panel F

Partial Balance Sheet

Cash	$ 3,000		
Inventory	6,000		
Equipment · · ·	6,000	Capital Stock and Paid-in Surplus	$15,000
Total Assets . .	$15,000	Total Equities.	$15,000

panel G

Partial Balance Sheet

Cash	$ 3,000	Accounts Payable.	$15,000
Inventory	21,000		
Equipment · · ·	6,000	Capital Stock and Paid-in Surplus	$15,000
Total Assets . .	$30,000	Total Equities.	$30,000

panel H

Cash	$12,000	Accounts Payable.	$15,000
		Notes Payable	9,000
Inventory .	21,000		
Equipment	6,000	Capital Stock and Paid-in Surplus	15,000
Total Assets . .	$39,000	Total Equities.	$39,000

Accounts and partial Balance Sheet

Cash			Accounts Payable	
Dr	Cr		Dr	Cr
15,000				15,000
	6,000			
	6,000			
9,000				

Inventory			Notes Payable	
Dr	Cr		Dr	Cr
6,000				9,000
15,000				

Equipment			Capital Stock and Paid-in Surplus	
Dr	Cr			
6,000			Dr	Cr
				15,000

- -

Jones Company, Statement of Financial Position, 12/31/6A

Assets			Equities	
Cash $12,000			Accounts Payable $15,000	
Inventory 21,000			Notes Payable 9,000	
Total Current Assets $33,000			Total Current Liabilities	$24,000
Equipment . . . $ 6,000			Capital Stock and Paid-in Surplus . $15,000	
Total Fixed Assets . $ 6,000			Total Net Worth.	$15,000
Total Assets $39,000			Total Equities	$39,000

---

panel J   income and retained earnings statements

Example of Income Statement (greatly simplified)
Jones Company, Statement of Income, year ending 12/31/6B

Sales	$600,000
Less: Cost of Goods Sold . .	450,000
Gross Profit	$150,000
Less: Other Expenses	110,000
Net Profit before Taxes . . .	40,000
Less: Income Taxes	15,000
Net Profit after Taxes	25,000

- -

Retained Earnings Statement
Jones Company, Statement of Retained Earnings, year ending 12/31/6B

Beginning Retained Earnings . . . . $ 0	
Net Profit after Taxes	$25,000
	$25,000
Less: Dividends Paid	4,000
Ending Retained Earnings, 12/31/6B . .	$21,000

Materials inventory, steel tubing

	Feet	Cost per foot	Total cost
Beginning Inventory	0	$0.10	
Purchase, 1/2.	500	$0.10	$ 50
Purchase, 1/6.	500	0.10	50
Purchase, 9/1.	1,000	0.12	120
Purchase, 12/1	2,000	0.12	240
Total available	4,000		$460
Withdrawal, 3/10.	500		
Withdrawal, 6/10.	500		
Withdrawal, 10/11	1,000		____
Ending Inventory.	2,000		$____

panel L manufacturer's income statement

Jones Company, Statement of Income, period 1/1/6B to 12/31/6B

Sales $600,000

Product costs
{
Cost of Goods Sold:
   Beginning Finished Goods Inventory (12/31/6A) . . . . . $ 25,000
   Cost of Goods Manufactured 440,000
   Cost of Goods Available for Sale $465,000
   Less Ending Finished Goods Inventory (12/31/6B). . . . 15,000
      Cost of Goods Sold 450,000

Gross Profit $150,000

Period costs
{
Operating Expenses:
   Selling Expenses. . . . . $ 60,000
   General Administrative Expenses 50,000   110,000

Net Profit before Taxes. . . . . $ 40,000
Less Income Taxes. 15,000

Net Profit after Taxes . . . . $ 25,000
Less Dividends Paid. 4,000

To Retained Earnings . . . . $ 21,000

panel M   schedule of cost of goods manufactured

Jones Company, Cost of Goods Manufactured, period 1/1/6B to 12/31/6B

Beginning Materials Inventory	$ 10,000
Add Materials Purchased	140,000
	$150,000
Less Ending Materials Inventory	5,000
Material Cost	$145,000
Direct Labor Cost	$100,000
Overhead Cost.	200,000
Total Manufacturing Costs.	$445,000
Add Beginning Work in Process Inventory	15,000
	$460,000
Less Ending Work in Process Inventory.	20,000
Cost of Goods Manufactured.	$440,000

panel N

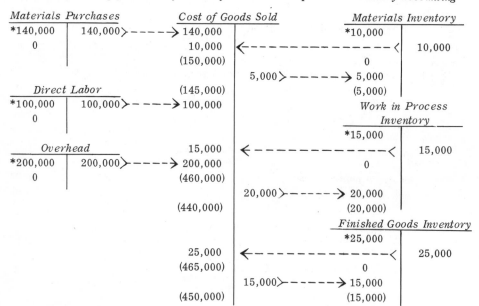

Inventory closing procedure for manufacturer under periodic inventory accounting

Starting balances marked *; progressive balances enclosed in parentheses.

panel O   break-even chart

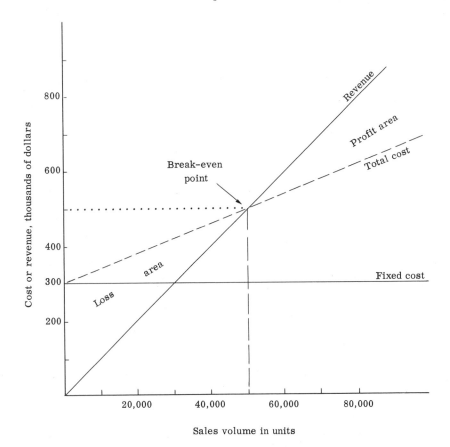

Sales volume in units

panel P   balance sheet

Jones Company, Statement of Financial Position, 12/31/6B

Assets			Equities		
Cash		$12,000	Accounts Payable.	$15,000	
Accounts Receivable $18,500			Accrued Wages and		
Less: Bad Debt			Salaries	5,000	
Allowance	500	18,000	Notes Payable.	9,000	
Inventory		40,000	Accrued Taxes	15,000	
Prepaid Insurance		1,000	Total Current		
Total Current			Liabilities.		$ 44,000
Assets		$ 71,000	Mortgage Payable	$20,000	
Land		$ 9,000	Long-term Debt		20,000
Buildings $15,000			Total Liabilities.		$ 64,000
Equipment	6,000				
	$21,000		Capital Stock		
Less: Accumulated			and Paid-in Surplus	$15,000	
Depreciation . .	6,000	15,000	Retained Earnings	21,000	
Total Fixed Assets		$ 24,000	Total Net Worth		36,000
Patents		5,000			
Total Assets		$100,000	Total Equities		$100,000

panel Q flow chart

Inputs   *Processing and recording*   *Outputs*

Timecards — sum hours — calculate payroll ← Payroll Master File

Salary Lists — To Journal → **Payroll Checks**

→ **Cost Analysis Reports**

Other Incoming Invoices — verify — To Journal → decision to pay → **Checks to Creditors**

Material Invoices — verify — To Journal

Receiving Records → **Inventory Control Records**

Purchase Order Copies

Transfer Notices (Stores Requisitions and Scrap Notices) — To Journal

Customer Master File — extend — To Journal → **Customer Invoices**

Shipping Notices — price ← Parts Master File

Customer Orders — summarize → **Sales Performance Analysis**

Budget Information → **Budget**

→ **Budget Performance Analysis**

Journal → Adjusting and closing entries / Journal entries from other inputs — post — Ledger → **Income Statement**

→ **Balance Sheet**

Checks from Customers — To Journal → to bank

Cancelled Checks; Bank Statements — reconcile with accounts

panel R

New Company ledger accounts for the year 196A

Cash

Accounts Payable

Inventory

Notes Payable

Land

Buildings

Capital Stock

Equipment

Prepaid Insurance

Organization Costs

panel S

Balance Sheet for New Company, 12/31/196A

Cash . . . . $ _ _ _ _
Inventory . . . . _ _ _ _
   Total Current Assets . . . . $ _ _ _ _ _ _ _
Land . . . . _ _ _ _
Buildings . . . . _ _ _ _
Equipment . . . . _ _ _ _
   Total Fixed Assets. . . . . $ _ _ _ _ _ _ _
Prepaid Insurance . . . . . . _ _ _ _
Organization Costs . . . . . _ _ _ _
   Total Deferred Charges . . . . $ _ _ _ _ _ _

Total Assets . . . . $ _ _ _ _ _ _ _

Accounts Payable . . $ _ _ _ _
Notes Payable. . . . . _ _ _ _
   Total Liabilities. . . . . $ _ _ _ _ _ _ _

Capital Stock . . . . . . _ _ _ _

   Total Net Worth . . . . $ _ _ _ _ _ _

Total Equities. . . . . $ _ _ _ _ _ _ _

panel T

New Company Ledger Accounts for the year 196B

Cash

(B) 23,000

Accounts Receivable

Bad Debt Allowance

Inventory

(B) 30,000

Buildings

(B) 40,000

Land

(B) 10,000

Prepaid Insurance

(B) 3,000

Equipment

(B) 24,000

Accumulated Depreciation–Bldgs.

Organization Costs

(B) 6,000

Accumulated Depreciation–Equip.

Accounts Payable		*Accrued Wages and Salaries*		*Notes Payable*	
	26,000 (B)				10,000 (B)

Taxes Payable		*Capital Stock*		*Retained Earnings*	
			100,000 (B)		

Sales		*Cost of Goods Sold*		*Payroll Expense*	

Depreciation Expense		*Insurance Expense*		*Bad Debt Expense*	

Loss on Equipment Disposal		*General Expense*		*Income Summary*	

New Company, financial statements for 196B
Income Statement, year ending 12/31/196B

Net Sales . . . . $_____

    Less Cost of Goods Sold . . . .

Gross Profit . . . . $_____

Other Expenses:

    Payroll . . . . $_____

    Depreciation. . . . . _____

    Insurance. _____

    General . . . . _____

    Bad Debt . . . . _____

    Loss on Disposal of Equipment . . . . _____

      Total Other Expenses. _____

Profit before Income Taxes . . . . $_____

Estimated Federal and State Income Taxes. . . . . _____

Net Profit after Income Taxes . . . . _____

Balance Sheet as of 12/31/196B

Assets		Equities	
Cash . . . . $_____		Accounts Payable. . . . $ _____	
Accounts Receivable. . $_____		Accrued Wages and	
Less Bad Debt _____		Salaries . . . . . . _____	
Allowance . . . . . _____		Taxes Payable . . . . . _____	
Inventory		Total Current Liabilities.	$_____
Total Current Assets . . . . $_____			
Land . . . . $_____			
Buildings . . . . $_____			
Less Depreciation . . _____		Capital Stock. . . . . . . $_____	
Equipment . . . . _____			
Less Depreciation . . _____		Retained Earnings . . . _____	
Total Fixed Assets. . . . . $_____			
Prepaid Insurance . . . $_____		Total Net Worth	$_____
Organization Costs. . . _____			
Total Deferred Charges . . . . . . $_____			
Total Assets . . . . $		Total Equities	$_____

New Company, Financial Statements for 196B
Income Statement, year ending 12/31/196B

Net Sales	$295,000
Less Cost of Goods Sold	192,000
Gross Profit	$103,000
Other Expenses:	
Payroll	$40,400
Depreciation	6,000
Insurance	1,000
General	1,000
Bad Debt	2,380
Loss on Disposal of Equipment	500
Total Other Expenses	51,280
Profit before Income Taxes	$ 51,720
Estimated Federal and State Income Taxes	22,000
Net Profit after Income Taxes	$ 29,720

Balance Sheet as of 12/31/196B

Assets

Cash		$ 53,500
Accounts Receivable	$38,000	
Less Bad Debt Allowance	380	37,620
Inventory		52,000
Total Current Assets		$143,000
Land		10,000
Buildings	$40,000	
Less Depreciation	1,000	39,000
Equipment	19,000	
Less Depreciation	4,000	15,000
Total Fixed Assets		$ 64,000
Prepaid Insurance	$ 2,000	
Organization Costs	5,000	
Total Deferred Charges		$ 7,000
Total Assets		$214,120

Equities

Accounts Payable	$ 55,000	
Accrued Wages and Salaries	300	
Taxes Payable	39,100	
Total Current Liabilities		$ 94,400
Capital Stock	$100,000	
Retained Earnings	19,720	
Total Net Worth		$119,720
Total Equities		$214,120

panel W

New Company ledger accounts for the year 196B

Cash			
(B)	23,000	195,000	(5)
(4)	270,000	30,000	(6)
		10,000	(10)
(14)	3,500	8,000	(12)
		53,500	(B)
	296,500	296,500	
(B)	53,500		

Accounts Receivable			
(2)	315,000	270,000	(4)
		5,000	(7)
		2,000	(17)
		38,000	(B)
	315,000	315,000	
(B)	38,000		

Bad Debt Allowance			
(17)	2,000	2,380	(18)
(B)	380		
		380	(B)

Land		
(B)	10,000	

Inventory			
(B)	30,000	195,000	(3)
(1)	215,000	1,000	(9)
(8)	3,000		
		52,000	(B)
	248,000	248,000	
(B)	52,000		

Buildings	
(B)	40,000

Equipment			
(B)	24,000	5,000	(14)
		19,000	(B)
(B)	19,000		

Accumulated Depreciation–Bldgs.		
		1,000 (13)

Accumulated Depreciation–Equip.			
(14)	1,000	5,000	(13)
(B)	4,000		
		4,000	(B)

Prepaid Insurance			
(B)	3,000	1,000	(15)
		2,000	(B)
	3,000	3,000	
(B)	2,000		

Organization Costs			
(B)	6,000	1,000	(16)
		5,000	(B)
(B)	5,000		

Accounts Payable			
		26,000	(B)
(5)	185,000		
(9)	1,000	215,000	(1)
(B)	55,000		
	241,000	241,000	
		55,000	(B)

Accrued Wages and Salaries	
	300 (11)

Notes Payable			
(5)	10,000	10,000	(B)

Taxes Payable			
(12)	8,000	15,000	(2)
		10,000	(6)
(B)	39,100	100	(11)
		22,000	(21)
	47,100	47,100	
		39,100	(B)

Capital Stock	
	100,000 (B)

Retained Earnings			
(10)	10,000	29,720	(22)
(B)	19,720		
		19,720	(B)

Sales			
		300,000	(2)
(7)	5,000		
(19)	295,000		
	300,000	300,000	

Cost of Goods Sold			
(3)	195,000	3,000	(8)
		192,000	(20)
	195,000	195,000	

Payroll Expense			
(6)	40,000	40,000	(20)
(11)	400		
	40,400	40,400	

Depreciation Expense			
(13)	6,000	6,000	(20)

Insurance Expense			
(15)	1,000	1,000	(20)

Bad Debt Expense			
(18)	2,380	2,380	(20)

Loss on Equipment Disposal			
(14)	500	500	(20)

General Expense			
(16)	1,000	1,000	(20)

Income Summary			
(20)	243,280	295,000	(19)
(21)	22,000		
(22)	29,720		
	295,000	295,000	

Smith Company, selected cost and other accounts, year 196A

Cash	
(B) 50,000	
(12) 32,000	

Taxes Payable	
	2,000 (B)

Accounts Payable	
	20,000 (B)

Materials Inventory	
(B) 30,000	

Factory Overhead	
(B) 15,500	

Factory Payroll Expense	

Work in Process Inventory	
(B) 16,000	

Materials Variance	

Labor Variance	

Finished Goods Inventory	

Overhead Variance	

Cost of Goods Sold	

Smith Company, selected cost and other accounts, year 196A

Cash			
(B) 50,000	12,740	(4)
(12) 32,000	40,300	(14)
	28,960	(B)
(B) 28,960		

Taxes Payable			
(14) 11,400	2,000	(B)
	8,260	(4)
(B) 1,120	1,260	(5)
	1,120	(B)

Accounts Payable			
(14) 28,900	20,000	(B)
	500	(1)
(B) 10,100	18,500	(13)
	10,100	(B)

Materials Inventory			
(B) 30,000	510	(2)
(1) 500	20,400	(3)
(13) 18,500	28,090	(B)
59,000	59,000	
(B) 28,090		

Factory Overhead			
(B) 15,500	22,900	(8)
(7) 7,400		
22,900	22,900	

Factory Payroll Expense			
(4) 21,000	15,000	(6)
(5) 1,260	7,260	(7)
22,260	22,260	

Work in Process Inventory			
(B) 16,000	52,200	(9)
(2) 500		
(3) 20,000		
(6) 15,000		
(8) 22,500	21,800	(B)
74,000	74,000	
(B) 21,800		

Materials Variance			
(2) 10		
(3) 400	410	(11)

Labor Variance			
(11) 140	140	(7)

Finished Goods Inventory			
(B) 25,520	51,040	(10)
(9) 52,200	26,680	(B)
77,720	77,720	
(B) 26,680		

Overhead Variance			
(8) 400	400	(11)

Cost of Goods Sold		
(10) 51,040	
(11) 670	
51,710	